A Practical Guide to Teaching English in the Secondary School

A Practical Guide to Teaching English in the Secondary School offers straightforward advice, inspiration and a wide range of tried and tested approaches to help you find success in the secondary English classroom. Covering all aspects of English teaching, it is designed for you to dip in and out of, and enable you to focus on specific areas of teaching, your programme or pupils' learning.

Fully updated to reflect what student and early career teachers see and experience when they enter the classroom, the second edition supports trainee and practicing teachers to teach in imaginative and creative ways to promote learning in English. Packed with ideas, resources, practical teaching activities and underpinned by the latest research into how children learn, the book examines the core areas of reading, writing and spoken English including:

- Plays, poetry, non-fiction, myths and legends, drama and Shakespeare
- Developing writing
- Creative grammar
- Talk and classroom dialogue
- Media and digital writing
- English across the curriculum
- Well-being through writing
- Literature and language post-16.

Including tools to support critical reflection, *A Practical Guide to Teaching English in the Secondary School* is an essential companion for all training and newly qualified English teachers.

Annabel Watson is Senior Lecturer in Language Education, School Direct Programme Leader, and Secondary English PGCE Course Leader at the University of Exeter, UK.

Ruth Newman is Senior Lecturer in Language Education teaching on the Secondary English PGCE and MA Ed in Language and Literacy at the University of Exeter, UK.

Routledge Teaching Guides

Series Editors: Susan Capel and Marilyn Leask

Other titles in the series:

A Practical Guide to Teaching Music in the Secondary School
Edited by Julie Evans and Chris Philpott

A Practical Guide to Teaching Science in the Secondary School
Douglas P. Newton

A Practical Guide to Teaching Design and Technology in the Secondary School
Edited by Gwyneth Owen-Jackson

A Practical Guide to Teaching History in the Secondary School
Edited by Martin Hunt

A Practical Guide to Teaching Modern Foreign Languages in the Secondary School
Edited by Norbert Pachler and Ana Redondo

A Practical Guide to Teaching Citizenship in the Secondary School
Edited by Liam Gearon

A Practical Guide to Teaching ICT in the Secondary School
Edited by Steve Kennewell, Andrew Connell, Anthony Edwards, Michael Hammond and Cathy Wickens

A Practical Guide to Teaching Computing and ICT in the Secondary School
Andrew Connell and Anthony Edwards with Alison Hramiak, Gavin Rhodes and Neil Stanley

A Practical Guide to Teaching Mathematics in the Secondary School, 2nd Edition
Edited by Clare Lee and Robert Ward-Penny

A Practical Guide to Teaching Physical Education in the Secondary School, 3rd Edition
Edited by Susan Capel, Joanne Cliffe and Julia Lawrence

A Practical Guide to Teaching English in the Secondary School, 2nd Edition
Annabel Watson and Ruth Newman

These Practical Guides have been designed as companions to **Learning to Teach X Subject in the Secondary School**. For information on the Routledge Teaching Guides series please visit our website at www.routledge.com/education.

A Practical Guide to Teaching English in the Secondary School

Second Edition

Edited by Annabel Watson and Ruth Newman

Routledge
Taylor & Francis Group
LONDON AND NEW YORK

Illustration: Sarah Hoyle

First published 2022
by Routledge
2 Park Square, Milton Park, Abingdon, Oxon OX14 4RN

and by Routledge
605 Third Avenue, New York, NY 10158

Routledge is an imprint of the Taylor & Francis Group, an informa business

British Library Cataloguing-in-Publication Data
A catalogue record for this book is available from the British Library

Library of Congress Cataloging-in-Publication Data
Names: Watson, Annabel, editor. | Newman, Ruth (Ruth Malka Charlotte), editor.
Title: A practical guide to teaching English in the secondary school / edited by Annabel Watson and Ruth Newman.
Description: 2nd edition. | Abingdon, Oxon; New York, NY: Routledge Books, 2022. | Series: Routledge teaching guides | Includes bibliographical references.
Identifiers: LCCN 2021026374 (print) | LCCN 2021026375 (ebook) | ISBN 9780367553340 (hardback) | ISBN 9780367553364 (paperback) | ISBN 9781003093060 (ebook)
Subjects: LCSH: English language–Study and teaching (Secondary)–Great Britain. | English literature–Study and teaching (Secondary)–Great Britain. | Education, Secondary–Aims and objectives–Great Britain. | Curriculum planning–Great Britain.
Classification: LCC LB1631 .P67 2022 (print) | LCC LB1631 (ebook) | DDC 371.33–dc23
LC record available at https://lccn.loc.gov/2021026374
LC ebook record available at https://lccn.loc.gov/2021026375

ISBN: 978-0-367-55334-0 (hbk)
ISBN: 978-0-367-55336-4 (pbk)
ISBN: 978-1-00-309306-0 (ebk)

DOI: 10.4324/9781003093060

Typeset in Palatino LT Std
by Newgen Publishing UK

Access the Support Material: www.routledge.com/9780367553364

Contents

Figures

Tables

Contributors

Barbara Bleiman was Co-Director of the English and Media Centre (EMC) and is now an education consultant there. She co-edits *emagazine*. She has written numerous articles, blogs and books about English teaching, including a book of her writings, *What Matters in English Teaching*, published by EMC in April 2020.

Susan Chapman is PGCE English tutor at Aberystwyth University. After working as an English teacher, head of department and senior examiner, she now works in higher education focusing on initial teacher education, undergraduate education studies and professional learning. Her research interests include curriculum reform, rural education and language awareness.

Joan Foley worked as Secondary English HoD in inner-city schools. She is now Senior Lecturer, PGCE Secondary English at University of West of England, and member of the English Association's Secondary Committee. She has co-developed projects promoting classical tales in English, for example, *Ovid in the West Country* and *Classics in Classroom Award* for new teachers.

Angela Goddard is a professor of English Language who has taught English at every level from primary to higher education. Angela is Chair of Examiners for AS/A Level English Language at a UK exam board, and has written extensively on many of the topics she raises in her chapter.

John Gordon is Reader in English Education at the University of East Anglia, Norwich. He researches with primary and secondary teachers in UEA's Shared Literary Reading course. His books include *Researching Interpretive Talk around Literary Narrative Texts* (Routledge), *A Pedagogy of Poetry* (IoE) and *Teaching English in Secondary Schools* (SAGE).

Lucy Kelly is a senior lecturer in Education at the University of Bristol, predominantly working as a university tutor on the English PGCE programme. Her main research interest is reflective practice as a positive tool for teacher well-being. She is PI for the 'Reimagining the Diary: Diary-Keeping and Well-being for Teachers' research project.

Judith Kneen is Programme Leader for PGCE English at Cardiff Metropolitan University. Having worked for many years as an English teacher and head of department, and also with Gloucestershire advisory service, she currently works in higher education, specialising in initial teacher education. Her research interests include cross-curricular study, curriculum change and teacher agency.

Andrew McCallum is Director of the English and Media Centre (EMC) and was formerly a teacher and a PGCE course tutor. In his current role he develops resources for teachers to use with their pupils, runs CPD and writes about a range of English-related topics. He has a particular interest in the creativity of language and how this translates to classroom practice.

Sharon Morgan is a lecturer in Education at the Graduate School of Education in the University of Exeter. She currently teaches on the MA Education Online and Secondary English PGCE programmes. Her research interests lie in improving students' writing through developing their metalinguistic knowledge and awareness of how grammar can be used to contribute to meaning.

Rhian Mulligan is a senior lecturer in Teacher Education at Cardiff Metropolitan University. She worked as a Secondary English teacher, with responsibility for mentoring PGCE students and NQTs, before moving into Initial Teacher Education. She currently teaches on the PGCE Secondary English and BA Primary Education programmes. Rhian is also a subject tutor for TeachFirst Cymru.

Debra Myhill is Professor of Education at the University of Exeter, and Director of the Centre for Research in Writing. Her research interests focus principally on writing and the teaching of writing, particularly linguistic and metalinguistic development, the composing processes involved in writing, the talk-writing relationship and creative writing.

Ruth Newman is a senior lecturer in Language and Literacy Education in the Graduate School of Education at The University of Exeter. Her research interests focus on the role of talk in the teaching of language and literacy, including the role of dialogic metatalk in the development of metalinguistic understanding and writing. Ruth teaches mainly on the Secondary English PGCE programme and MA in Language and Literacy Education.

Rachel Roberts is lecturer in Secondary English education and lead for the Secondary English PGCE at the Institute of Education, University of Reading. Rachel taught in secondary schools for ten years and was Head of Film & Media, prior to moving into higher education. She is Chair of the National Association for the Teaching of English (NATE). Her research interests include: the teaching of writing, media, mentorship and Initial Teacher Education.

Lorna Smith is a senior lecturer in Education and leads the PGCE English course at the University of Bristol. Her research interests include creativity, the past and future development of the subject 'English' and building teachers' confidence as writers through the National Writing Project.

Julia Sutherland taught English and was a head of department in comprehensives and sixth-form colleges, mainly in London. Julia teaches on courses including ITE secondary English at the University of Sussex and her research is on reading, dialogic classroom discourses, teacher development, practitioner research, equity and social justice.

Helena Thomas is Course Leader of the Secondary English PGCE at Bath Spa University and was formerly an English teacher and adviser in London. Her research interests include imagination and curriculum and she is currently writing a doctoral thesis on English teachers' experiences of curriculum.

Annabel Watson is Senior Lecturer in Language Education in the Graduate School of Education at the University of Exeter, having previously taught English and Media Studies in secondary schools. She leads School Direct and Secondary English PGCE courses and conducts research in the field of writing and linguistic/ metalinguistic knowledge, and teacher perspectives and experiences.

Jo Westbrook taught English in London secondary schools for over nine years, including as Head of Department, followed by VSO work in teacher education in Uganda. Jo works at the University of Sussex on reading and comprehension in the UK and on multilingual teaching and inclusive pedagogies in the Global South.

Acknowledgements

We would like to thank Dr Andrew Green for creating the original *A Practical Guide to Teaching English*, establishing such a strong remit for this edition. We would also like to thank the editorial and production team at Routledge for their assistance in preparing this manuscript, and the series editors for their invaluable guidance.

Abbreviations

AB	Awarding Body
AQA	Assessment and Qualifications Alliance
BoE	Board of Education
CCEA	Council for the Curriculum, Examinations and Assessment
CfW	Curriculum for Wales
CPD	Continuing Professional Development
CSE	Certificate of Secondary Education
DCSF	Department for Children, Schools and Families
DCMS	Department for Digital, Culture, Media and Sport
DfE	Department for Education
DfEE	Department for Education and Employment
DfES	Department for Education and Skills
EACEA	Education, Audiovisual and Culture Executive Agency
EAL	English as an additional language
EMC	English and Media Centre
ERA	Education Reform Act
ESU	English-Speaking Union
GCE	General Certificate of Education
GCEA	General Certificate of Education Advanced Level
HET	Holocaust Educational Trust
HMI	Her Majesty's Inspector
ICT	Information and Communications Technology
IT	Information Technology
ITE	Initial Teacher Education
KS	Key Stage (of the National Curriculum for England)
LATE	London Association for the Teaching of English
NACCCE	The National Advisory Committee on Creative and Cultural Education
NC	National Curriculum
NCTE	National Council of Teachers of English
NFER	National Foundation for Educational Research
OCR	Oxford and Cambridge Regional
OECD	Organisation for Economic Cooperation and Development
OFSTED	Office for Standards in Education
O level	Ordinary level
PGCE	Postgraduate Certificate of Education

PISA	Performance in International Student Assessment
PoS	Programme of Study (in the National Curriculum for England)
PSHE	Personal, Social and Health Education
QAA	Quality Assurance Agency
QCA	Qualifications and Curriculum Authority
QCDA	Qualifications and Curriculum Development Agency
QTS	Qualified Teacher Status
RfP	Read for Pleasure
TED	Technology, Entertainment, Design
WHO	World Health Organisation

With the exception of Chapters 16 and 17, where Advanced Level learners are referred to as 'students', the word 'pupils' has been used throughout this book to denote children in schools.

Introduction

This book is founded on the concept of principled practice, the idea that we should approach teaching with an informed understanding of pedagogy, how children learn, and what values drive what we do in the classroom. Smagorinsky describes how different this is to the 'silver bullet' notion of 'best practice' (2009, p.15). While the idea of 'best' implies that there might be a fixed set of approaches to teaching English that are always superior, the concept of 'principled practice' instead focuses on thinking about *why* we teach in certain ways. This focus on *why* invites you to make links between research and practice, to reflect on your own values, to unpick the hidden assumptions that can lie beneath the surface of any teaching activity and to consider how teaching and learning always operate in *context*.

Teaching English can be an utter joy – sharing texts that you love, seeing pupils debate ideas with authority and question each other with open-mindedness, enthusing a class about studying Shakespeare, or Dickens, seeing the creativity sparkle in their writing. It's also often a challenge, requiring you to handle a huge range of interrelated knowledge and skills in two separate but intertwined curriculum areas of language and literature. This book therefore looks at principles for teaching across a wide variety of dimensions of English – ranging from the nitty-gritty of developing comprehension, or the fundamental 'talk for learning', to the importance of attending to Media and Drama in English, and the opportunities to strengthen learning through cross-curricular synergies. The book is designed so that you can read individual chapters in isolation, but you'll also find recurring themes around concepts of creativity, explicit teaching, scaffolding learning, authentic texts and generating enthusiasm and engagement. Throughout the book, we offer you activities designed to help you to crystallise the 'principles' that will inform your 'practice'.

Above all, we invite you to view your knowledge of how to teach as an evolving, flexible entity. You are not accumulating a fixed and static body of knowledge about practice, ready to transfer into your teaching; rather, you are learning about evidence-informed, research-inspired approaches to English that you can try out, reflect on and *develop* in your own classrooms. Just as research is always marching

DOI: 10.4324/9781003093060-1

forward, as a teacher the way that you teach will likely evolve and change considerably over time. We offer here one synthesis of current knowledge about teaching English, but the principles that underlie your teaching will ultimately be your own.

Annabel Watson
Ruth Newman

Chapter 1 The English curriculum in context: A conversation through time

LORNA SMITH

INTRODUCTION

This book aims to support you in becoming an inspiring, engaging, expert English teacher, with each chapter containing suggestions to help you develop your subject knowledge, pedagogy and practice. Yet before heading into the future in this way, we want to start by taking you back in time. You are joining a community with a rich history. Understanding some of that history – and the debates that have taken place throughout – provides you with a basis for reflection, and so begins to nurture the English teacher you aspire to be.

For the purposes of this chapter, the focus is on secondary English in England. If you are based in Northern Ireland, Scotland or Wales, it would be interesting to investigate how the history of subject English in your jurisdiction led to the current Northern Ireland Curriculum (CCEA, 2007), Curriculum for Excellence (Education Scotland, 2010) or Curriculum for Wales (Hwb, 2020) respectively. Indeed, comparing and contrasting the national curricula across – and even beyond – the four countries of the United Kingdom provides an indication of some of the inherent tensions about what English *is* and what it is *for*.

The chapter begins, then, with a summary of how the subject of secondary English in England has evolved and been influenced by key historical, cultural, social, political and economic factors across the past 150 years, through the lens of government documents. These include major reports and guidance to teachers (1905–88), followed by the six iterations of the National Curriculum (1989–2014). Together, these policy documents are important indicators of how English was (and is) 'officially' seen and valued. Of course, the official view only tells part of the story – there are hundreds of publications written by teachers, academics and other interested parties that provide more depth and nuance, many of which you will become familiar with over the course of your training and beyond. However, the official view is an important starting point, not least because it indicates what has been sanctioned and publicly funded.

At the end of this chapter you should be able to:

- articulate your own understanding of the purpose of English;
- understand how curriculum policy is a product of its time that informs subject content and influences how the role of English is perceived;

DOI: 10.4324/9781003093060-2

- respond to some of the debates around speaking, listening, reading and writing that have been rehearsed over the decades.

Activity 1.1: What is English for?

Before reading on, jot down 10–12 quick-fire responses to the question *What is English for?* (Imagine how you might respond if a pupil asks you this in a classroom: it is a query you will undoubtedly be faced with sooner or later.) Write each point on a separately sticky note or jot them into a whiteboard app that enables each point to be moved independently.

For example: studying English enables you …

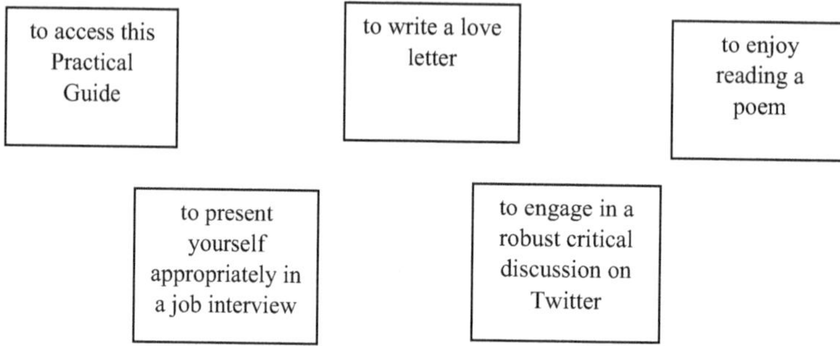

If you wish, revise or add to the list as you read the following historical overview. We return to your responses later in the chapter.

THE 1900S–1930S: SOWING THE SEEDS – THE BEGINNINGS OF SUBJECT ENGLISH

If you are asked to imagine a lesson in Victorian England, you might think of Charles Dickens' Mr M'Choakumchild and his boss, Mr Gradgrind, who aimed to fill their 'little pitchers […] full of facts' (1854, n.p.). Seeing such scenarios played out in life inspired the work of Matthew Arnold (1822–88), a respected inspector of government schools and critically recognised poet. Having observed first-hand the impact of payment-by-results, when the Revised Code of 1862 effectively forced Victorian teachers to practise learning by rote (as caricatured by Dickens), Arnold spent much of the rest of his life lobbying for all children in England – particularly the working class – to be culturally educated. He saw that '[i]t is in making endless additions to itself […] in endless growth in wisdom and beauty, that the spirit of the human race finds its ideal' (1869, p.47), and argued that if people could appreciate beauty through reading literature, they would become alive to opportunity, nourish their best selves and put the common good above personal gain; accordingly, appreciating culture is a means of 'growing and becoming' (1869, p.94) as individuals *and* a society. Arnold's beliefs inspired the development of the subject that became 'English'.

Around the turn of the twentieth century – in no small measure due to Arnold's work – the government recognised education as a national priority. The resulting Education Act of 1902 sought to strengthen the system for the local funding of elementary schools – the forerunners of the maintained system that served the majority working class – to ensure universal provision, and the school-leaving age was raised from 11 to 14 (although no distinction was initially made between primary and secondary phases). Elementary schools were free to develop their own curriculum (Shayer, 1972; Gillard, 2018). Meanwhile, middle- and upper-class children were educated in self-governing grammar or independent schools.

English was at that time gaining status as a university subject. Oxford opened a School of English in 1893; Cambridge followed suit in 1917 (Medway et al., 2014). Both offered English Literature; some graduates went on to teach English. However, English was mostly taught by generalist teachers without a university degree, particularly in the elementary schools. Official advice to support them was offered by the Board of Education in a new publication, *Suggestions for the Consideration of Teachers and Others Concerned in the Work of the Public Elementary Schools* (BoE, 1905/1912). It was emphasised that the advice given was tentative: it was for the teacher, as a trusted professional, to decide what was in the best interests of their pupils. The guidance promotes a child-centred, liberal approach, suggesting a teacher should promote 'active curiosity' and should 'know [...] and sympathise' with their pupils to 'adjust his (sic) mind to theirs' (BoE, 1912, p.11). In terms of English, it recommends that pupils be granted the 'liberty of free expression' (BoE, 1905/1912, p.12). It argues that confidence in oracy leads to a love of reading, and that freedom of choice of reading matter broadens pupils' perspectives. Decontextualised text-book written exercises are rejected in favour of written composition developed in parallel with the pupils' abilities and interests (BoE, 1905/1912). These approaches imply recognition of a link between creative practice, independent critical thought and the personal growth of individuals. The publication was so successful that it was frequently reprinted and launched a series. Nevertheless, the pedagogy that the *Suggestions* series advocated may not have been universally embraced, nor always effective: a letter to *The Times* complained 'The English boy cannot write English' (Fowler, 1910, p.1), and some were found to leave school functionally illiterate (Newbolt, 1921).

Many children educated in these early elementary schools would have become victims of the First World War (1914–18) which cost the lives of two million British soldiers (and wounded untold others) (Herbert, 2018). Yet, at its close, a more democratic society gradually emerged: women were finally given the vote, the strict class hierarchy began to dissolve, and white-collar jobs became available to the working class. The coalition government commissioned a report to consider 'the requirements of a liberal education, the needs of business, the professions, and public services, and the relation of English to other studies' (1921, p.4) as Britain began to rebuild. Sir Henry Newbolt, poet and civil servant, chaired the committee that led to the publication of *The Teaching of English in England* (1921). His report follows the humane approach of Arnold and the Board of Education in arguing that the most important result of education is not knowledge but 'experiences of human beings which are gained by contact with human beings' (1921, p.8). Newbolt places English as the 'keystone' (1921, p.6) in the centre of the educational arch, claiming English, an 'art, a means of creative expression, a record of human experience' (1921, p.11) is 'the true starting point and foundation from which all the rest [of the curriculum] must spring' (1921, p.14). He recommends a child-centred curriculum in which pupils are encouraged to question, engage in discussion, practise Drama. He encourages bilingualism, whereby pupils speak their local dialect (an important marker of personal identity) with confidence *as well as* become proficient in standard English. Pupils should read freely books chosen themselves, both canonical and contemporary – with guidance from the teacher, where necessary – and write critically and imaginatively for a real purpose and audience. The focus was on 'growing' the individual as a means of developing a cohesive society: Newbolt's aspiration was that future warfare could be prevented through enriched human understanding.

THE 1940S–1980S: CONTINUING TO CULTIVATE

Newbolt's optimism was sadly misplaced, as the Second World War (1939–45) began less than 20 years later. At its close, the Education Act of 1944 introduced the tripartite system (primary, secondary, further education), intended to rebuild the nation once again. There was no new subject guidance: individual schools continued to set their own curriculum. Evidence suggests that, in terms of English, Newbolt's recommendations were rarely practised: an His Majesty's Inspectorate report from 1951 found 'English in both grammar and modern schools to be competent but dull' (Medway et al., 2014, p.38). Textbooks and abstract grammar lessons dominated, perhaps because pupils at grammar or independent schools sat Ordinary levels (O levels) that were near-indistinguishable from those of the 1920s (Shayer, 1972); while the majority, destined for manual employment, did not sit school-leaving examinations at all. There was little pressure on teachers to inspire or pupils to achieve.

However, at around this same time, despite (or because of) a lack of official steer, practice in English developed markedly in some quarters. This post-war period saw the founding of the grass-roots London Association for the Teaching of English (LATE) in 1947 (Gibbons, 2013). LATE teachers – daringly – taught modern as well as nineteenth-century novels and began to publish pupil-friendly textbooks to replace formal grammar books (Medway et al., 2014). The movement spread: the National Association for the Teaching of English (NATE) was born in 1963.

The view that subject English should centre around the personal growth of the individual whilst developing their literacy skills was given fresh impetus in the 1960s when the incoming Labour government abolished the 11+ in most areas and introduced the Certificate of Secondary Education (CSE) for those not destined for O level. This resulted in the reinvigoration of the secondary English curriculum as all pupils (and teachers) had a tangible goal. Publications arising from a major international conference, including *Growth through English* (Dixon, 1967) and *Creativity in English* (Summerfield, 1968) – the titles of which indicate their child-centred, liberal perspective – became seminal texts for English teachers.

Nevertheless, despite the interest shown by educationalists in creative, child-centred learning, such practice was not universally accepted. The political establishment was fearful that school English was declining 'in a climate of unchecked creativity' (Bullock, 1975, p.6), which was one factor that led the education secretary, Margaret Thatcher, to commission the second major report on English teaching, *A Language for Life* (Bullock, 1975). Interestingly, the report advises *against* the prescriptivist approach Thatcher might have hoped for. Bullock – himself a distinguished, writer and academic – presents talking, listening, reading and writing as a 'unity' (1975, p.xxxv). The teacher's role was to develop pupils' confidence and fluency in language. Language development and learning are presented as heuristic, both dependent on 'discovery' (1975, p.50). In a striking metaphor, Bullock suggests language functions as a 'filing pin' (1975, p.48) capable of storing an infinite amount of information, enabling children to 'engage in critical and creative thinking' (1975, p. 79) to connect new knowledge to the familiar and the familiar to the new. The uncontextualised teaching of spelling and prescriptive grammar is discouraged: the report recommends that written work is a meaningful result of honed discussion and debate.[1]

THE 1980S: COMBINING PERSPECTIVES? TOWARDS A NATIONAL CURRICULUM

When Thatcher became Conservative prime minister in 1979, Britain was a new member of the fledgling European Economic Community but struggling with high unemployment and high inflation as traditional manual jobs were lost to automation. Seeking to improve Britain's economy and place in the free market, the government decided to introduce a free market economy into education: according to neoliberal orthodoxy, performance measures in the form of national testing would determine which schools should thrive and which should fail. Also, traditionalists in Thatcher's party voiced a desire for state control of curriculum content (Gillard, 2018). A national curriculum[2] could satisfy both needs.

The next two official reports on English teaching, *The Teaching of the English Language* (Kingman, 1988) and *English for Ages 5–16* (Cox, 1989a), were commissioned to support the development of the National Curriculum. Their contrasting messages are an interesting indication of the different perspectives on the place and role of English. In a departure from policy documents that preceded it, the semantic field in Kingman's report is strikingly authoritarian. Echoing the prevailing political mood, it promotes language as enabling humans to 'name [what] we have power over' (1988, p.7). It states that 'accurate use of the rules and conventions' are important 'to increase the freedom of the individual' and promote 'personal liberty' (1988, p.3). There is a focus on developing pupils' language skills to meet the needs of commerce. The teaching of 'our' literature is seen as necessary to develop pupils' vocabulary and English cultural knowledge rather than enrich their personal lives (1988, p.11). Themes that can be traced through previous reports are conspicuously absent: the noun 'growth' appears five times, but always concerning linguistic and intellectual growth, never 'personal growth'.

Professor Brian Cox, on the other hand – a poet, writer and academic – presents a broader view of English, seeking to unite the different constituencies (Cox, 1989a). However, his identification of the two underpinning core purposes of English is significant:

> First, English contributes to the personal development of the individual child because of the cognitive functions of both spoken and written language in exploratory learning and in organising and making sense of experiences [...] Secondly, **English contributes to preparation for the adult world**.
>
> (1989a, p.59; bold original)

So, while he stresses that they are interlinked, Cox follows earlier guidance in presenting the *personal development* of individuals foremost, with language as a means of *making sense of experiences* that ready the child for adulthood. He argues that English should take pupils beyond the core practical skills of Speaking and Listening, Reading and Writing to explore their own and others' linguistic and cultural identities, to use language for organisational purposes, to 'create and keep artistic artefacts – poems, plays, stories' (ibid.). This reinforces the notion that studying English should give pupils the ability and agency to deploy language *as they choose*. It is made explicit that 'multi-cultural, multi-lingual society' (Cox, 1989a, p.58) should be celebrated, whether or not the school is culturally mixed.

Cox and his committee conducted extensive research in the preparation of their report and were keen to represent teachers. The report identifies five 'views' summarising English teachers' thoughts on the purpose of subject English: personal growth, cross-curricular, adult needs, cultural heritage and cultural analysis (Cox,

1989a, p.60). These became popularly known as Cox's models, which we now invite you to explore through Activity 1.2.

Activity 1.2: Your positioning

Take the purposes of English you identified in Task 1 and arrange them according to Cox's models:

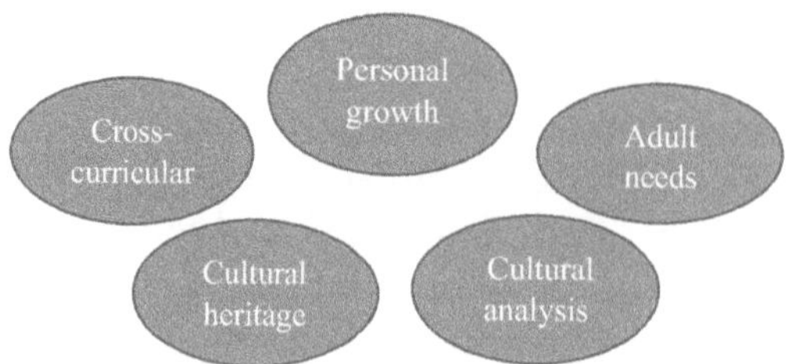

Does your view of English have a particular angle or bias? Do you see some views as more important than others? Compare your ideas with your course colleagues and discuss the similarities and differences.

1989–2014: ENGLISH ACROSS SIX NATIONAL CURRICULA – FROM PERSONAL GROWTH TO ENGLISH COMMODIFIED?

Cox's report provided the basis for the inaugural National Curriculum for English (DfE/WO, 1989). For the first time, English content was statutory, tested ultimately by the new General Certificate of Secondary Education (GCSE); and from 1992, it became subject to inspection by the Office for Standards in Education.

Cox's curriculum was 'generally welcomed' by the profession, but less so by the government (Marshall, 2000, p.6). For romantics, it did not sufficiently celebrate the canon of English literature (Cox had resisted calls to include lists of prescribed texts), while modernisers saw it as insufficiently rigorous in developing skills that could arrest Britain's relative economic decline in the more globalised market economy (Morgan, 2014). The curriculum was therefore replaced just a few years later by a slimmed-down, skills-based version. It introduced lists of prescribed texts from which teachers should select (DfE/WO, 1995).

In 1997 a New Labour government famously came to power on an 'Education, Education, Education' ticket. Cool Britannia was making social and cultural waves, and the dot.com boom was generating jobs and investment. A high-skills, high-trust education system was seen as necessary for this post-manufacturing economy to thrive (Morgan, 2014). However, there remained an uneasy tension between the growing understanding of the importance of developing a flexible, creative workforce (NACCE, 1999) and the need to succeed against global economic competitors. The government's response was cautious: it introduced a third curriculum (DfEE/QCA, 1999), even more prescriptive than that of the previous Conservative government, focusing specifically on work-based skills to 'raise standards' (1999, p.3) – the implication being that national prosperity would rise commensurately. Accordingly, this curriculum focused on preparing young people for employment: it foregrounds developing 'confidence in speaking [...] for *public and formal purposes*' (1999, p.31, my emphasis). Pupils should learn to read primarily to 'extract meaning' (1999, p.34) rather than for pleasure. There is a nod to personal growth in that 'creative, aesthetic and literary' (1999, p.39) writing is encouraged, but the general tone is formal. Even when this curriculum was revised five years later with a renewed focus on developing personal and creative skills across the curriculum (DfES/QCA, 2004), the English-specific orders were unchanged – formality and employability continued to dominate.

The next Labour government again revised the curriculum. This fifth iteration presents English through four key concepts: Competence, Creativity, Cultural Understanding and Critical Understanding. The inclusion of the Four Cs – as they were inevitably named – explicitly foregrounding creativity and understanding, suggests a partial return to the personal growth view. This is echoed in the emphasis that pupils should become 'enthusiastic and critical' (QCA, 2007b, p.61) readers for pleasure and write 'clearly and coherently [...] imaginatively, creatively and thoughtfully' (QCA, 2007b, p.67). However, ever-increasing pressure on teachers to ensure the highest possible examination results (Anderson, 2013; Smith, 2018) meant that genuine creative opportunities were, in practice, curtailed and constrained (Yandell and Brady, 2016).

When Conservative Michael Gove became education secretary on the election of the Coalition government in 2010, he could point to Britain's comparatively lowly rank on the Programme for International Student Assessment (PISA) tests[3] as evidence that Labour's approach was not working and so launched a wholescale programme of educational change. Although he retained and strengthened some Labour policies (including academisation and performance measures), he sought to change the National Curriculum as quickly as possible.

Gove positioned himself as the champion of a knowledge-rich curriculum based on ED Hirsch's arguments for cultural literacy and Michael Young's concept of 'powerful knowledge' (Morgan, 2014; Yandell and Brady, 2016). The idea of equity was reframed: rather than being concerned with personal development, or fitting a child with the creative, flexible skills needed for the world of work, Gove's mission was to increase pupils' access to employment through providing them with specifically sanctioned sets of 'essential' (DfE, 2014b, p.5) knowledge that would, in theory, level the playing field for those lacking 'cultural capital'. Gove's reading of Young is perhaps a misreading. For example, he advocated teaching 'a *permanent* body of knowledge which should be passed on from generation to generation' (*The Guardian* 09.05.08, my emphasis), seemingly ignorant of Young's recognition that powerful knowledge is flexible according to need (Burns, 2018). However, Gove brushed aside criticism from educationists, writers, subject bodies and even three of the four members of his own expert advisory panel (White and Brown, 2012; Mansell, 2012; Wintour, 2012). In the resulting sixth national curriculum (sic) for English, the word 'knowledge' appears 20 times, while 'creativity' (and any word with the 'create' root) is absent (DfE, 2014b). While this curriculum does claim to promote a 'love' (2014b, p.13) of reading, there is a sense that the requirement is more for pupils to appreciate the 'depth and power' (DfE, 2014b, p.18) of the English literary heritage than enrich their personal and broader cultural understanding, particularly as the texts examined at GCSE are exclusively British. 'Spoken Language' replaces 'Speaking and Listening' – with an emphasis on formal presentational English – and examination-specific writing skills are prioritised over expressive writing.

Proponents of this curriculum can claim success by pointing to PISA figures indicating a marked increase in pupil attainment in reading (NFER, 2019), with the UK rising from 27 to 14 in the 2018 rankings. However, the same PISA report notes that pupils in the UK are less happy than previously. Critics further suggest that the sheer volume of subject knowledge necessary to succeed in the revised GCSEs weighs down teachers and pupils more than ever (Bomford, 2018; Perryman and Calvert, 2020), with balance between content and accuracy reframed such that pupils attain higher grades if their work is boring and accurate, than if it has flair, originality and some errors (Smith, 2019). English teachers are concerned that the numbers taking Advanced (A) Level English Literature and A Level English Language are falling (Turner, 2019). This, coupled with evidence that fewer young people than ever are reading for pleasure (Videbaek, 2020), suggests that the current curriculum may be detrimental to subject English.

Activity 1.3: Creating a curriculum

This chapter has shown some of the tensions around how English is understood. It is a live, dynamic debate. As a beginning teacher of English, where do *you* think the emphasis should lie? Does the curriculum adequately represent your notions of the subject?

The statements in the boxes below summarise some of the different positions on what English is and what it is for. All have featured, variously, in the policy documents summarised above.

Based on your reading of this chapter and your wider reading:

i. place a mark between these contrasting statements to represent your position;
ii. in each case, add two or three bullet points to support your views. Can you suggest counter arguments that a colleague with a *different* perspective might offer?

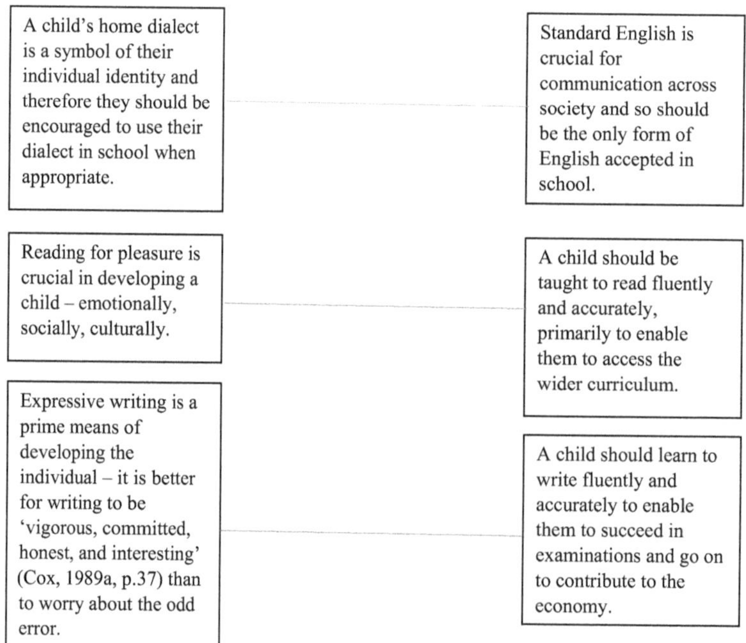

As you journey through the chapters of this book and consider the advice and recommendations therein, you could revisit this page and reconsider your perspectives, annotating the diagrams to justify your new positioning.

CONCLUDING THOUGHTS

Of course, the positions described above are not true binaries. Many English teachers would wish to help pupils succeed for all these reasons. However, the notion that remains the most popular with English teachers (Goodwyn, 2016; Smith, 2018) is the humanist, pupil-centred, personal growth view of English characterised by the statements in the left-hand column, as developed in the early policy documents (BoE, 1905/1912; Newbolt, 1921; Bullock, 1975; Cox, 1989a). Yet successive revisions to the National Curriculum – while intended to empower pupils to succeed in the employment market (and so meet political and financial imperatives) – have arguably limited the scope for this style of English to be practised. Ironically, it could be argued that opportunities for pupils to develop the collaborative, problem-solving and risk-taking skills crucial for success in the post-millennium economy (Barron et al., 1997; NACCCE, 1999) are curtailed as a result.

SUMMARY AND KEY POINTS

- English is rich and complex; it resists simple definition. English as presented in curriculum policy does not necessarily reflect how English teachers view the subject. You need to consider carefully what you believe English should 'be' and 'do' to inform your own developing practice.
- As a new teacher, you are becoming a member of a community that reaches back well over a century: to be an English teacher is to become part of a tradition.
- Understanding the arguments rehearsed throughout the subject's history helps orient you on the road to becoming a reflective, reflexive practitioner of the future.

KEY RESOURCES

1. For a comprehensive summary of education policy in England, with links to all the documents discussed in this chapter, see the excellent website *Education in England: A History of Our Schools* available at: www.educationengland.org.uk/history/
2. In *English in the National Curriculum*, chapter 2 of *English for Ages 5 to 16* (Cox, 1989a, pp.57–60), Cox sets out in detail what he sees as the place and role of English, drawing on the ideas of English teachers and education experts he consulted. To what extent do you agree?
3. Compare this to the parallel curriculum statement that opens the English curriculum under which you work, whether in England (DfE, 2014b), Northern Ireland (CCEA, 2007), Wales (HWB, 2020) or Scotland (Education Scotland, 2010).

NOTES

1. Another key recommendation was that English teachers should be properly qualified – at the time, there were few English specialists. Teachers of other subjects were given English classes on top of their other responsibilities. This is perhaps one reason why many did not engage with creative, pupil-centred approaches and resorted to textbooks.

2. The 'National' Curriculum was a misnomer from the start. It applied to only England and Wales and only to maintained schools. (The separate Curriculum for Wales was introduced after devolution in 1999.)
3. PISA was introduced by the Organisation for Economic Cooperation and Development in 2000. Testing takes place every three years.

Chapter 2 Spoken language and talk for learning

RUTH NEWMAN

INTRODUCTION

This chapter explores talk as a medium for teaching and learning, but also spoken language as an object of study in the subject of English. Focusing first on the theoretical value of talk for learning, the important role of the teacher in fostering interactions with pupils and the *repertoires* of talk available to teachers of English are explored. The chapter then reflects briefly on the somewhat chequered history of spoken language in the curriculum, and how spoken language features across UK curricula and examination syllabi. Finally, the chapter considers the characteristics of different spoken language forms, and strategies and activities to develop pupils' spoken language in the classroom are offered.

At the end of this chapter you should be able to:

- understand the relationship between talking, listening and learning;
- understand the concepts of authoritative and exploratory talk, as part of a *repertoire* of classroom talk;
- understand the curriculum expectations for spoken language;
- explore strategies for teaching spoken language.

Neil Mercer and Steve Hodgkinson point out in their introduction to the book *Exploring Talk in School* (2008), that while one of the challenges facing children as they grow up in the twenty-first century is how to become productive members of a technological society, we perhaps take too much for granted a more fundamental aspect of the human condition – our use of spoken language to communicate with each other. It is this human capacity for spoken language that enables us to talk constructively to those around us and to the 'physically disembodied contacts throughout the world' (Dawes, 2001, p.126); it is also 'central to both intellectual development and to becoming an effective member of society' (Mercer and Littleton, 2007, p.13), enabling us to coordinate activities and combine mental capacities (Mercer, 2000, p.105). Developing pupils' spoken language, therefore, is to prepare them for participation in an increasingly interconnected and unpredictable world.

DOI: 10.4324/9781003093060-3

A NOTE ON DEFINITIONS

In this chapter, the term 'spoken language' is adopted because of its use in the National Curriculum in England; it is used here interchangeably with the wider term 'talk'. It is important to note, however, that there is variation in terms used across UK curricula and that these terms have changed over time; what these terms imply about the nature and value of 'talk' is an ongoing subject of debate. These issues are considered briefly, later in the chapter.

TALK: A TOOL FOR TEACHING AND LEARNING

Talk is fundamental for learning – in English, and across the curriculum – and it is crucial to consider how you, as a teacher of English, can best utilise this educational tool. Take a moment to consider the many things that talk allows us to do: it enables us to communicate our ideas, interact and receive feedback (Howe, 1992). In the classroom, spoken language is the dominant language mode used by teachers, the dominant language mode used by pupils and, crucially, it is the medium for teaching and learning (Mercer and Littleton, 2007). For teachers, spoken language is an essential pedagogic tool.

A considerable body of evidence, gathered in over 40 years of educational research on classroom talk, demonstrates clearly the benefits of spoken language for learning and cognitive development (Resnick et al., 2015). And it is from some of this earlier, seminal work, that the famous and oft-cited claim that *reading and writing float on a sea of talk* arose (Britton, 1970, p.29). Much of this research on classroom talk is underpinned by Vygotksy's (1978) ideas about the socially constructed nature of learning: from this perspective, language is seen as fundamental to the process of constructing knowledge and shaping learning, and *interactions* between pupils and more knowledgeable others (e.g. parents, siblings, peers, teachers) are regarded as a mechanism through which knowledge is constructed and learning 'internalised'. Learning, therefore, takes place in the interactions between teacher and pupils. In the classroom, these interactions enable teachers and pupils to jointly construct knowledge, problem-solve and reason – all contributing to the development of pupils' thinking. The way teachers use questioning, respond to, build on and interconnect pupils' answers is crucial for the development of pupils' understandings.

You may have noticed how classroom talk so far has been characterised in dynamic terms – to *construct, problem-solve, reason, respond, build, connect* – and this highlights how it is the *active* participation in dialogue, between teachers and pupils or between peers, which supports the development of new knowledge. This characterisation of classroom talk – talk which can be described as 'exploratory' – is messy and unpredictable and, therefore, different from the type of talk you might use during, for example, a presentation. However, it is also important to stress that participating purposefully in learning dialogues also involves active *listening* from speakers (including teachers) – to make sure that ideas shared have been understood. There are also times during a lesson when it is just the teacher who does the talking – to explain a concept, deliver instructions or even steer a dialogue in a better direction – and this 'authoritative' input is also an important aspect of classroom talk which supports learning.

Teaching – in English, and across the curriculum – therefore, involves utilising a *repertoire* of talk, and this repertoire is fostered by what is called a 'dialogic' pedagogy – an approach to teaching which values and utilises classroom talk. Dialogic classrooms offer wide-ranging opportunities for pupils to listen to and engage in different talk forms, providing pupils with the best chance to develop learning talk repertoires on which different kinds of thinking and understanding are predicated (Alexander, 2018).

TEACHER-PUPIL INTERACTIONS

The section above points to the complexity of classroom talk and the skill involved in promoting and managing this. Whilst classroom talk comes in many forms, managing whole-class interactions is a major part of teaching. In high-quality whole-class interactions, teachers listen carefully to pupils' responses, question and extend pupils' thinking and coordinate peers' responses to foster dialogue.

You can see an example of this in the lesson below where the teacher draws out and extends pupils' ideas about Mr Wormwood, a character from Roald Dahl's *Matilda*: the teacher's aim here is for pupils to understand that the adjectives – 'small and ratty' – suggest something unpleasant about the character.

Activity 2.1

Read the transcript below and look for evidence of the teacher developing pupils' understandings.

TEACHER: [...] So, let's look at this quote now: (reads) Mr Wormwood was a small, ratty looking man [...] What kind of person do you think Mr Wormwood is? From that description?
SUZIE: He's small.
TEACHER: He's small [...] you've taken from the description. Read between the lines.
BROOKE: I think Mr Wormwood is a bit of a dirty man.
TEACHER: Ok, why do you think that?
BROOKE: In the text it says that he has a ratty moustache.
TEACHER: And what do you think of when you think of 'ratty', Sam?
SAM: Like he's really dirty [...] has a lot of food in it when he's been eating.
TEACHER: Now, Brooke and Sam are starting to infer. It doesn't say Mr Wormwood is a dirty man, it says that he has a thin, ratty moustache, and that has given the idea that all is not quite as it seems with this man.

This transcript is taken from an authentic classroom (see Newman and Watson, 2020), but edited very slightly to exemplify how teachers can coordinate turns.

At the beginning of this exchange, the teacher asks a **question** to elicit pupils' ideas about the character, asking 'what kind of person do you think Mr Wormwood is?' This **open question** prompts Suzie to say that he's 'small', but the teacher wants to develop this response to a more sophisticated inference, so she encourages pupils to 'read between the lines'. This prompts Brooke to suggest that Mr Wormwood is a bit of a 'dirty' man. The teacher picks up and **extends** this response through **exploratory questioning** – asking '**why**' Brooke thinks this. She then invites another pupil, Sam, to build on Brooke's response, **coordinating** a sequence of interaction and **extending** their ideas. She closes this exchange by reformulating pupils' responses in a clear authoritative explanation.

This short sequence illustrates how teachers can 'orchestrate' discussion in a way which develops understandings, and which organises the interchange of ideas. The teacher could have closed down the exchange sooner and provided her own explanation but, instead, she uses questions to support pupils in constructing and verbalising their own response. Asking pupils to elaborate on their responses, using *why* and *how* questions is a powerful way to develop pupils' thinking. It is important to note too that the way in which the teacher responds to pupils' suggestions, shows that she has **listened** – and we can 'see' this in the way she 'picks up' and reformulates ideas. It is through listening carefully to pupils' responses that teachers can determine levels of understandings or identify misunderstandings. This also helps teachers connect what pupils already know to new ideas or concepts.

As noted earlier, classroom talk comes in many forms and fulfils lots of different purposes. The sequence here is driven by a clear objective – the teacher wants pupils to recognise the effect of Dahl's word choice. If, for example, the teacher's aim was to recap prior learning, she might have used short, closed questions to check what pupils remember; or, if the teacher recognised misunderstandings in pupils' responses, she might have provided a lengthier, more detailed authoritative explanation. The point is that teachers use talk purposefully to serve different functions: they *adapt* their talk to suit the learning purpose, and in response to their pupils' needs and understandings – which is why it's a complex teaching skill which takes time to develop! Reflecting on the quality of your teacher talk is a useful thing to be doing throughout your training (and beyond!).

SPOKEN LANGUAGE IN THE ENGLISH CURRICULUM

Despite considerable evidence of its value and importance, spoken language in the curriculum has a fairly chequered history (see Jones, 2017 for extensive discussion). Spoken language is variously 'weighted' (in terms of value, content and assessment) across different curricula and examination syllabi, and its status has shifted over time. For example, it could be argued that the 2014 iteration of the curriculum in England downgrades spoken language and places comparatively greater emphasis on reading and writing. This perhaps reflects the view expressed by Robin Alexander in 2003 that oracy in England is at 'best a poor relation' to reading and writing. It is pertinent to relate this discussion too to issues of definition (noted at the beginning of the chapter): consider, for example, how 'spoken language' was referred to as 'speaking and listening' in previous iterations of the curriculum, how the Welsh curriculum refers to 'oracy' (2016), and how the Scottish curriculum of 2010 refers to 'listening and talking'. What do you think these differences might imply about the nature and value of 'talk'? 'Speaking and listening' and 'spoken language', for example, are terms that have been criticised for not capturing the importance of and the skills associated with 'oracy', a term which encapsulates spoken language as a more fundamental part of literacy (Wilkinson, 1965). And this provides only a flavour of the contested place of spoken language in curriculum and associated policy initiatives!

There is also quite considerable variation in the forms of spoken language featured across the curricula of England, Wales, Scotland and Northern Ireland. The curriculum for England (2014) places quite considerable emphasis on presentational types of talk – for example, presentation and speeches – and Standard English (SE), whereas the curriculum for Wales (see 2016) places emphasis on interacting with others, and notes other dialects and languages, in addition to SE.

Requirements for spoken language also vary across Key Stage 4 examinations, and tasks differ across specifications. For example, General Certificate of Secondary Education (GCSE) English Language pupils currently present information and ideas in a spoken presentation, but this spoken language endorsement is reported as a separate grade (Pass, Merit, Distinction or Not Classified) and does not contribute to the result of the GCSE qualification; in contrast, speaking and listening is an assessed component of the Northern Ireland Council for the Curriculum, Examinations and Assessment GCSE English Language, which involves presentation, discussion and role play. You need, of course, to make sure that you are clear about the curriculum expectations relevant to your context.

Activity 2.2

Find out how spoken language features in your curriculum and examination syllabi. You might then be interested to learn more about how, in previous iterations of the English GCSE, what was then called 'speaking and listening' was an assessed component. Concerns about marking and moderation led to its uncoupling from reading and writing assessments, but many felt that this move served to devalue spoken language and disadvantage pupils. Take a look at the articles and report to learn more about the debates:

- www.gov.uk/government/speeches/michael-gove-speaks-aboutthe-importance-of-teaching
- https://dera.ioe.ac.uk/17586/1/2013-04-25-gcse-english-consultation-on-the-removal-of-speaking-and-listening.pdf
- www.nate.org.uk/illuminate-making-speaking-and-listening-matter/

SPOKEN LANGUAGE IN THE ENGLISH CLASSROOM

We've considered so far the importance of talk for learning, and how spoken language features in curricula. The remaining sections of this chapter consider the opportunities the subject of English provides for utilising and developing spoken language, and offer practical approaches to the teaching of spoken language.

Activity 2.3

The list below shows a few of the many opportunities that the subject of English provides for utilising and developing spoken language. Can you think of any others?

- Debating an issue, for example, badger culling
- Role play, for example, question Macbeth and Lady Macbeth in 'Court'
- Presenting, for example, give a presentation to persuade an audience
- Collaborative talk, for example, in groups, discuss and rank characters from *An Inspector Calls* according to status
- Pair talk, for example, generate ideas for writing

These activities present significant opportunities for developing pupils' spoken language – for example, by developing pupils' ability to give a formal presentation or to participate constructively in group discussion. The activities here also illustrate how in the English classroom, spoken language is fundamental in the teaching of reading and writing. In English, then, spoken language is a *medium* for teaching reading and writing, but also the *object* of study.

It is important not to overestimate pupils' spoken language skills: not all pupils come to secondary school able to engage constructively in discussion and debate, or the other types of talk noted above and in curricula. Being able to 'talk' does not mean that pupils have the communication or interpersonal skills required to engage in constructive dialogues. As Mercer and Littleton say:

> social experience does not provide all children with the same language experiences, so we cannot assume that all children naturally have access to the same opportunities for developing their use of language as a tool for learning, reasoning and solving problems.
>
> (2007 p.2)

It's also important to consider the multilingual and multicultural compositions of many classrooms: pupils may well bring with them different cultural experiences and expectations of spoken language. These factors all have implications for your teaching, and particularly the way that you scaffold spoken language skills.

TEACHING SPOKEN LANGUAGE

When teaching spoken language, it's important to be clear about the type of talk that you are teaching – its characteristics – and its purpose. Douglas Barnes (2008) distinguished between the functions of exploratory talk (through which pupils try out ideas and organise their own thoughts) and presentational talk (where talk is adjusted to the needs of an audience). Giving a formal presentation is an example of presentational talk, as is telling a story, or delivering a speech. Presentational talk shouldn't be scripted, and should be adapted according to purpose and audience: a formal presentation, for example, requires Standard English, while we might draw more on different dialects and use more colloquialisms when telling a story – it is this 'code-switching', according to form and audience, that needs support. Group discussion – sometimes called 'collaborative talk' – is an exploratory type of talk which requires a range of interpersonal and communicative skills. It is extremely useful for pupils to engage in exploratory talk in *preparation* for presentational talk – for example, discussing and rehearsing lines with a partner, or working collaboratively to develop a key argument for a presentation. The remainder of this section suggests approaches to teaching presentation and collaborative talk.

Presentation

When working on presentations, you might decide to assign topics to pupils, or you might give pupils a choice. This decision is informed by your knowledge of your pupils; either way, give pupils plenty of time to research and talk their ideas through. You need to be clear about the purpose of the presentation: for example, is it to persuade an audience, or to explain an interest or hobby? You also need to be clear about the audience and level of formality required, because this should have a bearing on the language choices pupils make.

The teaching sequence below supports pupils to recognise the performance skills involved in delivering a presentation, and supports them to plan, structure and memorise key points. Note too how this sequence scaffolds pupils' awareness of the language used in presentations and provides pupils with an opportunity to reflect on and evaluate their talk. It is a sequence intended to scaffold learning but also develop confidence.

A focus on prior knowledge and experience

- At the beginning of a new topic, it's good to establish what pupils already know/ have experienced: for example, ask pupils what they think makes a good/bad presentation and collate ideas.

A focus on performance skills

- Watch a presentation on mute (e.g. *TED Talks* – link below).
- Ask pupils to discuss how the speaker uses body language and gesture to engage the audience.
- Watch the presentation again with audio.
- Ask pupils to pinpoint the key message.
- Discuss how performance elements are used to present and reinforce the key message, for example, use of pause, eye contact, varying tone.
- Build in activities to develop pupils' confidence with performance elements. For example, ask pupils to mimic a few selected lines from the presentation, focusing on pace, pause, tone and gesture; ask pupils to deliver a line in different ways – for example, slow/fast, varying tone/ monotone, placing emphasis on different words – and discuss the effect; to develop eye contact, one pupil can stand at the front of the class and 'lead' the rest of the group with their eyes – for example, looking down – pupils sit down; looking left – pupils move left (best done in a drama studio or outdoor space!).

A focus on structure

- Discuss the structure of the presentation.
- Draw out, for example, how speakers greet the audience/introduce themselves, introduce the topic; outline the presentation's goals and structure of the presentation; develop key points, each with a mini conclusion and transition point; finish with a strong conclusion, perhaps summing up what has been said and reiterating key messages; questions.
- Listen to the presentation one final time, this time, using audio only.
- Ask pupils to note and then discuss any particular words or phrases which the speaker uses to structure the presentation.
- Through questioning, support pupils to make connections between the speaker's language choices and their intended audience.
- Create a bank of phrases which can be used to structure a presentation, noting how choices alter the level of formality, for example, on behalf of; welcome to; hi everyone; I would like to take this opportunity to …; the purpose of this presentation is to …; let me start with …; to sum up …; I'd now like to move to …; turning our attention now to …; I'd like to expand on …; to return to the original point…; it should be emphasised that …; I am happy to answer your questions now …

A focus on planning and rehearsal

- After pupils have had time to research their presentation topics/collate ideas – ideally through exploratory talk with peers – ask them to sketch out their key messages.
- From this, pupils can begin to use the phrase bank above to sequence their messages. It's important that pupils do not write or rely on scripts, but are instead sequencing key messages, perhaps in bullet form.
- When first rehearsing and memorising the content and structure of the presentation, it can help to try to memorise just the phrases which lead into the key messages (e.g. firstly). Rehearsing a condensed version of the presentation in this way is helpful, reduces reliance on scripted versions and achieves a more conversational style.
- Once pupils are confident with the condensed version of their presentation, they can start to rehearse with more detail, paying more attention to performance elements.
- It's good to talk with pupils about what to do should they forget what they were going to say – for example, pause, take a breath, improvise, for instance by reiterating an earlier point.

A focus on delivery and reflection

- When it comes to pupils delivering their presentations, you might choose to stagger presentations over a sequence of lessons (listening to presentations for a whole lesson can be hard work!). You could also consider getting pupils to present to smaller groups.
- Before pupils deliver their presentations, it's a good idea to talk with the wider class about your expectations – pupils should be expected to listen carefully, maintain eye contact and think about a question to ask. It's really important to place importance on the role of the *listener*, not just the speaker.
- After the presentation, provide an opportunity to reflect. For example, ask pupils to point out what the presenter did well, and how these things match with their expectations of what makes a 'good' presentation.

Collaborative talk

You may have noticed how the sequence above draws pupils' attention to the conventions and language of presentations: the sequence uses 'metatalk' – talk about talk – to encourage pupils to think about the form and function of talk more explicitly (Newman, 2017). Observing and analysing examples of talk is a helpful way to promote metatalk, and enables pupils to see and hear how speakers fulfil the expectations of different talk types and adapt their language to an audience. Showing pupils examples of 'bad' talk can be a particularly effective springboard for discussion – it is often easier to identify what speakers do badly!

Thinking now about collaborative talk, the framework in Table 2.1 captures some of the interpersonal skills required for effective group discussion. The framework captures three interrelated dimensions of collaborative talk: *participating, understanding and managing*. You could use this framework to support analysis of collaborative talk, but also as a reflective tool, for example, asking pupils to compare their collaborative talk to the framework. The framework is intended to emphasise the importance of not only listening, but trying to understand what others have

Table 2.1 Framework for collaborative talk

	During collaborative talk, speakers:
Participating	Speak clearly and concisely Share experiences and challenge ideas without conflict Show respect for other people's ideas Build on other people's ideas
Understanding	Listen carefully in order to understand what's being said Listen with an open mind Use questions to explore ideas and ensure understanding Make sure that they and everyone in the group understand
Managing	Manage the talk to make sure that goals are met Keep the talk focused on the goal Manage challenges and objections with sensitivity Encourage others to contribute

Source: Newman (2017).

said – understanding that should be evident in the way speakers respond. In talk which is divergent or disputational, speakers often pursue their own agendas or arguments, instead of trying to understand and build on the ideas of others. The framework draws attention to the skill required in managing talk – in keeping the talk focused and achieving the task goal.

Activity 2.4

Sketch out a teaching sequence for collaborative talk that utilises the framework presented in Table 2.1 and provides an opportunity for 'metatalk'.

SUMMARY AND KEY POINTS

- Talk is a pedagogical tool for teaching and learning. Not only does fostering rich and varied classroom talk prepare pupils to participate in society, but it develops pupils' capacity for thinking and learning: as Halliday puts it, 'when children learn language, they are not simply engaging in one kind of learning among many; rather, they are learning the foundation of learning itself' (1993, p.93).
- Spoken language needs to be taught explicitly in the English classroom, with room for reflection and 'metatalk'.
- Talk is important not only for your pupils' learning but also your own. Dialogues which support you to reflect critically on your practice are a fundamental aspect of your initial teacher education, and beyond. Exploratory professional dialogues should expand your thinking by enabling you to consider your practice from different theoretical and contextual perspectives. We hope that your own experience of learning dialogues also helps you create 'communities of enquiry' (Mercer, 2000) in your own classroom, and exemplify the dialogic principle (Alexander 2018).

KEY RESOURCES

1. To learn more about 'dialogic pedagogy', read Robin Alexander's *Towards Dialogic Teaching: Rethinking Classroom Talk* (2017). Cambridge, UK: Dialogos, and his article Alexander, R. (2018), Developing Dialogic Teaching: Genesis, Process, Trial. *Research Papers in Education*. 33 (5), pp.561–98, which discusses a study that revealed the positive impact of a dialogic pedagogy on pupil learning: https://educationendowmentfoundation.org.uk/projects-and-evaluation/projects/dialogic-teaching/
2. Britton, J. (1970) *Language and Learning*. London: Penguin Books.
3. Mercer, N. and Hodgkinson, S. (eds.) (2008) *Exploring Talk in School: Inspired by the Work of Douglas Barnes*. London: SAGE.
4. Mercer, N. and Littleton, K. (2007) *Dialogue and the Development of Children's Thinking: A Sociocultural Approach*. London: Routledge.
5. Newman, R. (2017) 'Let's talk talk: Utilising Metatalk for the Development of Productive Collaborative Dialogues. *Thinking Skills and Creativity*. 26. pp.1–12.
6. To search for TED Talks and tips for great presentations:
   a. www.ted.com/recommends?gclid=EAIaIQobChMIl6K45PF6gIVWeDtCh3S0w6JEAAYASAAEgKOE_D_BwE
   b. www.ted.com/playlists/574/how_to_make_a_great_presentation

Chapter 3 Sharing a class reader

LORNA SMITH AND LUCY KELLY

INTRODUCTION

'Reading is a conversation', writes the author Mark Haddon (*The Guardian*, 2004). 'All books talk. But a good book listens as well'. The idea that reading is a conversation, and that books talk and listen, are central concepts in this chapter. Whilst the 'portable magic' (King, 2000, p.104) of books can be experienced independently, the *real* magic might happen when you communicate this externally to others. The oral tradition of storytelling exemplifies the importance of sharing a book through talk; silent reading was almost unheard of until the tenth century (Hall, 2014 in Brindley and Marshall, 2015). Interestingly, this reading pattern appears to be mirrored in school: pupils come from primary schools where reading aloud and talking about books is common practice yet, at secondary level, silent – or independent – reading seems to take over. Rather than being consumed in one go, reading often becomes 'distended and disrupted and [...] is experienced as an indigestible product' (Westbrook et al., 2019, p.67).

This shift in reading culture has implications. Performance in International Student Assessment (PISA) data (Videbaek, 2020) suggests reading for pleasure declines amongst secondary pupils. One explanation could be that pupils are not sharing stories in the same way as in their earlier schooling. When the dialogic practice of reading – talking about books and sharing them orally – is limited or absent, can pupils experience the same levels of engagement? Or, could a 'classroom community' (Bloome, 1986, p.71) fostered on shared reading prevent 'readicide' (the 'killing' of reading by schools) (Gallagher, 2009, n.p.)? These big questions cannot be answered within the parameters of this chapter; however, the popularity of adult book groups appears to demonstrate a desire to return to a shared reading experience as members of a reading community (Cremin, 2019), one that is a 'fully social activity' involving friends, family and pupils (Meek, 1991, p.41).

Therefore, in an era in which choice around texts may be limited, and pressures of time and accountability reduce the scope an individual teacher might have, this chapter offers research-informed, practical suggestions on how to approach a whole text and bring active learning into the classroom.

DOI: 10.4324/9781003093060-4

At the end of this chapter you should be able to:

- understand the impact of collaborative reading, including the affordances of reading together (and how to meet the challenges of reading together);
- celebrate the reading experience by sharing a text in as sustained, uninterrupted way as possible;
- understand how to reposition the teacher as reader, so that they are engaged in the reading process to explore, discover and find out alongside their pupils, as opposed to being seen as the 'expert';
- foster a reading culture through which individual interpretation is celebrated and avoid a prescriptive approach.

READING TEACHERS

It is generally assumed that English teachers are great readers (borne out through research suggesting most English teachers come into the profession because they are lovers of literature (Blake and Shortis, 2010). Whether or not this is true of your own route into teaching, you will certainly have read a lot of books. Many will have had a tangible or intangible impact on your *relationship* with reading, something of critical significance that will have changed you as a reader. Perhaps you remember the book that first consciously engaged you emotionally, or your first 'grown up' book with chapters that marked your growing maturity as a reader, or the book that prompted you to see something with a fresh perspective. Activity 3.1 now invites you to consider these in more detail.

Activity 3.1

My Life in Books *(inspired by Gabrielle Cliff Hodges' 'Rivers of Reading')*

- Think of ten books that have had a 'critical' impact on your reading history (Cliff Hodges, 2010, p.181). The list may include some of your favourite books but will not necessarily be restricted to these. Write the title and author of each on a separate sticky note (so that they can be easily moved around) or into a whiteboard app.
- In a different colour, note down *why* each book is important.
- Arrange the list in the order in which you read them, to reveal the 'story' of these critical incidents in your reading history. Cliff Hodges suggests using the metaphor of a river, which illustrates well the 'dynamic' power of reading (2010, p.184): rivers actively shape their course within the geographical context they are situated, just as readers can shape their future.
- What do your reflections on this process reveal? Does seeing your reading trajectory from this perspective offer any new insights about you as a reader?
- You might now try rearranging the texts differently, such as by (i) chronological order of publication; (ii) theme or by genre; (iii) how and where you read them. What additional insights does this provoke?
- Develop the sticky notes into a display or collage; if you are working electronically, you could develop a Prezi or PowerPoint, with one text per slide (see Key Resources, item 2, for examples).

This activity also works well in a classroom and is a good way to encourage pupils to articulate their own relationship with books.

It would be interesting to consider if any of the texts on your list in Activity 3.1 are those that you read in school. Yet even if some are, it is unlikely that any of your classmates experienced that text exactly as you did. You formed your personal interpretation, your own 'authentic' reading (Giovanelli and Mason, 2015, p.41); they will have formed theirs. These readings may have been similar but they will not have been (and nor should they have been!) identical: a single text is open to interpretation and ever-changing, depending on the reader. Those 'critical incidents' (Cliff Hodges, 2010, p.181) are the result of the interweaving of your context, your life experience and the text. It is through this 'exten[sion] of experience' that a reader is impelled – implicitly or explicitly – to question their assumptions and challenge preconceptions (Bleiman, 2020, p.154). From a classroom perspective, one of the reasons for teaching a shared text is because it enables us to stand in the shoes of others. Within the pages of a book, we can time travel to the past or future; we can explore new worlds and cultures; we can become different people.

Further, while the words on the page are fixed, perhaps their richness lies in the ambiguities, the 'gappiness' (Smith, 2020, p.3) between them. This makes them alive in unpredictable and changing ways, and each reader will interpret both the words and the gaps differently and dynamically. Through the shared experience of reading in the classroom we can together read between the lines, explore the ambiguities – the gaps – to co-create a version of the text. This offers an enriched, enjoyable, reading experience for all involved – whilst simultaneously enabling pupils' individual readings to be owned and celebrated. These readings are stored in pupils' personal 'narrative schemas' (their own independent mental 'scrapbook' for each text) (Giovanelli and Mason, 2015, p.45).

Thus, this chapter encourages reading together for enjoyment, pleasure and understanding – even with texts one has not chosen to read. We emphasise the value of creating a reading community (Cremin, 2020) within the classroom, one where we support each other to move forward in our 'reading apprenticeship' (Meek, 1991, p.31), and celebrate the diversity of readers (from committed, habitual readers to those less confident, less experienced) within the group.

DEVELOPING DIALOGIC READERS IN CONVERSATION WITH THE TEXT AND EACH OTHER

It is no light challenge for an English teacher to help perhaps 30 individual pupils simultaneously 'converse' with a text in a personal, meaningful way. They may appear reluctant, you are pushed for time, resources may be lacking. However, reading together, collaboratively, offers opportunities. In Activity 3.2 we look first at some practical considerations to help you set up shared reading in your classroom, then move on to suggest some activities that capitalise on the experience that a reading community provides.

Activity 3.2: Planning the reading experience

In Table 3.1, column 1 summarises some of the typical challenges that communal reading in a classroom might present, from both the perspective of the pupils and the teacher, while column 2 provides some suggestions to address these creatively. We invite you to use column 3 to consider what you might do in your classroom, inspired by your wider reading, practice and reflections. You could use the Key Resources at the end of this chapter as a starting point.

Table 3.1 Planning the reading experience

Challenges	Opportunities	In my classroom
Getting started		
The classroom context is not conducive to pleasurable reading	• Create an attractive reading environment – regularly replace book posters on the wall; establish a *Reading Recommendations* display. • Experiment with the classroom layout: arrange desks in islands, a horseshoe or circle to facilitate a supportive environment.	
Pupils resist the choice of text being made for them	• Offer your class a choice of text – read the first few pages of several texts; ask them to vote. If this is not possible, explain that the given text will be read, but ask pupils to recommend a book that *you* should read. Commit to reading it; devote some time to discussing it. • Encourage pupils to become agentive readers, more willing to experiment, by recommending texts to each other (Laurenson, 2015). Make explicit your own reading choices (Cremin, 2009a).	
Logistics: too much to read, not enough copies, too little time		
Limited time available	• As discussed in more depth below, plan to read the text as quickly as possible, avoiding spoilers or activities that deaden the thrill of the narrative (Westbrook, 2011; Giovanelli and Mason, 2015). • Rather than 'skipping' parts of the text to cram it all in, choose a shorter text. Short stories are an underused resource when it comes to teaching whole texts – search online by author or genre (e.g. Goodreads.com). • Watch a film version *before* reading, treating the film as a multimodal text that offers the full narrative arc and enables you to revisit key episodes in the text afterwards, drawing attention to the choices made by the scriptwriter and director in the adaptation.	
Limited access to texts means that pupils do not have a copy each, and school policy might mean texts cannot be sent home.	• Provide audio recordings or podcasts. Audio versions of most popular texts are commercially available, but you could record your own (a particularly valuable investment of time if you are likely to teach the text again). • Ask confident readers to record certain sections/chapters, individually or in small groups – the decisions they need to make regarding pitch, tone, voice, sound effects etc. inform their own critical appreciation too. • If the text is available online, download and share – in a suitably large font – via an interactive whiteboard (and/or pupils' phones). This also allows for a multimodal approach: illustrations and images can be included to add interest and support understanding (Kress and Van Leeuwen, 2001; Sacks, 2013).	
Accessing the text		
While reading round the class means that everyone can participate, the flow and audibility are often impeded.	• Read the text aloud yourself (having rehearsed properly first!). This model allows for a powerful shared experience (Rosen, 2019). • Do not *insist* that your listeners follow the text: perhaps allow them to doodle instead, inspired by what they hear. Comparing the images they produce is a useful 'way in' to discussion.	

Table 3.1 Cont.

Challenges	Opportunities	In my classroom
	• If the text has a lot of dialogue, individuals can take on roles, turning the classroom into a quasi-theatre. Invite the readers to the front; a background image on the board can set the scene effectively and provide a focal point for the audience. • Sections are read chorally, either by the whole class or groups, or sections are read aloud by groups with background music/sound effects added (Dymoke, 2009). • Allow pupils to choose their approach: they can listen to you reading, join a table group where pupils read to each other, or read quietly, independently. Dreyer (2003) recommends they should have the freedom to change groups when they wish.	
Pupils are unfamiliar with the context/ genre/author	• Contextual knowledge does not need to be taught before reading: almost always, context is revealed *through* the text (Westbrook, 2011; Bleiman, 2020) – the Latin *contexĕre* means 'to weave together, connect' (OED.com). Encourage pupils to consider the context *as they read:* instead of teaching about poverty in Victorian Britain before embarking on *A Christmas Carol*, read Stave One and ask pupils to discuss Dickens' perspective on the social conditions described. • Capitalise on cultural capital available in the class, gained either through their own life experience (a pupil might share how it felt to be newly arrived in the UK when reading *Pigeon English* (Kelman, 2012)) or their reading of other texts on similar themes.	
The vocabulary is antiquated or obscure	• Rather than pre-teaching unfamiliar vocabulary, gloss words as you go, so that new vocabulary is introduced in context; or read a section of text, check that pupils have got the gist, and *then* go back to clarify individual words. • Evoke pupils' morphological and semantic knowledge to speculate on definitions, before encouraging them to confirm using a dictionary.	

We now elaborate on some of the points in Activity 3.2 as we discuss how to create a rich, dialogic reading classroom. As suggested, it is dialogue and discussion that enable teachers to use their own developed 'narrative schemas' in a positive way with pupils coming to a text for the first time (Giovanelli and Mason, 2015, p.46). A classroom culture that celebrates a shared experience for all enhances authenticity and engagement because pupils are encouraged to continually share their developing schema through talk, using it to try out, develop and reflect upon their ideas in light of feedback from the other 'reading apprentices' (Giovanelli and Mason, 2015, p.46) in the room – including the teacher.

UNINTERRUPTED READING AND NURTURING INDIVIDUAL RESPONSES

You have used Activity 3.2 to help you plan the reading experience, set the scene, mindful of the importance of creating the right environment. The next challenge is to apportion reading time. Research suggests that it is more effective to read the text quickly over successive lessons, without interruption, rather than breaking it up. Getting through even complex novels in a swift, sustained manner repositions 'poorer readers' as 'good' readers because 'in a faster read, the text becomes coherent, reading experienced as a collaboratively constructed, active and engaged process' (Westbrook et al., 2019, p.67). Conversely, if the reading experience is slowed down and artificially chunked to fit pre-made activities, then a single 'authorised' (Giovanelli and Mason, 2015, p.53) view of the text is presented through which the teacher, a 're-reader', guides 'first-time readers' (2015, p.46). There is a danger that lesson tasks and teacher discourse – while expert and well-meaning – could hinder pupils' 'authentic engagement' (ibid.) with the text. We therefore recommend that to maintain engagement and support pupils in developing their own authentic readings, it is preferable to front-load the reading of the text at the beginning of a scheme of work and then revisit and discuss salient points when the pupils are also 're-readers'.

This approach avoids pupils being given 'manufactured' (Giovanelli and Mason, 2015, p.42) readings, either accidentally, through the framing of the lesson, or deliberately – albeit with the best of intentions – for exam purposes. It is easy to see why, in a climate of accountability, ready-made readings (and their written counterpart, Point/Evidence/Explain paragraphs) are sometimes prioritised in the English classroom (Gibbons, 2019), but this method is limiting. Instead, the oral rehearsal of ideas during and after the sustained reading experience improves pupils' writing about the text because it gives them the confidence to break away from the many 'constrained and constricted' (Gibbons, 2019, p.37) writing templates governing English classrooms: it enables them to see the 'bigger ideas' and the 'text in a larger sense' (AQA, 2018a, p.7). It is these *un*manufactured responses – rather than 'shoehorn[ed]' (AQA, 2018a, p 6) answers showcasing a 'reductive view of a literary text' (AQA, 2018a, p. 7) – that General Certificate of Secondary Education (GCSE) examiners look for.

PRACTICAL ACTIVITIES TO SUPPORT READERS AND RE-READERS

We now provide some examples of dialogue-rich strategies to help individual readers clarify, reflect on and deepen their understanding of a text, whether they are first-time readers or re-readers. These ideas can be easily developed and adapted for any secondary age group (and undergraduate level too).

FIRST-TIME READERS: ACTIVITIES TO ENGAGE, INTRIGUE AND INSPIRE

Although we are making the case for swiftly reading a text from start to finish, we would also suggest that devoting a single lesson to hooking pupils in through focusing on an interesting, short passage *before* the sustained reading starts can be very effective. It introduces them in a light-touch manner to genre, setting, theme, characterisation, plot – all aspects that they will need as they go on to explore and analyse the text – and gets them asking questions about what might come before or after. And, of course, given that some examination boards include an extract-style question, the following extract-based activities are also useful at the re-reading stage for GCSE preparation.

In response to the research revealing the lack of representation in the range of texts typically studied at secondary level (Smith, 2020), we have deliberately chosen for purposes of illustration a text written by a woman that features a man in a childcare role: George Eliot's *Silas Marner* (1861).[1] The eponymous Marner is a weaver, victimised for his religion. He comes to adopt a daughter, Eppie, when she wanders into his remote cottage as a toddler.[2]

This dramatic extract is taken from the middle of the novel when Marner fears he has lost Eppie. Before starting, engage pupils by asking if they have ever lost anything precious to them – what does it feel like? – and then read the passage together.

> The terrible fact burst upon him: Eppie had run out by herself – had perhaps fallen into the stone-pit. Silas, shaken by the worst fear that could have befallen him, rushed out, calling 'Eppie!' and ran eagerly about the unenclosed space, exploring the dry cavities into which she might have fallen, and then gazing with questioning dread at the smooth red surface of the water. The cold drops stood on his brow. How long had she been out? There was one hope – that she had crept through the stile and got into the fields, where he habitually took her to stroll. But the grass was high in the meadow, and there was no descrying her [...] The meadow was searched in vain; and he got over the stile into the next field, looking with dying hope towards a small pond which was now reduced to its summer shallowness, so as to leave a wide margin of good adhesive mud. Here, however, sat Eppie, discoursing cheerfully to her own small boot, which she was using as a bucket to convey the water into a deep hoof-mark, while her little naked foot was planted comfortably on a cushion of olive-green mud. A red-headed calf was observing her with alarmed doubt through the opposite hedge.
>
> (Chapter 14)

1. Ask readers to discuss in groups what they *like* or *enjoy* about this passage. You could then probe further: does Marner's rising panic remind them of their own emotions when realising something had been lost? Encourage them to question the text using 'how, what, why, where, when, who' question stems as prompts. Here, they might ask: *Why did Eppie wander off? How must Marner have felt when he found her? What sort of father figure is he?* Pupils can then discuss possible responses to the questions they pose. You as the re-reader should avoid providing the answers, thereby inviting the development of pupils' own authentic readings instead.
2. Alternatively, invite pupils to choose three words that interest them (you could be more specific, asking for a noun or adjective etc., depending on the text). Get them to compare and contrast their choices, then to drop a single word into a word cloud app such as www.worditout.com (see Figure 3.1). Duplicates are fine – even encouraged – as the size of the words in the cloud is proportionate to their frequency.

Figure 3.1 A word cloud created from 30 responses to the question 'Which noun interests you most in this passage?'

Ask pupils what they notice and discuss what is interesting. Here, they might contrast hope and fear, or notice the semantic field of nature. Challenge them to explore further by writing a 50-word story based on the cloud; share the stories – themes will emerge between them that are likely to be themes in the text itself.[3]

This focus on lexis prompts discussion on what sort of story they expect and is also an introduction to context: what do we learn about where the story is set, and when? Initial predictions will be progressively confirmed (or refuted) as reading progresses, and new questions will emerge.

By this point, pupils will have a flavour of the characters, plot, setting, context and theme. This passage can act as a fulcrum or reference point for the rest of the reading. You can now start at the beginning of the novel and read up to this point, pause and reflect, before continuing.

RE-READING: ACTIVITIES TO EXPLORE, CRITIQUE, CONSOLIDATE UNDERSTANDING AND PREPARE FOR EXAMINATION

We have argued that it is important to read the text quickly, to ensure that the reading experience retains integrity. Yet, at the same time – as readers ourselves who might turn down a page or highlight a passage on an e-reader – we know it is helpful to track the action, record salient moments. Writing about what has been read has the effect of ordering and 'harmonizing' (Britton, 1982, p.110) one's thoughts, so keeping a simple reading log, perhaps completed in the final ten minutes of a lesson, can be valuable.

However, we know that another reason why some pupils are reluctant to commit to books is because they assume that reading is the precursor to writing (Westbrook, 2011), and we want to retain the active reading dynamic. We therefore suggest in Table 3.2 some time-efficient activities that can be used during first reading and (more effectively) during re-reading, to provoke rich dialogue and thereby support 'active comprehension' (Cox, 1989b, p.135).

Not everybody should necessarily complete the same activity: by providing a menu of tasks from which pupils can choose, each creating outcomes which will be shared with peers, you can provide a subtle, inclusive means of differentiation. All these approaches enable pupils to develop deep understanding of how and why the author presents characters, plot and themes – the central elements of GCSE essay questions. Collated in a shared area online, the outcomes to the activities make invaluable revision resources.

Table 3.2 Multimodal activities to support active comprehension

Encourage pupils to:
• actively reflect on the text visually through images, diagrams, mind maps, storyboards, family trees, collages; and include their own reactions to these events;
• engage imaginatively through 'hot-seating' characters, inventing author interviews etc., perhaps recording the conversations on their phones;
• develop inference and analysis by posing each other further 'how, what, why, where, when' questions, focusing on what is known to the reader and what is inferred;
• analyse motivation and reaction by rewriting a given passage from another character's perspective;
• consider characters' and authorial perspectives by rewriting a given passage as a film script, including director's notes on characterisation, setting, mood, tone.

SUMMARY AND KEY POINTS

- '[R]eading without satisfaction is like the desperate attempts we make to keep a car going when it has run out of petrol' (Britton, 1982, p.35): it does not work. Fostering a reading culture where individual interpretation is celebrated and valued can recharge our pupils' reading batteries and put the 'satisfaction' (ibid.) back into reading.
- Using strategies that encourage engagement with the whole text and immersion within it will give pupils – and you as the teacher – the confidence to take ownership of the text, internalise it and make it their own (which will, where relevant, also lead to examination success).
- Creating a classroom environment founded on collaborative reading nurtures everyone's development as readers, writers, thinkers and humans.

KEY RESOURCES

1. Cox, B. (1989b) Appendix 6: Approaches to the class novel in English for ages 5–16. Available at: www.educationengland.org.uk/documents/cox1989/cox89.html

   Cox's (1989) 'Approaches to the class novel' remains one of the best collections of activities to prompt dialogue and engagement when reading a class novel.
2. Cliff Hodges, G. 2010. Rivers of reading: using critical incident collages to learn about adolescent readers and their readership. *English in Education*. 44 (3). pp.181–200, https://doi.org/10.1111/j.1754-8845.2010.01072.x

   In 'Rivers of reading', Cliff Hodges (2010) looks at the habits of committed, habitual readers, and thereby invites consideration of how to inspire others. Illustrated examples of pupils' Reading Rivers are effective models for your own classroom.
3. Cremin T. (2019) Reading communities: why, what and how? *NATE Primary Matters*. Available from: https://researchrichpedagogies.org/_downloads/Reading_Communities_TCremin_2019.pdf.

   Cremin (2019) builds on Cliff Hodges' work from the perspective of teachers in 'Reading communities: why, what and how?' with practical suggestions for how teachers can draw on their own reading for pleasure in the classroom.
4. Giovanelli, M. and Mason, J. (2015) 'Well I don't feel that': schemas, worlds and authentic reading in the classroom. *English in Education*. 49 (1). pp.41–56. https://doi.org/10.1111/eie.12052
5. Westbrook, J., Sutherland, J., Oakhill, J. and Sullivan, S. (2019). 'Just reading': the impact of a faster pace of reading narratives on the comprehension of poorer adolescent readers in English classrooms. *Literacy UKLA*. 53 (2). pp.60–8.

   Giovanelli and Mason (2015) in '"Well I don't feel that": schemas, worlds and authentic reading in the classroom' and Westbrook et al. (2019) in 'Just reading': *the impact of a faster pace or reading narratives on the comprehension of poorer adolescent readers in English classrooms* argue for a swift first reading of a text, referring to classroom-based research supported by evidence from both teachers and pupils.

NOTES

1. *Silas Marner* is offered as a GCSE text in the 2015 AQA and Edexcel specifications.
2. It would be interesting to compare *Silas Marner* to *Boys Don't Cry* by Malorie Blackman (2010), which also features an unusual father-daughter relationship

between teen father Dante, and the baby he did not know he had, Emma. It appears on the 2019 Edexcel GCSE specification.

3. Word clouds are also an interesting way to enable analysis. If you have access to an electronic version of the whole text, drop separate chapters into a word cloud, then compare them to explore how ideas and themes develop between chapters (Rank et al., 2011).

Chapter 4 Talk about texts: Discussion of literature in the English classroom

JOHN GORDON

INTRODUCTION

Reading and responding to literature dominate subject English. One pleasure of teaching English is the agency you have in how you talk about literature with pupils, even where the choice of texts is influenced by examination specifications or curricula. This chapter explores talk about texts, looking at examples of classroom discussion around literature and exploring the judgements teachers make in the moment-by-moment progress of conversations. For many people, reading outside school is a solitary activity, unless they choose to read together with others in reading groups (Duncan, 2012). In your English classroom, you frame the usually individual pursuit of reading to meet lesson objectives and pedagogic goals, making literature study a public and social event. Often this entails phases of reading texts together and aloud, interspersed by whole-class discussion. The teacher orchestrates talk about texts, guiding pupils' attention and eliciting their reactions to novels, plays or poems. The process can bring forth pupils' emotional responses to literature, inviting them to express thoughts that for individual readers would usually remain unvoiced. The activity also serves as induction to literary-critical discourse, introducing pupils to specialist terminology and methods of literary analysis. As an influential model to pupils in talking about literature, you have the privilege of creating environments where pupils can enjoy literature, helping them feel comfortable in sharing opinions about episodes, characters or ideas represented in literary texts.

At the end of this chapter you should be able to:

- recognise conceptualisations of reading (schemata) outlined in research literature and their relationships to classroom talk about texts;
- identify, in transcript examples, techniques teachers use to present and frame literary texts for pupils through teacher talk, and recognise how these techniques afford engagement, access and challenge for pupils;
- understand how teachers can gently elicit pupils' knowledge to inform whole-class and individual reading of literature;
- select subtle features of English teachers' talk for attention in your own observations of teachers at work, in mentoring discussions and in evaluation of your own teaching.

DOI: 10.4324/9781003093060-5

Throughout this chapter, rather than 'activities' you will find transcripts of teacher-pupil talk to analyse and reflect on.

CONCEPTUALISATIONS OF READING

Classroom conversations about any literary text lend you, the teacher, insights to what happens in the hearts and minds of pupils as they read. The convention of talking about texts in English assumes a connection between individual cognition and social interaction, consistent with social-constructivist theories of learning (Vygotsky, 1978). The choices you make in organising and conducting classroom conversations influence the responses of individual pupils, bridging public interaction with their inner thoughts, emotions and comprehension. In what teaching format will pupils encounter any text for the first time? Will they always read from pages, referring to their own copy of a book also available to everyone else in the class? Will they first hear a poem in the aural mode, or see a play in cinematic adaptation or filmed stage production? From these apparently simple decisions, the teacher begins to direct pupils' orientation to texts and foreground some text features over others, determining readings. These actions also influence the nature of interaction and speech around the literary works being studied.

Psychologists offer numerous accounts of the reading process and how readers perceive and organise information as they read, in frameworks known as schemata. These help us identify what knowledge individuals activate as they read. Prior knowledge schemata recognise personal experience as a factor influencing comprehension (Recht and Leslie, 1988). Cultural background schemata encompass the influence of different writing systems, conventions of grammar and patterns of discourse shaped by each reader's locality, ethnicity, class or religion (Reynolds et al., 1982, p.95). Knowledge of a topic or field can influence any reader's capacity to make inferences (Yekovich et al., 1990), as do knowledge of vocabulary (Nagy and Scott, 1990), discourse and genre (Graesser, Singer and Trabasso, 1994; Kucan and Beck, 1997). The expertise of teachers represents applied and practical knowledge of these, for instance as they diagnose the difficulties a pupil may have understanding an episode in a novel. The pupil may be struggling to understand, say, chapter 5 of *Frankenstein* (in which the creature is brought to life), because they find Mary Shelley's syntax unfamiliar, are unaware of the Gothic genre or have not yet studied electricity in physics. Teachers draw on several reading schemata concurrently, in assessing their pupils' comprehension and in making moment-by-moment judgements about what to foreground, what to explain and what to explore through questioning. These considerations shape pedagogies of reading, incorporated to talk about texts either in whole-class and teacher-led formats such as shared novel reading (Gordon, 2020), or in smaller group activity such as peer-to-peer 'guided reading' (Fountas and Pinnell, 1996; for a contemporary example, see Victoria State Government, 2020). Most of these formats include some sharing of literature, perhaps through reading aloud, some questioning by teachers or designated pupils, and extended discussion.

Nystrand's study of talk about texts in school literary study asserted that 'oblique rather than direct' (2006, p.393) modes of classroom discourse are best suited to effective literary study and successful educational outcomes. He identified 'patterns of interaction, categories of questioning, and approaches to discussion and small-group work' (p.403) as likely to aid pupils' reading comprehension, and expressed scepticism about approaches to reading based on 'tightly scripted direct instruction' (p.404). Talk about texts generates 'epistemic environments' (p.393), exploring knowledge and meaning in distinctive ways. These respond to literature's diverse affordances for expressing and conveying knowledge: each text embodies knowledge in a unique form. Talk about texts according to the conventions of literary studies is a form of academic literacy (Lea and Street, 2006), demanding of pupils specific academic language proficiency (Cummins, 1991), always sensitive to the idiosyncrasies of the focal literature. For these reasons, talk about text in your classroom merits careful consideration and planning: it is a mode of inclusive teaching. This chapter presents transcripts of talk about texts drawn from actual classrooms. They show how other teachers guide conversations and may prompt reflection on your own approach to reading conversations.

PRESENTING AND FRAMING TEXTS IN TALK

This first transcript represents an exchange where an experienced teacher of English involves a class of pupils (aged 11–12) in talk about the early pages of Penelope Lively's novel *The Ghost of Thomas Kempe* (first published in 1973, though the class uses the 2006 Egmont edition). They explore narrative voice relative to the story's protagonist 'James'. As you read the transcript in Activity 4.1, notice how the teacher alternates between reading passages aloud to pupils and eliciting their comments across turns in the conversation (each new turn is numbered).

Activity 4.1: First transcript

01 TEACHER I'm going to read a little bit more to you and I want you to be thinking about whether there's anything that comes up about language, interests or attitudes when I read this next paragraph.

We got halfway down page six last lesson and I'm just going to read a little bit more:

'They were almost home now. James could see the window of his attic room, staring over towards the church. The cottage was small, square and comfortable. Coming to live in it had been like putting on an old coat. It had a sagging slate roof, a bulge at one end where once there had been a bread oven, huge beams, creaking stairs, and stone floors with interesting cracks from which emerged, at night, large and stately black beetles. James was making a study of the black beetles. It was going to be called The Life Cycle of a British Beetle by Dr James Harrison, FRS, MP, DPhil, OBE. Helen preferred the new houses in the estate the other side of Ledsham, where she already had a network of friends'.

I think that's Mrs Harrison- '"Helen'. Already in that paragraph I think we've got something that we could answer. Yes, Ben?

02 BEN Helen's his sister.
03 TEACHER Oh, it's his sister, I beg your pardon, yes. We know he's got a sister, can we say anything about his language there?
04 EMMA No.
05 TEACHER Why not?
06 AYSHA He doesn't really...actually, he's quite formal.

07 LEON He didn't actually speak.

08 TEACHER He didn't actually speak, but it's interesting, because Aysha you're saying it's quite formal. Leon is saying he didn't speak, you're saying it's quite formal, and I think you're both right, because there's no dialogue there, there are no speech marks to say that he has spoken, but have a look at it.

Read through it again to yourself. Why does Aysha think it's quite formal and that that's got to do with James? Have just a read-through again now.

From turn 1, this teacher frames pupils' reading with cues for their attention, helpfully indicates to pupils where they should be looking on the page and provides an explanation of one character's relationship with the narrator. The teacher uses Ben's correcting contribution (turn 2) to draw attention to information that readers, the 'we' of the class, already know about the narrator and his world (turn 3). Here, with an open question, the teacher shifts pupils' reading position (Gordon, 2019a) from involvement to one of analysis, with the author's use of 'language' the focus. The teacher exploits the different and concise assertions by pupils at turns 6 and 7 to prompt whole-class reflection on the text's narrative voice. The teacher invites everyone, now alone, to negotiate the apparent contradiction (turn 8), paraphrasing the question again in new terms: 'I think Aysha is right in a way, that she said it is formal, and I think Leon's right that he doesn't say anything, but why are they both right?'

At turn 8, the teacher suspends the whole-class discussion to allow pupils brief opportunity to reread the focal paragraph privately and silently. Activity 4.1 invites you to reflect on the complex, efficient work of guiding literary reading presented so far.

After thinking time, the teacher invites her pupils to share responses, presented in the transcript in Activity 4.2 (numbering of turns continues from the conversation shown in Activity 4.1).

Activity 4.2: Second transcript

13 LUCY It's like he's thinking it. He's not actually saying it, but he's thinking it.

14 TEACHER He's thinking it. How do you know he's thinking it?

15 SAM Because it says...he's thinking of him writing stuff about the black beetle.

16 TEACHER Yeah, you're right, it doesn't actually say, 'James thought to himself...' but we know they're his ideas and he's come up with a title, which sounds quite formal, doesn't it? 'The Life Cycle of a British Beetle'. He's thinking of himself as a doctor, as a DPhil, an OBE, all this sort of thing, and that is very formal, isn't it? What does that tell us about James? What about the type of character? Emma?

17 EMMA Quite posh.

18 TEACHER Yes, quite well educated I would say. Probably from a middle-class family, yes.

Here the teacher elicits Lucy's view that the narrator is 'thinking it', and Sam's further warrant of textual evidence (15, 'it says'). The teacher then paraphrases Sam's remarks with even closer attention to the detail of the text (16), and allows Emma to respond to a new question, identifying the register of the narrative voice. The teacher's work is efficient, making the most of Lucy's first statement in the public arena of whole-class discussion. By paraphrasing, the teacher helps the whole class attend to the matter of 'thinking it', explaining and swiftly modelling the practice of warranting a statement about a literary text. The example mirrors widely taught formulae for writing about literature ('point-evidence-explain' and variants), expressed casually to maintain the flow of discussion. The importance of momentum is evident around David's further speculation about the narrator's social standing:

Activity 4.3: Third transcript

19 DAVID Didn't they say their house was quite big as well, so they'd have to be quite rich and formal?

20 TEACHER Possibly. Although when this was written, you could get a lot more for your money, especially in a rural area, so that's always a difficult one to judge. But you're right to be thinking about that sort of thing. So, we know that he's thinking it, but it doesn't actually say 'he thought …' Who is telling us these things? Hannah, who is telling us these things?

21 HANNAH What, who's telling us what he thought?

22 TEACHER Yeah.

23 HANNAH I thought it was the author.

24 TEACHER Not the author, you're close. What do we call the person that tells…Isaac?

25 ISAAC The narrator.

26 TEACHER The narrator, so the narrator is telling us this sort of thing. Is it a first-person narrative or a third-person narrative, if the narrator is telling us …?

27 PUPILS Third.

28 TEACHER It's the third-person, well done, and what does the third-person narrator enable us to understand about the different characters?

29 ISAAC Their personalities.

30 TEACHER All of them, exactly, well done. We can get into the heads of any character we like through the narrator, can't we?

This sequence covers a lot of ground, the teacher first validating David's inferential reading (turn 20), an important skill in literary reading. She maintains the discussion's momentum around the focal topic of narrative voice, and initiates exchanges that use more specific literary-analytic terminology (25, 27). These explore what different narrative perspectives can achieve in communicating information to readers (29, 30). These turns show the teacher responding to an inaccurate hypothesis (23), asking pupils to distinguish between categories of narrative voice they appear to have encountered before, and lightly underlining potential for narratorial omniscience.

In its entirety, this conversation represents several facets of talk about texts you are likely to consider when preparing, teaching and evaluating lessons. It shows interplay of 'live' judgements as the teacher organises pupils' contributions, steers progress through the text and balances reading literature with discussion of it. Additionally, the exchange demonstrates progress towards generic objectives which could underpin study of any narrative text, concerning identification and exploration of narrative voice, characterisation and features of style. It also makes clear the extent to which distinctive qualities of the focal text influence conversation, important to the nature and quality of the shared experience. For this class the lesson was also an early experience of reading a shared novel in secondary school, a form of a teacher-led induction. No secondary-phase teacher of English can assume that all pupils are familiar with the convention of reading in class in the same format. Anticipate that when pupils first join your lessons, you may need to provide deliberate, systematic induction to the formats for talk you use and their ground rules (Mercer and Edwards, 1987): previous teachers may have taken different approaches. Activity 4.2 invites you to consider the tacit ground rules and impact of talk about texts in another teacher's classroom.

ELICITING PUPILS' KNOWLEDGE TO INFORM READING AND INTERPRETATION

This example of talk about texts represents discussion about poetry during advanced-level study (ages 16–18). The group considers W.B. Yeats' poem 'Easter, 1916'. Participants in the conversation refer to the focal poem more obliquely than we found in the previous example.

In Activity 4.4, the teacher has just read the second stanza of Yeats' poem aloud to pupils, and now initiates an investigation to identify unnamed figures represented in the stanza. The pupils contribute suggestions informed by their broader cultural and historical knowledge (i.e. their 'cultural background' schemata), introducing information not presented explicitly in the poem.

Activity 4.4: Fourth transcript

TEACHER So we aim to get the kind of listing of the kind of people involved. Now you were saying you thought it was Maud Gonne?
SIOBHAN I th- think it's like, like an almost a metaphorical approach to like Ireland I (suppose).
TEACHER Right.
SIOBHAN On the whole kind of like a classic (mirror) image of Maud Gonne 'cos that's, was always (unclear – he?) always had it in somewhere in any poem so I think like he's actually like personifying Ireland as a woman.
TEACHER That's very interesting because that was done at the time, yeah.
SIOBHAN Mm, a lot.
TEACHER Lots of her iconography, erm, if we – before I do tell you who I think this is, and there are links as well to the same classic Maud Gonne (audio is unclear here – 'image'?). What other things would give you clues in there as to who this is, does anybody know who this is?
HELEN Is it Countess Markievicz?
TEACHER Yeah, it's Countess Markievicz. What do you know about her?
HELEN Erm, I know that she was involved in the Easter Rising.
TEACHER Yeah.
HELEN And then she was arrested.
TEACHER Yeah –

HELEN And they wouldn't try her because she was a woman and that she was also involved in Daughters of Ireland.
TEACHER Good, yeah, and do you know how – how Yeats knew her?
HELEN No, was she – was she not just from the same social circle of Belfast?
TEACHER She was, absolutely.

The exchange builds from Siobhan's suggestion that the figure is Maud Gonne, a woman Yeats knew, loved and wrote of frequently. In this context, however, the hypothesis is incorrect. Nevertheless, the teacher does not correct the proposal, instead allowing conversation to develop from the contribution. The teacher simply acknowledges the point, and with the 'you were saying' formula encourages the pupil to offer more comment. The pupil's response takes the reflective talk into new territory, speculating that the focal figure is a personification of Ireland. This contribution and a later hypothesis that the figure may be another woman, Countess Markievicz, rest on knowledge the pupils bring to their interpretation. The pupils share with their teacher and therefore the whole class information not available to them in the poem. These are details that are useful for all present to be aware of, items that delineate the context of the poem and its production in ways that might aid understanding of other stanzas and of the poem in its entirety.

The teacher's role in eliciting these is important not only for helping pupils understand the significance of the figure in the stanza, it also models a mode of speculation. The teacher initiates and encourages a way of thinking about poetry, across a conversation heard by the whole group, that can gently influence how individual pupils approach their private poetry reading. That this is a judgement on the part of the teacher, rather than an accidental occurrence, is revealed in the teacher's aside 'before I do tell you this'. The comment indicates that withholding the correct information is tactical, also highlighting the distinctiveness of classroom dialogue and its ground rules. The pupils do not contest the action, which in talk outside a classroom might be considered unusual, instead accepting the 'move' as a normal element of talk for learning in literary study.

It is possible to view the exchange as an instance of pupils' 'cultural literacy' coming to bear on their reading. In this respect, the teacher's skill in eliciting what they know relates to topical debates in education and literary study about the nature of disciplinary knowledge. This teacher's approach with the poem is one that allows for pupils' expertise. This pedagogy recognises readers bring experiences to texts (Rosenblatt, 1978). It does not represent a 'transmission' mode of teaching where an explanation of the poem's meaning is presented to pupils. The distinction goes to the heart of current educational debate, and is likely to raise important questions for your consideration as you prepare talk about text for your pupils. What are the values and assumptions that lie behind your approaches to literature? How do you judge when to invite pupils' speculation about texts, and when to make unequivocal statements that influence their interpretation of novels, plays or poems?

CONCLUSION

The examples of talk about text presented in this chapter signal teachers' influence in shaping the 'epistemic environment' for reading, sometimes tacitly and sometimes directly. On occasion, alteration between tacit and direct methods is evident even in single turns of teacher talk, as in this example drawn from a lesson (ages 14–16) on Stevenson's *The Strange Case of Dr Jekyll and Mr Hyde*. Letters A to D in the transcription mark discrete moves in the teacher's utterance, each point guiding pupils' reading attention in a different way or to different information:

> So as we come into that paragraph on pathetic fallacy we already appreciate how the characters are feeling (A). They are going to Jekyll's house now to find out what on earth is going on (B). We don't know – as a character – we don't know what is happening, okay, (C) but we do know that Jekyll's been locking himself up again, and we know that Poole is very, very afraid (D).

The teacher directs pupils' orientation to the novel by switching between a distanced perspective (A and C), which describes features of the narrative using literary-analytic jargon, to one of immersion in the world of the story (B and D). This example of exposition signals the potential of teacher talk to model literary discourse for pupils, inducting them to the academic and disciplinary literacy of English. The turn combines specialist vocabulary likely to support pupils' academic language proficiency with paraphrased episodes from the narrative, framing the text's narrative for consideration in the classroom. Elsewhere, I have called this additional narrative work on the part of the teacher pedagogic literary narration, distinctive to literary study (Gordon, 2019a).

These fragments maintain the presence of the text and the world of its story in the conversation. Often the most efficient means of maintaining the text's presence is through quotation, as in this commentary about Dr Jekyll:

> he talks about – later on, on page 44 – 'The evil side of my nature. Even as good shone upon the countenance of one, evil was written broadly and plainly on the face of the other', then he goes into great detail about the character of Hyde and even though it was an 'ugly idol', it was 'a leap of welcome'. He welcomed Hyde; he embraced him. 'This too was myself. It seemed natural and human.'

Again, the teacher embeds the narrative, now verbatim, in speech which weaves the teacher's words and those of the novel. Remember, pupils do not see the quotation marks you have just seen on the page: this is continuous expression. These spoken quotations bridge the individual experience of reading from the page with the public arena of the classroom, and transpose the mode of print to fleeting verbalisation.

Whenever you do this as a teacher, you place the literary work in conversation before your pupils as an object of public attention. The action is a key move in talk about texts, lifting words from the page into the public space. Spoken quotation is a powerful pedagogic resource to support pupils' involvement in the text, and to support their later capacity to recall text details and direct quotations (Gordon, 2019b). In your earliest teaching, you may find this fluency does not come easily. With time, and probably with some deliberate concentration on the skill, you will soon weave texts into your own expression instinctively. Creating 'epistemic environments' through talk about texts is as much about these small details as it is about lesson planning, a balance Activity 4.3 invites you to consider (see also Resource 5.10). In your own teacher talk you model and embody for pupils what it is to be a literary reader, so that they may speak confidently about literature themselves.

SUMMARY AND KEY POINTS

- Talk about texts where pupils participate enthusiastically and with insight can appear spontaneous and self-sustaining, but is likely to result from the teacher's care and skill.
- Effective talk about texts arises from the teacher's careful preparation, close knowledge of the text (at the level of the passages considered) and subtle exercise of judgement during teaching.
- Teachers can shape talk about texts to influence pupils' enjoyment of reading and enjoyment of discussing their reading.
- Talking about texts in the classroom inducts pupils to academic literacy in literary studies: the teacher is always an influential model of how to talk about texts.
- Bring texts into speech: make texts present in the room and on the air, through spoken quotation in talk.

KEY RESOURCES

1. Gordon, J. (2020) *Researching Interpretive Talk around Literary Narrative Texts: Shared Novel Reading*. New York and Abingdon, Oxford: Routledge. The transcripts presented in this chapter derive from research presented in this book. The book also provides an outline of research methods and a theoretical framework for researching talk around texts in primary schools, secondary schools, higher education and informal reading groups. The book provides resources for teachers and mentors in its final chapter.
2. https://litlanglearn.org/ This website presents transcripts and audio files representing real talk about texts in English lessons in the UK. The examples are presented for use in continuing professional development for English teachers, allowing reflection and discussion around instances of 'talk about texts'. The site invites visiting teachers to upload audio files of short sequences of talk drawn from their own teaching, contributing to a shared professional corpus of 'talk about texts'.
3. www.education.vic.gov.au/school/teachers/teachingresources/discipline/english/literacy/readingviewing/Pages/teachingpracguided.aspx#link94 This website from Victoria State Government details web resources for organising Guided Reading, a distinctive form of talk about texts you may want to try.

Chapter 5 Reading comprehension

JULIA SUTHERLAND AND JO WESTBROOK

INTRODUCTION

Young children initially learn to think, express themselves and understand the world through speech: talking to parents/carers, peers and community develops children's vocabulary, language, concepts and understanding. But once children learn to read, their learning intensifies as written text, fiction or non-fiction, typically contains more challenging vocabulary and syntax, and introduces new knowledge, narratives and ways of thinking about the world. So, becoming a successful, motivated reader, able to tackle increasingly challenging texts in school and independently, is fundamental to pupils' learning and achievement across the curriculum: 'reading can make you smarter' (Cunningham and Stanovich, 2003, p.1; 1998). Sadly, approximately a fifth of adolescents in the UK do not develop adequate reading literacy, according to international reading surveys (e.g. OECD, 2019) and, for example, in England, 30% of pupils consistently do not achieve the national literacy benchmark, Level 4 in General Certificate of Secondary Education (GCSE) English (DfE, 2019). Leaving school with weak reading skills hinders young people's ability to progress to higher education and employment, negatively affecting future earnings, health, personal fulfilment and even mental well-being (Clark and Teravainen, 2018).

This chapter supports you in how to develop all your pupils' reading abilities, giving them the best chance of succeeding in education and their future lives, and nurturing their interest in reading.

At the end of this chapter you should be able to:

- recognise the interrelated components of reading – decoding, fluency and comprehension – and key strategies that enable pupils to develop these;
- identify the different reasons why some KS3 pupils struggle with reading comprehension and select teaching strategies to support their development;
- recognise the importance of motivating pupils to read, and of increasing their reading of whole texts, by planning engaging lessons, reading culturally diverse, stimulating texts and supporting pupils to read for pleasure (RfP) independently;
- appreciate the importance of dialogic, small-group and class talk in developing comprehension and higher levels of interpretation, enabling pupils to become

DOI: 10.4324/9781003093060-6

capable, enthusiastic and critical readers, who enjoy exploring texts in a reading community.

HOW DO READERS READ AND COMPREHEND TEXT?

Before you read this chapter, reflect on the questions in Activity 5.1 to start you thinking about what comprehension is and how we do this.

Activity 5.1

Reflect on these questions and write some notes:

1. How do readers read and comprehend text?
2. What makes a 'reader'? If these two questions are different, in what way?
3. Is reading only an internal, cognitive process? Or is it also sociocultural, nurtured by cultural contexts and conditions?
4. If so, which language and other contexts support children and young people to become capable and enthusiastic readers? Do all children have equal access to these?
5. Which kinds of texts might engage and challenge the diverse pupils in your KS3 and KS4 classes? Have you read many of these?

Reading involves two main components: first, word recognition or decoding – the ability to read and correctly pronounce written words out of context, applying letter-sound knowledge and achieving automaticity. The second element is language comprehension, the ability to understand words, sentences and whole texts. This depends on early readers' oral language experience. Pupils may have difficulties in either reading component or both: for example, dyslexics are weak at decoding, and 10% of children at the start of secondary school have specific difficulties with comprehension, but may be competent decoders (Oakhill et al., 2015).

DECODING AND FLUENCY

Learning to read entails enhancing oral language and learning to decode print. Enhancing oral language is achieved through encouraging children to talk and listen to many oral stories and other texts, while also learning to distinguish phonemic sounds at the beginning and in the middle of words ('sand-pit'; 'sand-wich'). Decoding is learning to crack the code of letters and syllables that make up each written word, matching phonemes (letter sounds) with their written representation as graphemes (Nag et al., 2014). Decoding in English is not, however, straightforward since English has an opaque, complex and disjunctive orthography with no direct association between a phoneme and its written equivalent: there are 26 letters of the alphabet but 44 different combinations of sounds that are represented by letters and combinations of letters. It takes up to three years for children with English as a first language to learn all those sounds. Hence, there may be some pupils who still find decoding difficult at secondary school, and so English teachers need to know how to diagnose where their particular difficulties lie and how to teach basic decoding. But decoding continues even with skilful, fluent readers as we all slow down and fixate on an unfamiliar word as we read, in order to understand it. So how do we decode?

A systematic synthetic phonics approach is strongly promoted at Reception and KS1 in the National Curriculum (DfE, 2014a), so that young children learn to read c-a-t or st-o-p from left to right. This is helpful in cracking the alphabet code but is only one of several possible decoding strategies, especially for older pupils who may have found just using phonics problematic.

Segmenting words into their onset and rime, such as 'st-op' or into syllables such as 'car-pet' or 'ele-phant' gives larger units of meaning for readers to work with, as does learning the whole words as one visual block. The shape of the words 'elephant' or 'dinosaur' are easily recognisable because of the different long stems above and below the line and perhaps because they are familiar words. Learning high-frequency words (listed in the KS1 curriculum) is helpful, particularly for words which do not obey phonics rules, and there are many in English, such as 'said' or 'fish'. Using rhyme and analogy also helps, such as 'light', 'sight', 'might' where the 'gh' is silent. Syntax offers further clues as English has a distinctive sentence pattern, for example, article-noun-verb-preposition-article-noun (the cat sat on the chair), so there are limits to what the end word can be, that is, something a cat will sit on. Context and collocation within a text also greatly support inferential word reading so that if a text is about football, then a young Leeds United fan will more easily read connected words such as 'supporter', 'goal' and 'crowd'.

Fluency, both reading aloud and 'silently' in your head, is important in understanding a text. Pupils need support in reading aloud fluently to reach levels of effortlessness and automaticity that free up their cognitive capacity to comprehend what they are reading, not merely to parrot the text (Oakhill et al., 2015). Findings by Hasbrouk and Tindal (2006) show that some readers read more slowly but this does not prevent them from comprehending at the same level as others, with a wide range, from 100 to 200 Words Correct Per Minute at KS3. Reading rate varies depending on the familiarity, difficulty and interest in the topic of the text (a difficult text is one that has one in ten unknown words) and the security of the reading environment (Hasbrouk and Tindal, 2006). Readers also need to read for at least two to three minutes to 'get into' the text and understand what is going on, as reflected in their fluency and prosody of expression.

READING COMPREHENSION, INFERENCE AND BUILDING MENTAL MODELS

Comprehension involves an additional, higher-level set of language skills and processes to decoding and also relies on readers' existing knowledge, for example, of vocabulary, grammar, syntax, 'world' and text knowledge, including understanding how narratives and other texts are structured. This is because reading is an active process involving readers constructing meaning, by applying relevant knowledge at key points to 'fill in the gaps' or make the required inferences, and integrating meaning across the whole text. Indeed, inference is one of the most important elements of comprehension as readers need to make inferences at the level of words, sentences, paragraphs and whole text (Oakhill and Cain, 2012). For example, as a reader reads, they first need to activate word meanings, but skilful readers can also infer unfamiliar vocabulary from the context (Cunningham, 2005), a skill you can teach all your pupils, as discussed below. The reader also has to make inferences and connections across sentences, for example, noun/pronoun, literal inferences, for example, linking the name of a female character, 'Varsha', at the start of one sentence, to 'She' in the next. The final main type of inference – 'knowledge-based' – requires the reader to apply personal, contextual/world or textual knowledge to create meaning (described to pupils as: self-text, world-text or text-text knowledge, Westbrook, Sutherland, Oakhill and Sullivan, 2019).

As the reader starts reading a non-fiction or fictional text, they build a mental model (Kintsch, 1998) or representation, integrating their inferences and making text connections, while continuing to apply their knowledge. They must constantly adapt their model as they read, either to accommodate new information, or indeed to revise their model, if the new information challenges this. Crucially, this means that readers must also constantly monitor their comprehension, clarifying any 'blocks' and finding a strategy to resolve these. For example, they may question a text in their heads to recall some prior information, skim back to identify a missing name or recall an event, reread a whole section, look up some unfamiliar vocabulary or Google contextual information, for example, about the 2008 riots in Johannesburg when reading *Now Is the Time for Running* (Williams, 2012). Finally, the reader should achieve global coherence or a satisfying, complete understanding at the end of the text.

In this active reading process, being able to draw on knowledge of text structure, for example, how to utilise subheadings, diagrams, captions and an index in non-fiction, or story structure in fiction, also supports readers' comprehension. For example, if you have read a detective story or one of Dahl's *Tales of the Unexpected* (1979), you will be looking out for surprising plot twists and 'red herrings', though you may still not predict that the murder weapon in one tale is a frozen leg of lamb! A reader who has never encountered the detective or thriller genres will find navigating these texts much more challenging.

When we asked you to reflect earlier on your knowledge of reading, this was based on the above reading theory. Briefly eliciting what pupils already know about a topic or the setting of a new novel is likely to engage them, and makes them conscious of the class's shared knowledge that they can apply to the text as they read, supporting comprehension and motivation. But if you've chosen an engaging novel, immersing the class in this, by reading a few chapters quickly, is also crucial, so keep pre-reading activities brief!

WHY DO STRUGGLING READERS FIND READING CHALLENGING?

You will now appreciate the complexity of reading and the multiple cognitive processes that need to occur simultaneously. Research (e.g. Oakhill and Cain, 2012) has shown that of all the skills outlined above, three of the biggest predictors of later success in reading comprehension with younger children are: the ability to make inferences; be aware of and be able to apply knowledge about text structure; and be able to monitor one's comprehension. Other studies (e.g. Perfetti and Stafura, 2014) have also identified depth of vocabulary knowledge, that is, knowing how a word such as 'table' can be used in different contexts, not just vocabulary breadth (knowing many words), as important for comprehension.

So why do KS3 'struggling readers' find these processes so challenging? First, they may have poor short-term memory and weaknesses in language processing (Moats, 2009). If struggling readers also lack fluency, they may expend too much of their processing capacity on decoding, leaving inadequate capacity to develop comprehension. Therefore, these readers may never reach the stage of building a mental model and embedding this in their long-term memory, a process they also find challenging (Compton et al., 2014). Second, some pupils have difficulties with inference, in addition to lacking the required general knowledge to make inferences (Oakhill et al., 2015). Lastly, struggling readers typically have poor self-monitoring skills: when reading independently, they are not aware of the precise moment when they reach a 'sticking point' and need to apply a strategy to be able to read on. Instead, they become utterly 'lost' in the text and lose motivation to continue.

Struggling readers' difficulties, including weaknesses in vocabulary and understanding how to apply knowledge of other similarly structured texts, are compounded by their lack of reading. Reading many extended texts independently, is highly correlated with developing comprehension (Mol and Bus, 2011). This is a strong argument for encouraging pupils' independent reading for pleasure (RfP, Cremin et al., 2014). Cunningham and Stanovich (1998) call this the 'Matthew Effect': the rich ('good readers') get richer, the poor ('struggling readers') poorer. 'Good' readers typically read more whole texts independently, thereby developing their vocabulary, knowledge, fluency and comprehension skills, all elements enabling and motivating them to read increasingly challenging texts afterwards. This virtuous cycle also develops good readers' positive reader identity or 'reading self-concept' (Retelsdorf et al., 2014): their belief that they can overcome challenges and that reading is rewarding, which also makes them try hard when the reading gets tough! Inevitably, struggling readers experience the opposite, damaging cycle: failure in comprehension, reading anxiety and negative reading self-concept lead to not reading independently, exacerbating comprehension weaknesses.

TEACHING COMPREHENSION

The best way to develop comprehension at KS3, especially for struggling or reluctant readers often in low sets, is by reading complete, engaging, challenging texts and exploring these with plenty of talk and whole-text connections (Fletcher, 2014; Westbrook et al., 2019).

Excessive microanalysis of literary features in extracts and drilling in written 'PEEZ' (Point-evidence-explanation-zoom) paragraphs has dominated many KS3 English lessons, understandably, because of GCSE pressures on performance, although even GCSE examiners do not advocate this (AQA, 2018a). But there is no evidence that this motivates reading or supports sophisticated whole-text comprehension; indeed, declining numbers taking A level English suggest the need to re-emphasise reading engagement at KS3 and KS4.

The list of teaching strategies below can help you create an encouraging and rich reading culture in your classroom in which pupils can learn to comprehend:

- Build on pupils' existing oral and literacy practices, making connections between home, school and primary school.
- Include your pupils' online and multimodal literacies, for example, watching films develops understanding of narrative structure, which is transferable to comprehending a novel (Kendeou, 2008).
- Create trusting, collaborative classrooms, where pupils who may not see themselves as 'readers' appreciate that they already 'read' every day and can discuss books with peers and teacher in groups and whole-class.
- Support your pupils from more disadvantaged backgrounds who have had fewer opportunities to access books, read and be read to in class.
- Present culturally relevant books in school, where pupils from diverse backgrounds can see themselves, identify with characters and become absorbed in reading: choice of texts is critical.
- Read a wide, eclectic range of novels yourself to make informed recommendations for a pupil who shows interest in a particular writer or theme.

- Dedicate time to individual reading (as you would for individual writing) at the end of a shared reader, in the library, or 'Drop-everything-and-read' (DEAR) time.
- Create your own small class library for browsing or to plant a suitably engaging book in a pupil's hand.
- Bring in a whole selection of texts that are thematically related to a completed shared reader for pupils to choose one to read independently (Westbrook, 2013).

READING ALOUD: WHOLE-CLASS AND SMALL-GROUP

You need to give pupils ample opportunities to practise reading aloud and silently. Interestingly, listening to a skilled reader, or teacher, read a text aloud fluently, at adequate pace and expressively also supports pupils' decoding, fluency and comprehension, scaffolding less experienced readers as they follow the same text with their eyes, leading them through it at greater speed so they can enjoy the story (Kuhn, 2010; Westbrook et al., 2019). You can stop at known 'sticking points' and model how to decode an unfamiliar word or to check that all are following the plot briefly, for 30 seconds.

It is helpful for pupils to read the first four to five chapters of a novel aloud together to ensure pupils understand the basic plot, characters and setting and avoid the discombobulation that happens in the opening pages. As the novel progresses, more inferences need to be made in the second half as the reader (and writer) looks backwards, infilling, as the end comes in sight, so a solid understanding at the beginning supports this. Once immersed in the novel, small groups of pupils can read aloud to one another, avoiding the public nature of the 'round-robin' class reading that so many pupils fear. This reading also helps readers develop their 'inner ear' of the text when they then read silently, on their own.

DIALOGIC GROUP TALK AND DEVELOPING PUPILS' COMPREHENSION STRATEGIES

Another way of ensuring your pupils become confident comprehenders is to teach or recap research-based, comprehension strategies: questioning, clarifying, summarising/recalling information, predicting, inferring, developing vocabulary, making whole-text connections and monitoring comprehension (EACEA, 2011; Scammacca et al., 2016). You can model how to use a strategy, by 'thinking aloud' as you read with the class: 'I'm not sure what "xeno/phobia" means here, but the context is Zimbabwean refugees arriving in South Africa – and I know what "phobia" means because I'm claustra/phobic, so I'm inferring it may be fear of ...?' Then ask pupils to practise using these strategies in small peer groups, while reading the next chapter, particularly monitoring their comprehension and asking spontaneous questions of their group, if anyone gets 'stuck'. In our 'Faster Read' study, one teacher gave her Year 8s key rings, representing six key strategies, to which they fixed their own images. She explicitly taught each strategy over a series of lessons: by week four, pupils had internalised these and would spontaneously display their key rings to illustrate which strategies they had found useful that lesson (Sutherland et al., 2020).

Use group talk to embed these strategies and make pupils metacognitively aware readers, who can choose flexibly from this range. Extensive evidence shows that talk supports reading comprehension, interpretation and motivation (Applebee et al., 2003; Okkinga et al., 2018; Soter et al., 2008; Sutherland, 2015; Sutherland et al., 2020). Use pair and structured group talk to support reading and induct pupils in how to be dialogic (equal and inclusive, inviting others to contribute) and how to ask good questions of texts (from literal – 'Who does "he" refer to?' – to inferential 'Why is Deo sad here?' and analytical 'Why does that mockingbird keep appearing?'). Model 'all questions in reading are good questions' using the interactive whiteboard, displaying texts and asking pupils to stick Post-it questions they would like to ask the text/author. Groups should create 'group guidelines': for example, respect all opinions; build on each other's ideas about texts; respectfully challenge; use tentative talk to tease out meanings ('Could it mean …?'); use reasons or textual examples to support points; and reflect afterwards on the quality of their group talk and their understanding of the book (Sutherland, 2015). Use drama activities, for example, hot-seating and conscience alley, to empathise with characters and deepen interpretation.

DEVELOPING INFERENCE, ASKING QUESTIONS AND BUILDING MENTAL MODELS

You need to teach pupils how a short, simple text is knitted together through literal inferences (Oakhill et al., 2015), developing metacognition in pupils' reading. Activity 5.2 sets out a simple exercise you can do with your pupils to show them how literal inference works.

Activity 5.2

Draw arrows between the nouns and their pronouns in this short story:

The lion was tired and lay down to sleep.
A mouse came out of the bush and jumped around over her.
'Grrr!' she roared.
'Sorry! I didn't see you there', the mouse squeaked.

Misunderstandings can arise over who 'her' and 'she' and 'you' refer to, but there are clues in the 'Grrr' and 'roar' and 'squeaked' that help readers draw on knowledge of the world to make sense of who says what. It is helpful to do the first two lines of this exercise together:

The lion was tired and lay down to sleep.
A mouse came out of the bush and jumped around over her.
'Grrr!' she roared.
'Sorry! I didn't see you there', the mouse squeaked.

An example is done for you here in Figure 5.1.

The lion was tired and lay down to sleep.
A mouse came out of the bush and jumped around over her.
'Grr!' she roared.
'Sorry! I didn't see you there', the mouse squeaked.

Figure 5.1 'Lion and Mouse' annotated

The next task in Activity 5.3, with a longer, whole text, shows how readers make knowledge-based inferences, by asking questions and making connections between clusters of words, while applying their 'world' knowledge. Please find Alice Walker's 'The Flowers' (1973), available online. If you've read this already, try an unfamiliar short story, for example, O'Brian's 'Samphire' online.

Activity 5.3

1. Read the title and the opening two paragraphs and pause:
   - Infer where the story is set
   - Predict what might happen next, and the end of the end of the story (start building your mental model)
   - Predict the tone of the story and any ideas it may explore (a hard question!)
2. Now read to the end. Ask two to three questions as you read – things that are puzzling or you want to know more about.
3. Were any of your predictions correct? How on earth did you make these, based on such short opening paragraphs? What knowledge were you drawing on?
4. Do you still have any questions that might be answered by a second reading? What do the flowers symbolise?

You will have experienced that the opening paragraphs of 'The Flowers' required you to connect related words – 'pigpen', 'harvesting', 'corn', 'cotton', 'peanuts', 'squash' and especially, 'smokehouse' and 'sharecropper cabin' – drawing on your knowledge of crops and specialist tenant-farming vocabulary to infer the setting as probably the American South, although this is never explicitly stated. Was your initial mental model of a carefree child running through the countryside? At what point did you have to adapt this to accommodate new information or clues given about the context, combining this with your own knowledge – the history of African Americans' persecution – to comprehend this story? Did you predict the tone would change so radically? If yes, were you applying knowledge of other, similar texts?

These kinds of metacognitive activities allow your pupils into the 'secret' of reading, enabling them to understand how to infer, ask questions, make predictions and create meaning in the text. Comprehension is sometimes regarded as a lower-level skill than analysis, but understanding what the 'flowers' in Walker's title may symbolise shows that comprehension and interpretation are not distinct, but on a continuum. Spending more time on whole-text comprehension enables your KS3/4 pupils to excitedly discover for themselves the patterns, motifs, oppositions and parallels in narratives.

ASSESSMENT OF READING

Assessment of reading should take different forms, be formative in function as you move your pupils through a text, going almost unnoticed by pupils, and should not interrupt or curtail the flow of the narrative or discussion. Leave formal written work and literary analysis for final tasks. Do explicitly value using exploratory group and class discussion, and drama tasks, making notes (Post-it Notes are good) as you quietly listen to a group, or audiotape group talk for later assessment. Groups can 'hot-seat' a character or explore an assigned chapter together, developing character, plot, theme, mood and narrative voice and do a group presentation of key aspects to the class. To assess individual pupil recall of key events, characters or thematic development, use Google Docs quizzes or ask pupils to do tweets by a character or a 'Role on the Wall'. Visualisations of the plot using graphic organisers support whole-text structure, similarly, mapping out timelines, or event maps, and using pictures or photos to create family trees of characters or tension and emotion graphs. More conventional written assessments – a review, commentary or rewriting an event from the viewpoint of a character, pupils' own stories on similar themes or simply an analytical essay – will be richer for all the above activities. And try to avoid asking pupils to write the diary of a character – old, tried, and does not work!

Experiencing the importance of leading KS3 struggling and reluctant readers through a whole, challenging, engaging text for the first time, a recent student teacher, Andy Bates, said: 'If you've never climbed a mountain, how would you know that the view when you reach the top is fantastic?'

SUMMARY AND KEY POINTS

- Focus on motivating reading and developing pupils' comprehension and analysis, by reading a class reader quickly enough for pupils to follow the narrative and want to know what happens next!
- At KS3, read a minimum of two whole, challenging, culturally diverse, typically modern texts every year to engage pupils and develop their reading. Expect pupils to read three+ independently per year of KS3.
- Read expressively aloud to classes and encourage pupils to read in groups.
- Focus on whole-text inference and comprehension, not just analysis of literary features in extracts.
- Use exploratory group talk and drama activities.
- Set activities to support understanding of narrative structure, for example, graphic organisers.
- Support vocabulary development, through pupils reading many texts, becoming skilled at inferring unfamiliar words.
- Assess reading through group and class talk and imaginative writing tasks.

KEY RESOURCES

1. Follow the United Kingdom Literacy Association's Children's Book Awards – the only book award judged by teachers! https://ukla.org/ukla_resources/the-ukla-book-awards-2020-winners/. Follow the Carnegie and Kate Greenaway Medals, and Good Reads website (www.goodreads.com/?ref=nav_home) to identify great young adult (YA) fiction for you to read as a class and to recommend to pupils. Set up YA book groups with colleagues – and pupils – to explore new fiction together and write blogs about it for other pupils and teachers.
2. Browse English & Media Centre publications, blogs and Continuing Professional Development events for ideas on engaging, culturally relevant texts and stimulating approaches to teaching reading and developing comprehension and interpretation at KS3 and KS4, for example, www.englishandmedia.co.uk/publications/diverse-shorts-literature-to-promote-critical-thinking-print.
3. Read this accessible book on theories of how pupils develop their comprehension and implications for your teaching of reading: Oakhill, J., Cain, K. and

Elbro, C. (2015) *Understanding and Teaching Reading Comprehension: A Handbook.* London: Routledge.

4. Excite pupils to read by watching the author talk about why they wrote the book, for example, Alex Wheatle: www.youtube.com/watch?v=prNcqQJQdac.

   Encourage pupils to write to authors about why they enjoyed their book and invite local authors to your school to keep the dialogue going: www.booktrust.org.uk/books-and-reading/tips-and-advice/reading-in-schools/how-to-arrange-an-author-visit/.
5. Read *Why Closing the Word Gap Matters: The Oxford Language Report* (2018). Oxford: Oxford University Press, to understand pupils' different starting points with vocabulary in Year 7 on, and what you can do to support their vocabulary development, thereby supporting their comprehension: https://global.oup.com/education/content/dictionaries/key-issues/word-gap/?region=uk
6. Bleiman, B. (2020) *What Matters in English Teaching: Collected Blogs and Other Writing*. London: English & Media Centre. Bleiman's chapter on reading emphasises the importance of motivating and engaging KS3 pupils in reading with some stimulating approaches for you to experiment with.
7. Keep up to date with national trends in reading and how you can support the most disadvantaged pupils with their reading, by browsing the National Literacy Trust's website, https://literacytrust.org.uk/research-services/research-reports/children-and-young-peoples-reading-in-2020-before-and-during-the-covid-19-lockdown/.
8. Read this book, showing engaging ways of approaching reading and ideas about how to research reading in your classroom: Cliff Hodges, G. (2016) *Researching and Teaching Reading: Developing Pedagogy through Critical Inquiry.* London: Routledge.

Chapter 6 Teaching the process of writing

DEBRA MYHILL

INTRODUCTION

Mary Pipher makes a strong argument for the transformative power of writing:

> Words are the most powerful tools at our disposal. With them writers have saved lives and taken them, brought justice and confounded it, started wars and ended them. Writers can change the way we think and transform our definitions of right and wrong.
>
> (Pipher, 2006, Cover Copy)

But how many secondary pupils have a classroom experience of writing that empowers them as agentic and autonomous writers? More commonly, many pupils see writing as a chore, a necessary evil, heavily constrained by the expectations of assessment. This chapter foregrounds the process of writing, rather than the written text, and sets out to support you in teaching writing with confidence, creating engaged communities of writers in your classroom.

This chapter explores what research in cognitive psychology tells us about the writing process – what happens in our head when we write. Firstly, it outlines the first cognitive models of the writing process and in particular, consider the processes of planning, drafting and reviewing. The differences between developing writers and skilled writers are explored, and throughout the chapter a range of practical ways to build an attention to the writing process into the teaching of writing are shared.

At the end of this chapter you should be able to:

- understand cognitive theories of the process of writing;
- understand the cognitive concepts of planning, drafting and reviewing processes;
- recognise that the writing process is recursive, not linear, staged steps;
- know how teaching can integrate attention to writing as process.

But first, how much have you thought about what happens when you write yourself? This chapter is punctuated by a series of opportunities for you to work on a piece of writing of your own, and to reflect on the process of writing that you

DOI: 10.4324/9781003093060-7

adopt. Please don't skip these, as they tie in to the concepts and the ideas that the chapter explores.

Activity 6.1: Time to write

Think of a place that is very special to you, somewhere that you feel happy. It can be an indoor place or an outdoor space. Take a few moments, closing your eyes if it helps, to revisit this place in your mind's eye. Imagine yourself in this place and look at all the details. What can you see: what colours, shapes, light and shadows, people, objects etc.? What can you hear: nearby, in the distance? Are there any smells or textures that you associate with this place? How do you feel when you are in this place? Recall all the details of your special place, as though you are filming it.

Now you are going to free-write. Free-writing is when you write without worrying about whether what you are writing is any good, or whether the spelling is correct. The key thing is to keep writing, just letting the words and ideas flow. You just get your ideas and images and feelings down onto the page, and let your pen take your imagination for a walk. No one will read this free-writing – it is just for you.

Give yourself five minutes to do this free-writing: try to keep writing throughout, recalling all the details of your special place. And no evaluation of whether what you have written is any good!

THE FIRST COGNITIVE MODEL OF THE PROCESSES INVOLVED IN WRITING

The first attempt to map out what happens in our heads when we try to move from thoughts to words and sentences on the page was a study by Hayes and Flower (1980a). They investigated the processes involved in the act of writing by asking mature writers to undertake a piece of writing and at intervals through the writing, to say what they were thinking – a research process known as 'think-aloud'. Their analysis of these data led to their development of the first model of the cognitive processes of writing (Figure 6.1). They represent these as Planning, Translating and Reviewing, but importantly the model reminds us that these processes are influenced by two other factors, the Task Environment and the Writer's Long-Term Memory, and what we know about the topic and the writing expectations for that kind of writing. So asking pupils to write a personal narrative about a time when they felt fear draws on personal experiences of being frightened and their familiarity with narrative. In contrast, asking pupils to write an argument about the need for action on single-use plastics requires knowledge of a range of facts and opinions about single-use plastic and understanding of how to write an argument. When teaching writing, we need to consider both of these factors in our planning, summarised in effect as two key planning questions:

- what are the demands of this writing task in terms of the topic, and the writing type/genre?
- what do pupils in this class know about this topic and the expectations of this writing type/genre?

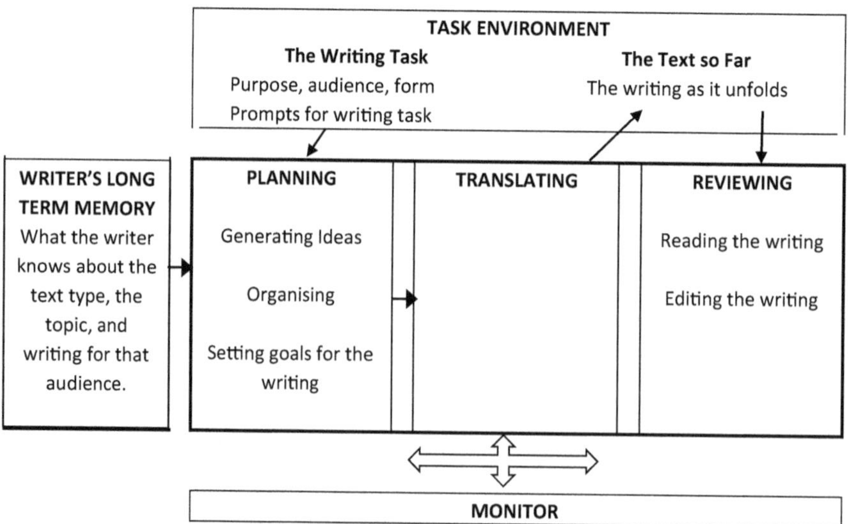

Figure 6.1 An adapted version of Hayes and Flower's (1980a) model of writing processes

A crucial element of Hayes and Flower's model was that they did not see the writing processes of planning, translating and reviewing as sequential, occurring one after another, but recursive, interacting with each other. They suggested that a mental monitor constantly switches a writer's attention across the three mental processes. So if you are creating a written outline of your text to help you organise your writing, you are inevitably evaluating that as you develop it, deciding what structure to use, what ideas to include and so on. As you write, you may pause and reread the text produced so far, which might generate new ideas for where you want to go next, or may trigger you to revise something you have already written. So let us pause at this point, and revisit your free-writing.

Activity 6.2: Time to write

Go back to your earlier free-writing about a special place. Reread it, underlining words and images which seem to capture the essence of that place. As you do this, you may well want to change some, or you may come up with new images or descriptions, so you can add those too. Don't worry about how messy your page may look – this is not about neat, polished writing!

PLANNING, DRAFTING AND REVIEWING

Since Hayes and Flower's first model, there have been several other versions, all making modifications to this original version (e.g. Flower and Hayes, 1981; Scardamalia and Bereiter, 1987; Berninger and Swanson, 1994; Hayes, 1996; Kellogg, 1996; Berninger et al., 1996; van den Bergh and Rijlaarsdam, 1996). Each of these modifications refined or elaborated on particular elements of the original model, or added in new factors influencing writing, such as motivation, working memory and the social context. But, in a nutshell, common to all the cognitive models are three key processes of planning, drafting, and reviewing, which are likely to already be familiar to you as terms frequently used in the writing classroom. It is worth looking at these in a little more detail.

The planning process, as represented in cognitive psychology, is not simply the practice of creating a written plan for a piece of writing, which is the general way of thinking about this in school. It is a much broader, messier process of preparation that includes mulling over ideas and incubation, clarifying what needs to be done, setting goals for the task and generating ideas. The first writing task that you did involved planning processes, by using free-writing, defined by Elbow and Belanoff (2000) as writing, without pausing, capturing any ideas or thoughts that come to mind. It is a practice advocated by many professional writers and writing teachers because it separates 'the producing process from the revising process' (Elbow, 1998, p.14). For writers and teachers, the benefit of this is usually linked with freeing up imagination and creativity without the judgement of evaluation and revision. For cognitive psychologists, free-writing is an example of an activity which reduces cognitive 'load', the burden you are placing on your working memory, by not asking it to manage generating ideas at the same time as evaluating and revising them. The more usual school view of making a plan, or an outline, for a piece of writing is, of course, part of the planning process, and there is evidence that writing plans can help improve the quality of the writing, provided the plans are effective. Hayes and Flower found that 'Good writers appear to have more flexible, high-level plans and more self-conscious control of their planning than poor writers' (1980b, p.44).

Effective plans do not address only the content of the piece of writing – what to say – but also the rhetorical and structural plan for the text – how to say it. However, a plan is a set of initial intentions, not a precise summary of the final text: 'Good plans are rich enough to work from and argue about, but cheap enough to throw away' (Hayes and Flower, 1980b, p.43). I wrote a careful plan for this chapter, covering both content and structure, but already the chapter has evolved to be something rather different. The writing of a text often triggers a re-evaluation of the plan and modifications and changes. This is another example of the recursiveness of the writing process: planning is not time-limited to a period before writing a draft, it recurs throughout the whole process. In the classroom, we can support writers' understanding of the planning process by drawing attention not only to making a written plan but also to other aspects of the planning process such as: how to think through what the writing task is asking them to do in terms of audience and purpose; how to consciously consider what they know about the characteristics of the genre they are writing; and thus how to plan for the rhetorical and structural aspects of the text as well as the content. Using free-writing regularly can help pupils generate ideas and find writing more approachable, but make sure they understand that it is a tool for generating ideas, not a first draft!

Drafting refers to the mental process of moving from thoughts in the head or an outline for writing to producing the text itself. It is not well researched in cognitive psychology. Hayes and Flower rather problematically called it 'translating' in their first model (Figure 6.1), as though drafting were a simple process of translating words in the head into words on the page. But it is much more complex than this. Often we have incomplete or half-thoughts and it is through writing that we clarify what they are and how to express them. Later research divides drafting into formulation and execution (Kellogg, 1994, p.31; Alamargot and Chanquoy, 2001, p.71), where formulation is shaping the preverbal message into words, and where execution is the transcribing of those words as written text. Nonetheless, the key and most relevant aspect of drafting is that it represents the process of producing a version, or multiple versions, of the written text. Teaching pupils to pause periodically to read what they have written while drafting, and to revisit any plans they made, helps make drafting more purposeful with the goals of the writing task in mind. Likewise, oral rehearsal, where a writer speaks aloud (or 'aloud in the head') the next clause or sentence they are about to write can help reduce the cognitive load of producing verbal text, and at the same time allow the writer to hear the text they are composing. Of course, it also reinforces the interaction of planning and reviewing with the drafting process.

In contrast to the drafting process, there has been a considerable body of work on the reviewing or revising process (e.g. Sommers, 1980; Chanquoy, 2001; Keen, 2020), largely because it is much easier to research changes to a written text through revision than it is to capture what is happening in the brain as text is produced. Most researchers distinguish between evaluating the written text, which is about thinking and judgement, and revising the text, which is about making changes. This is a helpful distinction for the classroom, as often it is the evaluating, deciding what is good and what needs changing, which pupils find difficult, as it relies on knowledge about writing which they may not yet have. In the second writing activity above, you were engaged in the reviewing process, as I invited you to evaluate the images in your free-writing and to revise the images by making changes. If you added any new images, you were also using generating ideas, part of the planning process – another salient reminder of the recursiveness of the writing process.

The journey from research to classroom practice is often inspired by a professional desire for teaching to be research-informed, but can also lead to misunderstandings of the research which do not help pupils' learning or teachers' teaching. This is very much the case with these cognitive understandings of the mental processes of writing. Planning, drafting and reviewing are cognitive processes, but curricula and classroom teaching materials nearly always make them stages or steps in the writing process. As processes, they interact with each other, and mature writers cycle recursively between planning, drafting and reviewing throughout the process of writing. There are fuzzy boundaries between them: if you added a new image to your free-writing, it is generating an idea, but it has occurred because you were reviewing your images. In the classroom, planning, drafting and revising are too often treated as chronological, linear steps in the task of producing a finished piece of writing, which neither draws accurately on the research nor helps pupils become more adept at managing the writing process. Find ways, through your teaching plans, to disrupt the plan-draft-revise sequence, such as drafting and revising a character description before planning and writing the full narrative.

Having just considered each of these writing processes, let us return to your own writing, and begin to develop it.

Activity 6.3: Time to write

Revisit and reread your free-writing, and the changes you make to the images. Now write (draft) just one paragraph where you try to recreate for your reader both the sense of place and your feelings about it.

DIFFERENCES BETWEEN MATURE AND DEVELOPING WRITERS

One significant strand of modification of the early cognitive models of writing processes investigated how these models related to younger and more inexperienced writers (e.g. Bereiter and Scardamalia, 1982; Berninger and Swanson, 1994;

Berninger et al., 1996), recognising that models based on the thinking aloud of mature writers may have some limitations if applied to developing writers. This, of course, is particularly important from a teaching point of view. For children just beginning to write, a lot of their memory capacity is taken up just getting words onto the page, and thinking about letter shaping and word spacing. Alarmargot and Chanquoy (2001, p.49) explain that younger writers do not manage organising operations in writing

> because their planning and processing abilities are weaker and more limited and also because the load associated with the writing task is heavier than for experts as they have not yet automatised the low level writing operations (such as graphic transcription).

In other words, they are not yet fluent writers.

The concept of 'writing fluency' recurs in the research on writing development, because children who are not fluent have little cognitive attention available to think about what they are writing, or what they will write in the rest of the text. Writing fluency is a somewhat slippery concept to define as for some it is simply about writing with speed and accuracy (Johnson and Street, 2013; Hier et al., 2019), but in general, it refers to the ability to generate written text with ease with a high level of automaticity (Brand and Brand, 2006). When you were free-writing in the first Time to Write activity of this chapter, you were probably demonstrating writing fluency. You were letting words and ideas flow from your head onto the page without having to think about spelling, vocabulary and sentence structure. Because writing fluency means the writer has more cognitive 'space' to think about the bigger picture of writing – the ideas, the structure, the whole text – there is a relationship between writing fluency and writing quality (Dellerman et al., 1996; Graham et al., 2012; Gillespie and Graham, 2014). For many secondary pupils, other than those with specific learning difficulties, transcription and writing fluency is not usually a problem. However, for writers with English as an Additional Language (EAL), a lack of writing fluency may be impeding their capacity to progress. For pupils with EAL, writing fluency may be reduced for two reasons. Firstly, if the script of their first language is not alphabetic, they have to master the automatic shaping of English letters. Imagine how much easier it would be for you to copy a line of Italian, compared with a line of Urdu or Mandarin, which are not alphabetic languages. But also, generating text in a second or additional language can be more difficult than in a first language (Chenoweth and Hayes, 2001) because you need to have access to the vocabulary and the syntactical or grammatical structures which enable you to communicate in English. To support EAL writers with writing fluency, create opportunities for them to talk about their ideas and develop the key vocabulary they need before they write, and when they are getting their ideas down onto the page, encourage them to use words from their first language if they need to, and return to them later to find out the appropriate English word.

You may also find that some of the weaker writers in your classes also have limited writing fluency. Make time to observe pupils as they write, and note if they seem to be particularly slow at generating text. Various timed exercises have been shown to increase writing fluency (Datchuk, 2017), but if you use these in a secondary classroom, be creative about adapting to make them more like games, as they can be a little dull and not likely to excite a teenager who is already struggling with writing! But free-writing can be a real help in fostering writing fluency in secondary school because it is not evaluated and it encourages letting the ideas flow. Another strategy can be helping writers to use 'oral rehearsal' – the process whereby you speak aloud or aloud in your head what you are going to write next, as a way of rehearsing the shape of a clause or sentence. It can also be valuable for some writers to learn to touch-type and to word-process their writing, as this too can assist writing fluency.

However, writing fluency is only one difference between writers of different levels of proficiency. Another key strand is how well developing writers can manage the recursivity of the writing process, and this has very real implications for secondary pupils. Berninger et al. argued that 'in skilled writers, planning, translating and revising are mature processes that interact with one another. In beginning and developing writers, each of these processes is still developing and each process is on its own trajectory, developing at its own rate' (1996, p.198). In your secondary classroom, you probably find that your better writers are already planning, drafting and reviewing in an interactive way. But you also have writers who are much more inclined to deal with each process as a separate stage, and in practice often not review and revise their work, and may not plan either. It is worth noting whether there are pupils you teach who simply draft a piece of writing, put the final full stop and sit back, finished. Unlike very young writers who simply do not have the mental capacity to manage the writing process recursively, in secondary schools, pupils who just draft and complete have learned this behaviour and they need help and support in handling the writing process more strategically (Harris et al., 2015). Explicitly teach pupils the words that reflect the writing process, such as generating ideas, free-writing, evaluating, revising and proofreading so they can become a shared language for discussing the writing process, and scaffold each of these processes carefully. You might also consider adopting a portfolio approach, where pupils collect finished drafts of writing over a term, and then work on revising two or three of them at the end of term.

CONCLUSION

This chapter has offered an overview of the writing process as understood in cognitive psychology, and drawn attention to the implications of this for the secondary writing classroom. What the chapter has not done is consider sociocultural perspectives on the process of writing which position writing as a social practice, situated within communities of writers, and where the writing process can be shared and collaborative, which you will find discussed in more detail in Chapter 9. In research, these are very separate fields of inquiry, but in the classroom they are both equally important. We need to think about how our teaching supports pupils in becoming increasingly aware of how they manage their own writing process, and increasingly adept at switching between planning, drafting and revising. But at the same time, this needs to be located within classrooms where writing is valued, where writers' voices are heard, and where there is time and space for writing.

Activity 6.4: Consolidating your learning

1 Reflect on the three episodes of writing that you have undertaken alongside reading this chapter, and reread your writing. Now consider how what you have done aligns with the ideas raised in this chapter. Write a 200-word reflection which makes direct connections between the theoretical

concepts in cognitive psychology and your own practical experience of writing.

2 Look at the National Curriculum for writing relevant to your teaching: can you find examples of how it incorporates the writing process into the curriculum?

3 Prepare a sequence of four to five lesson plans addressing writing, thinking as you plan about how to draw on the ideas in this chapter. Annotate the completed sequence with the writing process concepts you are addressing.

SUMMARY AND KEY POINTS

- Cognitive research on the writing process reminds us that it is not simply the writing itself that needs to be considered but also the environment for writing, and what writers already know about writing.
- Planning, drafting and reviewing are common to almost all writing models, but these are process, not chronological steps or stages. Mature writers manage these processes recursively, switching repeatedly between them.
- Very young writers use up a lot of mental capacity simply getting writing onto the page; for them transcription is effortful. As writers mature, they should achieve writing fluency, where they can write with reasonable speed and accuracy because transcriptional aspects of writing have become automatised.
- Less proficient, or less motivated writers in secondary school may simply draft their writing with no meaningful planning or revision.

KEY RESOURCES

1. Cremin, T. and Myhill, D. (2012) Laying the Foundations for Writing (chapter 1). In *Writing Voices: Creating Communities of Writers*. London: Routledge. This chapter gives an accessible overview of different theoretical perspectives on writing and the writing process.
2. Flower, L. and Hayes, J. (1981) A cognitive process theory of writing. *College Composition and Communication*. 32 (4). pp.365–87. This is one of the earliest articles outlining the cognitive model of writing, and worth reading in full.
3. Keen, J. (2017) Teaching the writing process. *Changing English*. 24 (4). pp.372–85. This article complements the present chapter very well, exploring the writing process and how it can equip secondary writers to be more capable writers
4. YouTube. Anne Haas Dyson. *Place of Childhoods in School Writing Programs: A Matter of Ethics*. Available from: www.youtube.com/watch?v=Nm2CQXgHzu8&t=5s. Anne Haas Dyson is one of the most eminent researchers who looks at writing from a sociocultural perspective. It also draws on research in early years classrooms, and it is important for you, as secondary teachers to understand the learning trajectories your pupils have followed.
5. YouTube. *Ian McEwan on His Writing Process*. www.youtube.com/watch?v=q0ZEE9_iZRk
6. Arvon website: www.arvon.org/. Arvon is a creative writing charity, which includes as part of its work running writing residentials for children and young people, and they often work specifically with young people from disadvantaged

backgrounds. Look at their Learning pages, especially the Learning Resources page with free teaching materials for creative writing, including a specific resource for bilingual or multilingual writers. Look also at the Arvon values on the About page, and consider how you might recreate these in a secondary classroom.

Chapter 7 Creative grammar for creative teachers

DEBRA MYHILL

INTRODUCTION

Creative writers have long recognised the power of control over grammar as an essential aspect of becoming an adept writer. Former poet laureate, Ted Hughes, reflected that 'conscious manipulation of syntax deepens engagement and releases invention' (Hughes, 1987), making a direct connection between grammar (syntax) and creativity (invention) in writing. Significantly, he also uses the word 'conscious', indicating that this creative use of syntax is something the writer is aware that he or she is manipulating. A similar link between grammar and shaping text was made by novelist, Ursula Le Guin, who, lamenting the loss of grammar teaching in schools, argued that:

> Somehow we're supposed to be able to write without knowing anything about the equipment we're using. We're supposed to 'express ourselves', to squeeze out the orange juice of our souls, without being given anything to do it with, not even a knife to cut the orange [...] Writing a sentence that expresses what you want to say isn't any easier than plumbing or fiddling. It takes craft.
>
> (Le Guin, 2015, pp.13–14)

And yet there are also many creative writers who argue passionately that it is perfectly possible to be a good writer without knowing any grammar, and some denounce grammar as anti-creativity. The subject of grammar provokes strongly dissenting perspectives which even after more than 50 years of debate are still not reconciled.

This chapter briefly addresses why teaching grammar has this long history of disagreement concerning its value in the teaching of writing. It then outlines the important difference between tacit and explicit grammatical knowledge, and why this is relevant to teaching. The principal focus of the chapter, however, is the explicit teaching of grammar through a functionally oriented pedagogy, which positions grammar as a creative and constructive resource in the teaching of writing. In this way, through making meaningful connections between a grammatical choice and its rhetorical or communicative effect in a text, pupils develop

DOI: 10.4324/9781003093060-8

understanding of the craft of writing, and the potential power of their own grammatical choices.

At the end of this chapter you should:

- understand why 'grammar teaching' provokes differing views;
- be able to distinguish between tacit and explicit knowledge of grammar;
- know how a view of grammar as choice supports the teaching of writing;
- be able to plan effectively for embedding grammar within the teaching of writing.

GRAMMAR TEACHING: A CONTROVERSIAL ISSUE

So why is grammar such a contested topic? In part, it is because the word 'grammar' means different things to different people, both lexically and emotionally. Moreover, there are different types of grammar in the field of linguistics – generative grammar; computational grammar; functional grammar and so on. Perhaps, even more relevant to the controversy about teaching grammar is that people's experiences of being taught grammar shape their view of what grammar teaching is, or should be. For some, it is about understanding correctness, and applying rules to language use to avoid making errors, thus making writers more proficient. For others, it is about crushing writers' creativity by focusing only on the mistakes they make. For yet others, it is about a curiosity and an interest in how language works as a communicative resource. And for those, including many English teachers, who were never taught about grammar, the idea of grammar provokes shame, fear and anxiety (Watson, 2012). As a consequence, the debates and arguments can often be frustrating as contributors are commonly discussing the subject from very different perspectives.

At the same time, the debates within the teaching profession about the place of grammar in the curriculum have also been shaped by the empirical evidence. Until recently, the only empirical evidence that considered the possible learning benefits of grammar, largely a series of meta-analyses, concluded that it had no impact (Braddock et al., 1963; Hillocks, 1984; Hillocks and Smith, 1991; Andrews et al., 2006; Graham and Perin, 2007). Indeed, the seminal quotation from Braddock et al.'s 1963 study, that teaching grammar had 'a harmful effect on the development of original writing' (Braddock et al., 1963, p.37) has reverberated through the debate ever since. But there is a real problem with this research, which links back to the varying views of what grammar is. The studies taught discrete, form-focused grammar lessons where pupils learned the structure of the language but did not look at written texts to consider how the grammar was used, nor did they teach it in the context of helping pupils understand the effect of the grammatical choices they made in their own writing. It is hard to imagine why teaching pupils to name and identify nouns, or subordinate clauses, on Tuesday might make them more adept writers in the writing lesson on Thursday! For discussions about the grammar debate from different national perspectives, you might look at Kamler (1995), Kolln and Hancock (2005) or Myhill and Watson (2019). More recently, however, there is a growing body of research internationally pointing to new and effective synergies between teaching grammar and teaching writing, all with the common foundation of looking at how grammar is functioning in specific contexts. This chapter builds on this contemporary research.

Activity 7.1: Grammatical subject knowledge

As noted above, many teachers were not themselves taught grammar and can feel very anxious about it. Test out your own grammar knowledge and build your confidence using this website – www.cybergrammar.co.uk/ – designed for teachers.

TACIT AND EXPLICIT KNOWLEDGE OF GRAMMAR

Another misunderstanding which muddles thinking about the teaching of grammar is confusing tacit and explicit knowledge of grammar. Just look for a moment at these sentences and consider whether you think there is anything wrong with them, and if so, how you would explain the problem.

- She bought his wife a leather red small handbag.
- I am knowing my language very well.

The chances are that you could correct the 'error' in each of these sentences easily, but your ability to explain the error (problems with adjectival word order; and use of present progressive rather than present simple) depends on your explicit grammatical knowledge. The concept of tacit and explicit knowledge relates to all learning, not just grammar, and Polanyi (1966) is usually credited with the first exploration of these concepts. He argued that 'we can know more than we can tell' (1967, p.4), drawing attention to the fact that we all have knowledge which we cannot verbalise or explain. He uses the example of how we recognise the face of someone we know – we can all do it, but we cannot explain how we do it.

All language users, except those with specific language impairments, learn how to use the grammar of their first language without being taught the rules. The rules are acquired tacitly through social interactions and contextual experience. Young children learning to talk demonstrate this perfectly: they make mistakes which show they are learning the rules, and in time, those mistakes disappear. For example, many young children add '-ed' to form the past tense of an irregular verb (gotted; thoughted; putted), because this is the rule for regular verbs. This is tacit knowledge. But they certainly cannot say, at about age three, that the past tense on regular verbs in English is formed using '-ed'! To verbalise this requires explicit grammatical knowledge which they do not have. This tacit knowledge of grammar is an immense resource, and if we had to rely on being taught all the rules of language, we would be much slower at developing proficiency as speakers and writers. It is also acknowledged in the National Curriculum for English in England (Primary):

> The grammar of our first language is learnt naturally and implicitly through interactions with other speakers and from reading. Explicit knowledge of grammar is, however, very important, as it gives us more conscious control and choice in our language.
>
> (DfE 2013a, p.64)

When pupils learn to name and identify a noun (explicit knowledge), they have already been proficient users of nouns for years, as it is impossible to talk or write without nouns (tacit knowledge). This raises an important 'why bother' question – if pupils already have tacit knowledge of grammar, why do we need to teach it to them explicitly? One reason is because tacit knowledge depends on the kinds of language experiences you have had, including your reading experience. Writing is not speech written down (Perera, 1987), and one very real challenge for pupils in secondary classrooms is to understand the diverse and different ways written texts are constructed compared with spontaneous speech. Explicit grammatical knowledge can help build this understanding. It is also important to remember that pupils with English as an Additional Language (EAL) may need explicit grammatical knowledge to help them strengthen their use of English grammar constructions, especially those that are not paralleled in their home language. Tense and aspect are often challenging for pupils with EAL, as is adjectival word order, and seemingly random patterns of how we use prepositions ('aim at' or 'aim to') or articles ('the law' but 'society') in English.

GRAMMAR AS CHOICE

Whilst we cannot ignore the importance of tacit grammatical knowledge, explicit knowledge is particularly valuable in a classroom context. Because it is accessible, usable knowledge and can be verbalised, it generates possibilities for direct teacher input about language, for whole-class or peer-to-peer sharing and discussing of language, and for independent decision-making about language. None of these things are possible with tacit knowledge. Due to a growing recognition of these possibilities, there has been a developing body of research advocating the benefit of explicit grammar teaching in the past ten years. Researchers at the Centre for Research in Writing at the University of Exeter have shown through both large-scale quantitative studies and in-depth qualitative studies that grammar can have a beneficial effect on pupils' capacities as writers (Myhill, Jones, Lines and Watson, 2012; Jones, Myhill and Bailey, 2013; Myhill, Jones and Lines, 2018) and as readers (Myhill and Watson, 2017). Research in Australia (Macken-Horarik and Sandiford, 2016); in Canada (Nadeau, 2017); in the United States (Schleppegrell and Moore, 2018; Klingelhofer and Schleppegrel, 2016, and in Spain (Fontich and Garcia-Folgado, 2018) similarly highlights the learning power of explicit grammatical knowledge. Common to all of this research is a rejection of a prescriptivist view of grammar as imposing rules on languages users, and a much more creative sense of grammar as a resource for recognising the possibilities of language. In the classroom, this plays out in lessons where attention to grammar is embedded within relevant points for learning.

Let's pause at this point and explore what this means in practice with an example that we have repeatedly used in continuing professional development sessions with teachers. Look at the sentence below, read it aloud and think about where the emphasis might come in the sentence. Can you create other versions of this sentence, rearranging the words in different ways (using all the words and adding no new ones)?

And out of the mists came a figure in flowing green walking across the water.

Now look at the sentence below, which is one of many possible rearrangements, and compare it with the first one. How do they differ? If you were filming the two sentences, how might you manage the camera shots?

And a figure in flowing green came walking across the water out of the mists.

For many readers, the first sentence foregrounds the mists and establishes suspense or mystery as the emerging figure slowly becomes clearer and more distinct; in the second, it is the figure who is prominent from the start and the mists are relegated to a backing position. The first sentence is taken from Michael Morpurgo's children's book *Arthur, High King of Britain*, at a key moment in the narrative, and the second is the rearrangement. The point, however, is not that one sentence is better than the other – and of course they are both grammatically correct – but that the grammatical choices we make can alter how we communicate with our readers. Here, the first sentence uses a fronted adverbial (out of the mists) to foreground the mists, and by putting the subject of the sentence (a figure in flowing green) after the verb (came), a delay is created before the subject is revealed. In the second sentence, the subject is in its common position in English at the start of the sentence and before the verb. This is the 'conscious manipulation of syntax' that Hughes noted as linked with creativity, and it is this kind of understanding which our approach to the teaching of grammar seeks to foster.

This way of thinking about grammar turns traditional views of grammar and traditional ways of teaching grammar on their head and, in contrast to decontextualised grammar lessons where pupils learn to name and identify grammatical structures and undertake drills and exercises, this approach makes meaningful learning connections for pupils between grammatical choices and their impact on the crafting of text. This new direction in grammar pedagogy draws on the theoretical thinking about language of the linguist, Halliday (1978, 2003), who argued that grammar is a crucial resource for making meaning. He signalled the need for a change in how we think about grammar: 'our traditional compositional thinking about language needs to be, if not replaced by, at least complemented by a "systems" thinking whereby we seek to understand the nature and the dynamic of a semiotic system as a whole' (Halliday and Matthiessen, 2004, p.20). This is a functional approach to grammar, focusing on what the grammar is doing in the text, rather than a form-focused approach, which concentrates on identifying the grammatical structure. In other words, grammar is not about breaking down language into its component parts, but looking at how those parts – at word, phrase, clause and text level – work together holistically to shape meanings. And at the heart of an understanding of the interrelationship of grammar as meaning is enabling pupils in our classrooms to

GRAMMAR AS CHOICE: INTERNATIONAL PERSPECTIVES

The point of grammar study is to enable pupils to make choices from among a range of linguistic resources, and to be aware of the effects of different choices on the rhetorical power of their writing.
Israel: Lefstein, 2009 p.382

Every choice carries a different meaning, and grammar is concerned with the implications of such choices.
UK: Carter and McCarthy 2006 p.4.

Encourage writers to recognize and use the grammatical and stylistic choices available to them and to understand the rhetorical effects those choices can have on their readers.
US: Kolln and Gray 2016: Introduction

We need to understand how our ideational choices construct participants, processes, and circumstances from a particular perspective; we need to attend to our choices of mood and modality, which encode relations of authority and agency between writers and readers; we need to think about how textual choices work to foreground and background ideas, to construct cause and effect, to position information as old or new.
South Africa: Janks, 2009 p.130

We can make explicit how choices of visual and verbal resources privilege certain view points and how other choices of visual and verbal resources could construct alternative views.
Australia: Unsworth 2001 p.15

Figure 7.1 International voices advocating the concept of grammar as choice

Table 7.1 The LEAD principles

Acronym	Principle	Rationale
LINK	Make a ***link*** between the grammar being introduced and how it works in the writing being taught	To ensure a learning purpose for addressing grammar, connecting grammar with meaning and rhetorical effect
EXAMPLES	Explain the grammar through showing ***examples***, not lengthy explanations	To avoid mini-grammar lessons, and to allow access to the structure, even if the grammar concept is not fully understood
AUTHENTIC TEXTS	Use ***authentic*** texts as models to link writers to the broader community of writers	To illustrate the language choices made by published writers and emphasise the connectedness of reading and writing
DISCUSSION	Build in dialogic ***discussion*** about grammar and its effects	To foster metalinguistic understanding about language choices, and thus develop independence in making those choices

have explicit understanding of the effect of the grammatical choices they make in their own writing. There is now growing international advocacy of the importance of enabling developing writers in our classrooms to become more adept at the craft of writing through greater capacity to make choices, as indicated in Figure 7.1.

Let's think a little more now about what this means in practice in a secondary English classroom. The fundamental principle underlying a functional approach to grammar is that it is situated naturally within the teaching of writing at a point where a meaningful connection can be made between the grammar and the writing. There are many different ways that you could do this, but to support teachers new to this way of thinking, we have developed four pedagogical principles, the LEAD principles, as a scaffold for designing lessons. These are laid out in Table 7.1 above.

Activity 7.2

Look at the texts, including poems, that you teach for General Certificate of Secondary Education and A level, and consider how you could make more connections for pupils between the grammatical choices writers make and the pupils' own writing choices.

Focusing on the L (Link) of the LEAD principles, select some examples of authorial grammatical choices and write down how you would articulate to your pupils how that choice is working in the text.

An example of a learning sequence using the LEAD principles

Below is an example of one possible learning sequence that could be embedded into a writing lesson, where pupils are learning about how to depict a setting in a narrative, and about how the choices made in describing that setting can influence how the reader responds to that setting. The lesson uses Dickens' description of Coketown in *Hard Times*:

> It was a town of red brick, or of brick that would have been red if the smoke and ashes had allowed it; but as matters stood, it was a town of unnatural red and black like the painted face of a savage. It was a town of machinery and tall chimneys,

> out of which interminable serpents of smoke trailed themselves for ever and ever, and never got uncoiled. It had a black canal in it, and a river that ran purple with ill-smelling dye, and vast piles of building full of windows where there was a rattling and a trembling all day long, and where the piston of the steam-engine worked monotonously up and down, like the head of an elephant in a state of melancholy madness. It contained several large streets all very like one another, and many small streets still more like one another, inhabited by people equally like one another, who all went in and out at the same hours, with the same sound upon the same pavements, to do the same work, and to whom every day was the same as yesterday and to-morrow, and every year the counterpart of the last and the next.
>
> Charles Dickens *Hard Times*

- Begin by sharing the reading of this paragraph, discussing pupils' initial thoughts and feelings about Coketown, and inviting pupils to consider the question: *How should the reader react to Dickens' description of Coketown?*
- Draw attention to the following noun phrases in the first three sentences:

'a town of red brick'
'a town of unnatural red and black like the painted face of a savage'
'a town of machinery and tall chimneys'
'interminable serpents of smoke'
'a river that ran purple with ill-smelling dye'
'vast piles of buildings full of windows where there was a rattling and trembling all day long and where the piston of the steam-engine worked monotonously up and down, like the head of an elephant in a state of melancholy madness'

Invite pupils in pairs to look closely at these noun phrases and discuss the following questions:

- How does Dickens' choice of noun phrases to describe Coketown appeal to the reader's senses of sight, sound and smell?
- What do these vivid sensory details tell us about life in Coketown?
- How should the reader react to this?

In feedback and discussion you might draw out: the visual impact of the descriptive noun phrases with the harsh, unnatural colours, smoke and ashes, painting a vision of hell; the reference to the 'ill-smelling' atmosphere and the implications for the health of Coketown's inhabitants; the references to the incessant noise, emphasising there is no respite for the workforce; how the sensory description builds in intensity throughout the description, through deliberate repetition of key words and their synonyms across sentences and through progressively expanded noun phrases.

- Now display the long final sentence of this paragraph and read it aloud, so pupils can hear the rhythm of the sentence. Hand out envelopes containing the sentence cut up into the segments marked by the punctuation, and invite pupils in groups to line the segments in order in a column one after another, and then to discuss these questions:
  - How has Dickens made this sentence so long and so repetitive?
  - What does the repetitive nature of this sentence reinforce about life in Coketown?
  - How should the reader react?

In feedback and discussion you might draw out: the number of phrases and coordinated clauses joined with 'and', so that the rhythm of the sentence reinforces the idea of the interminable monotony of lives and actions; a view of people as machines stuck in repetitive routines; repetition and intensification of similar phrases suggesting the uniformity of people's surroundings and dullness of daily routines, coupled with monosyllabic words which create a metronomic beat.

- Lead a short plenary point where you draw out the learning point of this sequence – that we see here how Dickens' choice of noun phrases and sentence structures shapes how the reader reacts to it and emphasises the monotony and unnaturalness of the industrial landscape; and that as writers, we too can think about how our language choices when describing a setting can influence our readers.
- Invite pupils to think about the setting they have chosen for their own narrative: what do they want readers to think or feel when they read it? Does the detail in their noun phrases help achieve this? Are there any possibilities for exploring sentence structure to achieve this? The pupils are then given time to reread and revise the description of the setting in their own narratives.

How the LEAD principles are addressed in this sequence:

Link: exploring how your choice of noun phrases and sentence structures can help shape how your reader reacts to what you have written.
Examples: the relevant noun phrases highlighted in colour so they can be discussed; the long final sentence cut up into its punctuated segments.
Authentic Text: the description of Coketown in Dickens' *Hard Times*.
Discussion: teacher-facilitated and peer-to-peer discussion of Dickens' use of noun phrases and repetitive structures in the long sentence to convey the monotony and unnaturalness of the industrial landscape.

Activity 7.3: Exploring a persuasive text

The Dickens example draws on a narrative text, but the LEAD approach is equally applicable to non-fiction texts.

Look at the text of Barack Obama's 2008 election victory speech (*Yes we can*), freely available on the internet. This is a text full of classical rhetorical devices. But look at it through a different lens and annotate it with comments where you can see a link between a grammatical choice and a rhetorical effect.

CONCLUSION

A significant element of a functional approach, embedding grammar *within* the teaching of writing, is that it is making visible and explicit how grammatical choices can support the shaping of meaning and the meeting of rhetorical intentions. This explicitness gives access to understandings that not all pupils have tacitly, and may be particularly enabling for disadvantaged pupils (Janks, 2009; Myhill, 2018), addressing the 'larger goals of emancipatory teaching' (Micciche, 2004, p.717). Indeed, Martin makes the point that

> bright middle-class children learn by osmosis what has to be learned [while] working class, migrant, or Aboriginal children, whose homes do not provide them with models of writing, and who do not have the coding orientation to read between the lines and see what is implicitly demanded, do not learn to write effectively.
>
> (Martin 1989 p. 61)

However, our research has also highlighted the importance of teachers' subject knowledge of grammar (Myhill, Jones and Watson, 2013), and teachers' pedagogical skills in managing effective dialogic discussion are critical to successful implementation of this approach (Myhill and Newman, 2019; Myhill, Newman and Watson, 2020; Tracey et al., 2019).

SUMMARY AND KEY POINTS

- Grammar as choice makes meaningful learning connections for pupils between grammatical choices and their impact on the crafting of text.
- There is an important difference between tacit and explicit grammatical knowledge.
- Explicit teaching of how to craft writing may be particularly significant for disadvantaged pupils.
- Teacher knowledge of grammar and their skills in managing dialogic discussion are critical aspects of effective implementation.

KEY RESOURCES

1. An extensive set of resources for teaching grammar as choice can be found on the Centre for Research in Writing website: http://socialsciences.exeter.ac.uk/education/research/centres/centreforresearchinwriting/grammar-teacher-resources/
2. Reedy, D. and Bearne, E. (2020) *Teaching Grammar Effectively in Primary Schools*. Leicester: UKLA.

   Although written for primary, this book is full of practical ideas which can easily be adapted to the secondary classroom, especially by using different texts.
3. To understand the grammar debate, read Myhill, D. (2018). Grammar as a meaning-making resource for improving writing. Contribution to a special issue: Working on Grammar at School. *L1-Education: Empirical Research across Linguistic Regions. L1-Educational Studies in Language and Literature*. 18. pp.1–21.
4. Visit the Englicious website for subject knowledge support and teaching resources: www.englicious.org/
5. For a reference book for grammar subject knowledge, look at Myhill, D.A., Jones, S.M., Watson, A. and Lines, H.E (2016) *Essential Primary Grammar.* Oxford: OUP, which was written for teachers.

Chapter 8 Reading and writing poetry

ANNABEL WATSON AND RHIAN MULLIGAN

INTRODUCTION

Poetry, in all its forms, challenges us. Pupils (and teachers!) can often be intimidated by poetry, seeing it as something opaque, difficult and more detached from everyday life than other forms of literature (Sigvardsson, 2020; Dymoke, Lambirth and Wilson, 2013). Poetry analysis is often associated with the pressure of high-stakes exams, and teachers can struggle with how to assess poetry writing, particularly given that as a form it often privileges personal expression and creativity over more easily evaluated features such as generic conventions (Dymoke, 2003). However, the key message we want you to receive from this chapter is that poetry is a gift for English teachers. A poem gives you the opportunity to explore language in its most highly crafted form, and to share with your pupils a completed text, in its entirety, within a single lesson. Poetry is also language in its most playful form, and this ludic quality is one of the most important factors for engaging and enthusing pupils. Poetry is unparalleled in its potential for developing creativity and providing an opportunity for our pupils to enjoy exploring language. It provides a platform for self-expression and a means to address ideas that might be more difficult to explore in prose or a play.

Whatever your own experiences, as an English teacher you already appreciate the significant cultural, intellectual, social and emotional transitions captured by poets across the ages, presented to us in accessible and entertaining ways. Poetry 'lifts the veil from the hidden beauty of the world, and makes familiar objects be as if they were not familiar' (Shelley, 1840). Poets invite us to empathise, sympathise and challenge accepted ideas: the form, structure and content might differ but the purpose of poetry is constant – it gives the writer a voice. Use it to ignite the flame of intrigue in your pupils!

At the end of this chapter you should be able to:

- understand how to find 'ways in' to poetry that engage and motivate pupils;
- know how to develop personal and critical responses to poetry;
- understand the value of poetry writing, and how to use text models and the drafting process to support pupils' creative poetry writing.

DOI: 10.4324/9781003093060-9

Activity 8.1: Preparing to teach

- Consider your skills, knowledge and experience: do you have a favourite poet/style of poetry? Which poems have you previously taught?
- Consider purpose: what relationship do you need your pupils to have with the poetry you teach? Are you exploring the poem as part of wider body of work? Are you exploring themes, formal features, use of language? Is it for an exam?
- Read and annotate the anthologies or collections you will be teaching: familiarise yourself with the poets' backgrounds and some key themes.
- Develop your own poetry glossary, including not just definitions of key terminology but also examples from real poems and interpretations of the effect or impact of the language, devices and structure used in the poem.
- Talk to your colleagues in the department about the poems you will be teaching and what works for them.

WHERE TO START?

Despite the fact that poetry can seem intimidating, you can quickly develop pupil confidence with purposeful, exciting and creative inquiry tasks. Pupils need to critically engage with all aspects of language, structure, form and tone as well as the potential impact on the reader. Adding historical context to this mix might seem daunting, but it is important for engaging with narrators who are both present in their experiences and spectators in their own lives.

As with Shakespeare, it is important to help pupils to find a 'way in' to a poem, so that what might initially appear difficult becomes a creative or intriguing challenge. Below, we offer some suggestions for how to engage pupils at the outset.

Start with the big picture

Few poems are published as stand-alone artefacts, so considering how a poem sits within a wider collection can be a useful starting point. For example, knowing that Seamus Heaney's 'Mid-Term Break' is taken from *Death of a Naturalist* (1966), a collection that explores events of Heaney's childhood – both idyllic ('Blackberry Picking') and tragic ('Mid-Term Break') – helps pupils develop a better understanding of individual poems. If working with an anthology or collection of poetry, pupils could create a 'bird's-eye view'. Figure 8.1 is a beautiful example from ©FlipsCo that focuses on themes; the same principle could be applied to formal, literary or linguistic features to support comparison across poems or a holistic understanding of a collection.

Alternatively, you could ask pupils to create a cento by using words and phrases from other poems in a collection, then consider how the new poem links to it. This encourages pupils to engage with the poems as a collection (and has some overlap with 'found poetry' and digital montage texts, as discussed in Chapter 15).

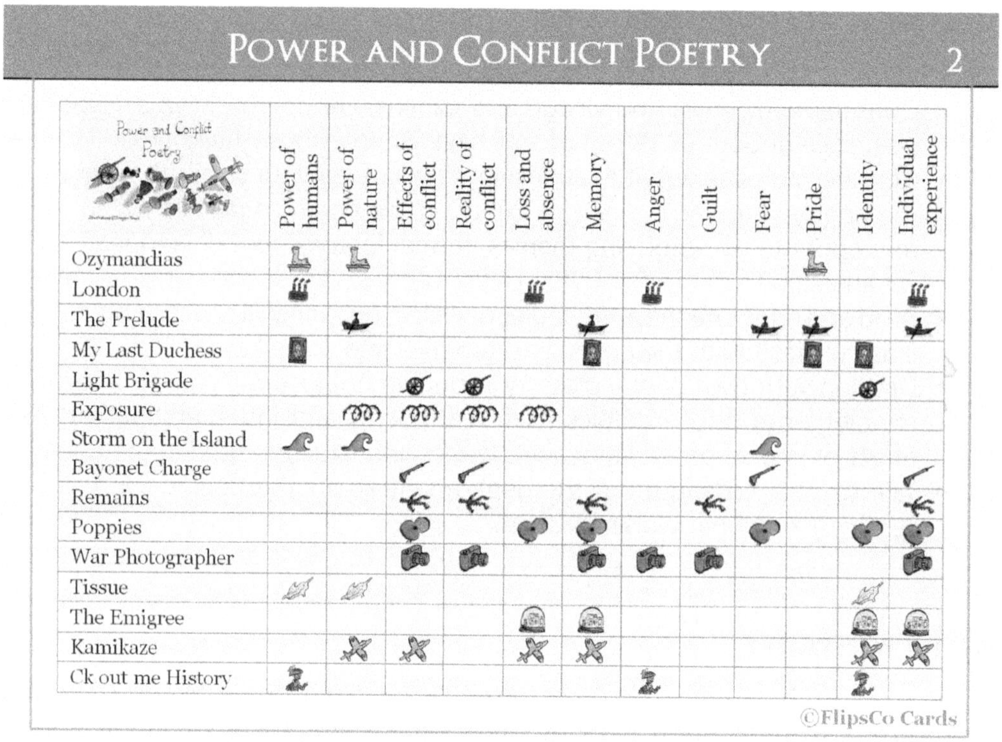

POWER AND CONFLICT POETRY 2

Power and Conflict Poetry	Power of humans	Power of nature	Effects of conflict	Reality of conflict	Loss and absence	Memory	Anger	Guilt	Fear	Pride	Identity	Individual experience
Ozymandias												
London												
The Prelude												
My Last Duchess												
Light Brigade												
Exposure												
Storm on the Island												
Bayonet Charge												
Remains												
Poppies												
War Photographer												
Tissue												
The Emigree												
Kamikaze												
Ck out me History												

Figure 8.1 Revision card sourced from the Power & Conflict set of FlipsCo Cards

Oracy and use of visual prompts

Poems have developed within an oral tradition, and reading them aloud to pupils is an immediate way to engage pupils in active listening and makes the content accessible. As pupils listen, you could also give them a visual prompt which helps them to identify and explore key imagery. For example, pupils could compare images of a garden spade and a pen as a 'way in' to Heaney's 'Digging', leading to a discussion about family relationships or what it means to feel a sense of purpose in your life. Another idea for using paintings to develop understanding of poems is explored in Chapter 18, which considers how poetry might interact with art as an aspect of English across the curriculum.

Start 'close up'

In contrast to the 'big picture' approach, sometimes starting 'close up' can offer a playful, non-intimidating approach to a poem. You can tailor the activity to emphasise the features you want to prioritise – themes, key vocabulary, particular linguistic, literary or formal features, for example. You could:

- Introduce the poem as a word cloud and ask pupils to deduce themes and ideas. You might draw out specific semantic fields or word classes as a way to start identifying how language is used before seeing it in full context.
- Use prediction activities which start with the title, or a phrase or line with key words removed.
- Offer an accessible cloze activity – the missing vocabulary could present challenges in meaning, a thread of imagery or a particular theme. Explore pupils' responses as a way to compare interpretations and make predictions

about the poem, and then discuss the correct answers and address errors and nuances of meaning.
- Develop understanding of form with shorter poems by asking pupils to create their own. Pupils can engage with the humour of Anglo-Saxon riddles or kennings by inventing some, and the seemingly simple structure of haiku poems can unlock discussions about the close connection between structure and content.

Lift the poem off the page

Steele (2015) argues for the importance of reading poetry aloud. You need to become an expert in performing poetry – bringing it to life for your pupils by giving your voice to the words. Think about the rhythm and sounds of the poem as you prepare to read – and make sure that you practise! Reading well helps pupils disentangle complex syntax and hear metrical patterns. Involving pupils in performing poetry themselves is also important for developing their sensitivity to sound and rhythm, as well as supporting their understanding of themes, imagery and tone.

In summary, exploring poetry brings a range of challenges and requires supported, scaffolded learning. In your planning and preparation think about how to give pupils a 'way in' to a poem: for example, if pupils have understood a key point in the poem from an image before reading, they will then be able to 'hook' this into their analysis and critical thinking. Supporting pupils as they engage with close analysis, using some of the strategies suggested above, will help them develop confidence and understanding as they explore key ideas in greater depth.

DEVELOPING INTERPRETATIONS

Once pupils have engaged with a poem, they need to develop personal responses which consider the impact of the poem on the reader. A poem, as a microcosm of a world, presents an opportunity for pupils to make meaningful connections to their own lives, explaining their unique perspectives and comparing these to their peers. Pupils bring a diverse set of interpretations to a discussion, but always check pupil understanding: they sometimes misread homophones or homonyms; they might avoid or misunderstand challenging vocabulary; they might come to a poem with an interpretation already in their minds or they might simply have been engrossed in a challenging group activity and focused more on the outcome of the task rather than developing their understanding of the text. Try to avoid saying 'there are no wrong interpretations', and instead support pupils as they explain their views and gently correct their misconceptions while allowing for dialogic exploration. 'Mantle of the expert' tasks, 'Envoy' and 'Jigsaw' tasks can give assigned groups the responsibility of exploring different aspects of a poem – interpretation then becomes a creative, collective experience that can lead to greater insight.

Pupils need to be able to explain and justify their personal responses, something which you need to scaffold through modelling and dialogic activities in which they explore and discuss different ideas. This requires pupils to think about the interaction between the ideas and formal features present in the poem, and their own associations, experiences and expectations. If you would like to know more about this, you could read about Text World Theory (Giovanelli, 2016; Cushing, 2018), which is based on the idea that meanings are created through a combination of the linguistic and formal properties of a text, and the knowledge and experience which readers bring to bear as they interpret it.

You also need to prepare your pupils to be critical readers by challenging them to ask questions, explore unfamiliar language and to think about what the poet is really saying. You need to address this alongside the formal and technical features of poetry – ranging across metre, layout, rhetoric, imagery, sound and indeed poetic forms. Remember, as always with English, that 'feature-labelling' is not as important as being able to discuss the impact that these choices have. Explicit teaching of the vocabulary of analysis is useful here – particularly vocabulary which describes tone (e.g. amused, belligerent, celebratory, defensive, desperate, empathetic, excited, hopeful, irate, nostalgic, scathing, urgent) and vocabulary which links form to effect (e.g. connects, conveys, emphasises, evokes, suggests, recalls, relates to).

Less confident pupils might seek to quantify terminology or evidence in a response by asking things like 'how many quotations do we need?' or 'how many techniques should we write about?' Although these questions signify very valid concerns, encourage them to move away from a checklist approach and instead consider the beginning, middle and end of the poem. Pupils can become reliant on acronyms like PEE (Point/Evidence/Explain) and variations (PETER/PETAL), which can limit their analysis. Try to avoid using checklists or formulae that encourage pupils to spot and quantify formal features, and instead use dialogic talk, modelling and model responses to support their understanding of the relationship between form and effect and their ability to structure a formal response to a poem. Focus them on 'what, how, why' for deeper thinking.

You might like to consider the following different types of analysis. Comparative analysis entails comparing poems, and this sometimes reveals themes that might have been previously overlooked. Pupils need to confidently establish connections between poems, so this needs to start with a firm understanding of the original poems. You might try comparing a poem pupils have studied to an unseen poem, or comparing a printed poem to one which pupils have to recall from memory, depending on the requirements of the examination for which you are preparing them. Holistic analysis invites pupils to 'look at the whole' from different points of view (Petty, 2006, p.330). This might involve developing different responses to a character – such as finding evidence that shows the refinement of the speaker of Robert Browning's 'My Last Duchess' as well as his monstrous side – or creating contrasting interpretations of the viewpoint present in a poem. An example of this could be in the close analysis of the frozen figures in John Keats' 'Ode on a Grecian Urn': pupils could select a range of quotations that suggest the excitement of anticipating a wonderful dance and, contrastingly, language that suggests the realisation of the observer that the figures are frozen forever in their separate moments, never to speak nor dance with one another. Atomistic analysis is perhaps the most traditional approach to teaching poetry, and asks you to 'cut up the topic into discrete bits and look at these one at a time' (Petty, 2006, p.328). This might typically involve considering different formal characteristics of a poem separately (for example, structure, metre, imagery), and might involve close analysis of a single word or phrase before relating this analysis back to the overall tone and meaning of the poem. You can scaffold this through the use of a grid such as that developed by Frayer et al. (1969). This model graphic organiser supports word-level analysis by asking pupils to explore definitions, facts, synonyms and antonyms (see Figure 8.2).

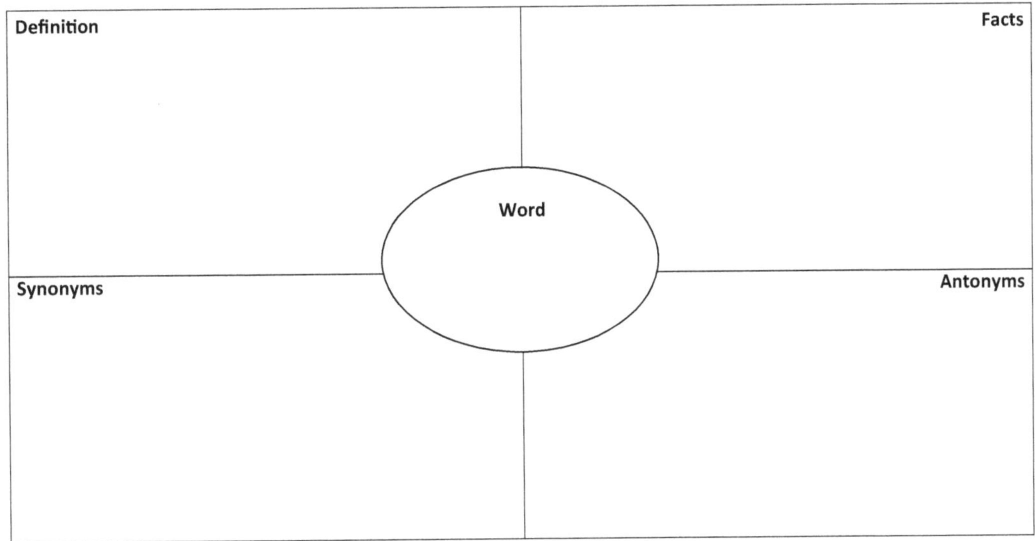

Figure 8.2 Example of a Frayer graphic organiser

Activity 8.2: Approaches to poetry analysis

Take a poem that you are likely to teach. Consider how you might approach it through each of the methods of analysis outlined above. What are the benefits and drawbacks of each one? What understandings do they each foster?

CONTEXTUAL KNOWLEDGE

Exploring literary traditions or significant, historical contexts such as First World War poetry in Wilfred Owen's 'Exposure' or the more distanced perspective of war in Ted Hughes' 'Bayonet Charge' engages pupils in broader analysis and opens the door to deeper understanding. Debating whether John Donne's 'Hymn to God, My God, in My Sickness' was written from the poet's deathbed or during the throes of a fever seven years earlier in 1623, invites pupils to consider contextual attitudes to religion, especially considering Donne's extraordinary anticipation of being made into God's 'music'. Including context tasks in preparatory work focuses pupils on the links between content and context from the beginning. There is huge scope for valuable context tasks that prepare pupils to confront challenging themes: the brutality of a faceless regime depicted in Niyi Osundare's 'Not My Business' requires a clear understanding of the context for pupils to fully understand why the speaker tries to ignore the terror inflicted on the people around him. It also helps pupils understand the mindset of the poet and makes their experiences more accessible. Osundare sets the horror and pain clearly present in his poem to 'a tune that is simple, accessible, topical, relevant and artistically pleasing' (1990, cover copy).

Exploring context in poetry also presents a valuable opportunity to reflect the diversity of contemporary classrooms and to open up understanding of different experiences across the world. There is often considerable flexibility for teachers to choose the poems that they teach, especially at Key Stage 3 – you don't need to buy 30 copies of a class reader! Given the poor track record of diversity in current children's literature and in the texts studied in UK secondary schools (Centre for Literacy in Primary Education, 2018; Smith, 2020), it is important to consider diversity and representation as you select poems to teach. Think also about how to explore the poetry of diverse social and ethnic groups and cultures in a respectful, empathetic and celebratory way.

Building cultural and historical knowledge is important, but steer pupils away from writing a purely contextual paragraph in their introductions. Avoid context that is either detached from analysis, or only loosely associated with links between form and effect – always remind pupils to link features of the poem with relevant context as opposed to the other way round. For example, a detailed account of the corruption in commerce and the monarchy during William Blake's lifetime would not be an effective introduction to an analysis of 'London'. Instead, encourage pupils to explore the imagery of the 'blackning church' through the duality of the physical corruption of an ancient building in an increasingly industrialised world and its overt failure to protect the children of a morally corrupt world.

LINKING READING TO WRITING: DESIGNING POETRY

The word 'poet' means 'creator' or 'maker', and poetry is language in its most artistic and crafted form. Writing poetry can be motivating and liberating: it foregrounds creativity above technical accuracy, it offers opportunities for artistry in that it can be performed aloud or presented as concrete artwork, and it doesn't require extended writing. However, poetry writing is unlikely to be a major component of external summative examinations, so is often neglected (at least post-Key Stage 3). Despite this, poetry writing is important in both allowing pupils to be creative, and in helping to demystify the poems that they read.

Writing is often conceptualised as a 'problem solving' activity (Kellogg, 1996). We have an aim when we write – something which we want to communicate, or generate, or release, even if we're only writing for ourselves – and we make choices in our writing with that aim in mind. The concept of writing 'as an act of design' (Sharples, 1999) emphasises this idea of the writer as a purposeful designer, selecting from their repertoire of words, phrases and structures as they craft their text. This is a particularly useful way to frame poetry writing for pupils, helping them see themselves as artists who are designing and shaping their poems to have a particular impact on their reader. Creativity theory also posits that being creative is a problem-solving activity, requiring us to apply knowledge inventively to a situation; seeing or doing things differently (Craft, 2003) – something which resonates clearly with the concept of writing as design. Start, then, by helping pupils articulate their intention in writing their poem. What do they want to achieve? Who is their reader? What do they want them to understand, or to feel? It is tempting to want to allow full freedom of expression when asking pupils to write poetry, setting them off with no limits, but it's worth noting that constraints – much like a scaffold – can actually help pupils be creative. Defining the 'problem' and setting the design specifications is important. In the words of Rollo May (1975, p.115):

> Creativity arises out of the tension between spontaneity and limitations, the latter (like the river banks) forcing the spontaneity into the various forms which are essential to the work of art or poem.

With this in mind, using poems as models for imitation and experimentation can foster a strong understanding of the relationship between form and effect, providing clear 'limitations' which help channel pupils' creative impulses into a carefully shaped written product. Theodore Roethke's 'Child on Top of a Greenhouse' is a great example of a poem to imitate – a list of noun phrases, it expresses the exhilaration of the speaker's escape to the rooftop of the world through a series of visual images that exist, verblessly, outside of time. As a pattern to play with, this offers all sorts of opportunities to explore how to evoke the atmosphere of a particular moment. Pupils can draw ideas from model poems to expand their repertoire of language, poetic forms and devices, and you can plan developmentally across Key Stages to build up their knowledge of a wide range of literary and linguistic resources which they can use selectively in their own writing (Myhill et al., 2013).

Activity 8.3: Creative responses to poetry

Choose a poem that you think will work well as a model for pupils' own writing. Think about the best 'way in' to the poem, and then about how to develop their interpretation and analysis, then about which features they could mimic and experiment with. Then plan and teach a lesson or short sequence of lessons in which pupils read, respond to and write in the style of the poem. Is there room for further creative responses – maybe a performance of their poems, or an artwork?

THE DRAFTING PROCESS

Thinking of writing as an act of design also allows you to emphasise the writing process as you teach (see Chapter 6). Planning for an emphasis on drafting – both in terms of generating ideas and careful evaluation and revision of work – will help pupils hone their writing with a focus on how a reader might respond (Dymoke, 2003), also helping them develop an identity as a poet, a crafter of words. Showing pupils the drafts of published poems is a good way to reveal the laborious process that underpins most successful poetry writing (there are many readily available, for example on the British Library website), and the sight of original manuscripts complete with ink blots, scribblings and crossings out is a great way to demystify poetry.

It can be hard, as a teacher, to assess poetry in a way which respects pupils' expressive choices while also providing useful feedback. It can be difficult to avoid superficial responses which focus on technical features such as consistency of rhythm or accurate use of punctuation without really developing pupils' understanding of the impact of the different choices that they make. Emphasising formative rather than summative assessment, ideally integrated as part of a drafting process and incorporating peer or self-assessment, may be particularly relevant for poetry (Dymoke, 2003). Where summative assessment is required, consider asking pupils to annotate their poem to explain their design choices and the messages and feelings that they wanted to communicate. You might then focus your feedback on the annotations, and separately provide your own personal response to the poem as a reader, recognising the pupil as 'owner' of their poem.

Look also for opportunities to link from writing back to reading. There is evidence to suggest that pupils find it easier to explain the impact of writerly choices in their own writing compared to texts which they read (Watson and Newman, 2017), so this might act as a scaffold for exploration of other writers' poetry. If pupils are able to explain that they have chosen to use sibilance to create a sinister atmosphere, or that they've used a dactylic rhythm to create a sense of urgency, this may also help them identify and explain the impact of similar features in poetry that they read.

SUMMARY AND KEY POINTS

- Challenge assumptions that poetry is 'difficult'. Make it an exciting, creative and liberating experience for readers and writers by finding creative and engaging 'ways in' to poems.
- Include a range of approaches to analysis with your pupils, be confident in correcting misconceptions and explore context in order to unlock deeper interpretations.
- Consider representation and diversity in the poems that you select to teach. How can you use poetry to broaden horizons, promote empathy and understanding?
- Make links between reading and writing, helping pupils find their voice by identifying the message they want to communicate, and building a repertoire of language, structures and devices that they can use in their own poetry.
- Integrate formative assessment as part of the drafting process, and encourage pupils to annotate and explain the choices that they have made in their writing.

KEY RESOURCES

1. Dymoke, S., Lambirth, A. and Wilson, A. (eds.) (2013) *Making Poetry Matter: International Research on Poetry Pedagogy*. London: A&C Black. This is the most comprehensive synthesis of research perspectives on poetry education.
2. Dymoke, S., Barrs, M., Lambirth, A. and Wilson, A. (eds.) (2015) *Making Poetry Happen: Transforming the Poetry Classroom*. London: Bloomsbury Publishing. This publication is linked to 1 above, but has a particular focus on pedagogy – how to put the research into practice in your classroom.
3. https://poetrysociety.org.uk/ – boundless resources, blogs, videos and poetry writing competitions for young people. Your pupils can join the network of young poets too: https://poetrysociety.org.uk/young-poets/young-poets-network/
4. https://childrens.poetryarchive.org. This offers an archive of poems read aloud, browsable by age and supported by further resources (e.g. interviews with authors).
5. www.scottishpoetrylibrary.org.uk/ This is specifically for Scottish poetry, browsable by place, curriculum level or theme, with banks of learning resources.
6. www.bl.uk/catalogues-and-collections/catalogues The British Library provides access to many poetic manuscripts, including drafts.
7. https://flipscocards.com. This website allows you to download (for a small fee) beautifully designed revision cards which use visuals to support poetry analysis.

Chapter 9 Teaching non-fiction reading and writing

SHARON MORGAN

INTRODUCTION

According to Paulo Freire (1985, p.21), a key question presented to us as teachers is 'how not to separate reading the word and reading the world, reading the text and reading the context'. This privileging of broader contextual factors where 'reading the word' also requires us to read 'the world' can be seen as a nod towards critical literacy theory which considers our language choices to be inseparable from the culture and society in which they were made. Therefore, what we read, write, hear and say can never be 'neutral or value-free' (Wray, 2004, p.3). This concept, where language choices have potential to influence audiences and shape meaning, is at the very centre of this chapter's focus and is linked to how we read and how we write non-fiction texts.

As a result, this chapter considers the reciprocal relationship between reading and writing non-fiction through a sociocultural perspective where textual meanings, and text-type value, are negotiated through our shared understanding as members of a community (Nystrand, 1989; Cremin and Myhill, 2012). We consider how genre, alongside purpose and audience, can be used to facilitate our understanding of how language, grammar and structural features can be used to convey meaning and influence intended audiences. The symbiosis of reading and writing also provides us with opportunities to consider how authentic model texts can be used for textual analysis purposes to support pupils' reading of non-fiction, as well as scaffold the writing process, particularly when writing in unfamiliar genres for unfamiliar audiences. Interwoven into these sections are practical activities for you to try out and take into your classrooms. These activities are centred on exploring writer's language choices and how they have been crafted to convey meaning to the implied reader.

At the end of this chapter you should be able to:

- develop understanding of the sociocultural views of reading, writing and genre;
- understand the reciprocal relationship between reading and writing;
- develop knowledge and understanding of how model texts can be used to explore real writers' uses of language, as well as scaffold pupils' own writing;

DOI: 10.4324/9781003093060-10

- develop knowledge of the ways in which language, grammar and structural features can be used to convey meaning.

NON-FICTION ACROSS UK CURRICULA

If you take a moment to consider the range of non-fiction texts which circulate in our communities, it becomes evident that the list is an incredibly long one. From formal newspaper articles to celebrity 'insta' captions, non-fiction texts permeate our daily lives – informing us, advising us and most definitely persuading us! Therefore, it is of little surprise that non-fiction reading, and writing, is embedded in curricula across the nations of the UK. All curricula highlight the need for pupils to read and write for 'a variety of purposes and audiences across a range of contexts' (DfE, 2014c, p. 3) and develop 'an understanding of how meaning is created' (CCEA, 2017). As a result, this synergy across the four corners of the UK indicates the importance non-fiction plays in our society, and given how new media technologies grant us (and at times bombard us with) constant access to online content, there is little wonder why twenty-first-century pupils need experience analysing and evaluating non-fiction texts where potentially biased statements and 'fake news' can be presented as verifiable truths and facts. Furthermore, not only do pupils need to recognise how the language choices of real writers are shaped to convey meaning, but they also need to be equipped to creatively and purposefully craft their own texts and have the skill to adapt their writing to suit various contextual factors such as genre, audience and purpose.

SOCIOCULTURAL PERSPECTIVES AND GENRE

Given the emphasis of various curricula on teaching pupils to read and write a range of non-fiction texts from different genres, purposes and audiences, it is useful to consider how genre approaches to writing stem from sociocultural views which focus on the function of language in social contexts (Nystrand, 1989; Hacker et al., 2009). Unlike the cognitive model of writing explored in Chapter 6 which sees the writer as a 'lone individual' (Cremin and Myhill, 2012, p.18) this theoretical perspective considers writing as a social act which is influenced by our shared cultures and use of language (Hacker et al., 2009; Vygotsky, 1991; Bahktin, 1981). As a result of this shared understanding, textual meaning is jointly constructed through the writer-reader relationship (Nystrand, 1989; Cremin and Myhill, 2012). When we read, we bring our own broader contextual and prior knowledge with us, and it is this which helps us mediate our understandings of the meanings created through the writer's choices of language. With this in mind, you may well need to consider any cultural implications associated with particular words or concepts for English as an Additional Language pupils. Metaphors and idioms, which often have culturally dependent meanings, might cause particular challenges for this cohort of pupils (Hessel and Murphy, 2019).

So, what kinds of genres and writing purposes do school curricula value? The 2016 Welsh KS3 curriculum for English provides us with a list of possibilities which you might find useful when beginning to consider the wide range of writing purposes available to you as a teacher: 'recount, instruct, inform, explain, argue/persuade, discuss/analyse, evaluate, narrate, describe, empathise' as well as writing in a variety of forms including 'letters, diaries, articles, stories, reports, speeches, short plays and scripts, leaflets, advertisements, posters, web pages, questionnaires, reviews, soliloquies' (CfW, 2016, p.23). As you can see, the list includes a range of text types, including multimodal media ones such as advertisements and posters (though do seek out the National Curriculum relevant to your area).

However, this list is not definitive and there are many more non-fiction texts circulating in your pupils' lives than the ones cited here – particularly in a multicultural classroom. Furthermore, not all pupils are familiar with all school genres, and there is likely to be some disparity in terms of the range of genres experienced outside of school and in their homes (Swales, 1990; Myhill, 2005a). After all, not all genres appear to be equal and therefore, as Myhill (2005a, p.292) states, 'Consideration of the nature and extent of children's prior knowledge of written discourses ought to be a key principle in the framing of the teaching of writing'.

READING NON-FICTION TEXTS

Bearing this in mind, and that you are more than likely educating a diverse range of pupils for jobs which don't currently exist, you might find it useful to collect a selection of broader genres and text types which pupils are likely to encounter in and out of their outside-school lives, for example, blogs, social media campaigns, fake news items and online pop-up adverts. Alongside collecting different genres or forms of writing, also collect texts which are aimed at different target audiences and constructed for different purposes, demonstrating cultural diversity and social inclusion (these can also be used as model texts when teaching how to write non-fiction texts, as outlined further on in this chapter). It can be particularly useful to source two texts from the same genre and purpose, and explore how the use of language and presentational features have been chosen to convey different meanings to different audiences, as demonstrated in Activity 9.1.

Activity 9.1: Analysing the language of European referendum campaign posters

Vote Leave: 'There are 35 million potholes in Britain. But your money is being spent on a bridge like this in Greece'. (Image of bridge is shown on the poster.)
The Green Party: 'We're fairer, safer and greener in Europe'.

To give you some contextual information (because as we have already identified, context is important in terms of how we read and write non-fiction), the sentences are taken from two different European Union (EU) referendum campaign posters. Whilst they both have the same purpose (to persuade), they are targeted at different audiences, that is, people who either want Britain to remain in the EU or leave. Before analysing the sentences, we might also want to acknowledge that there are other possible contextual factors at play here which might impact on the readers' interpretation and processing of this information. For instance, one poster is from the Green Party, and the other Vote Leave. If we have any prior knowledge of the Green Party, will we be drawing on that wider contextual knowledge and will this impact on the meanings we derive from this poster? If we know anything about Boris Johnson or Michael Gove (who led the Vote Leave campaign and are members of the Conservative Party), will this also influence us? As a teacher, you want to consider at the lesson planning stage possible differences in your pupils' broader cultural and contextual knowledge – some pupils live in households where topical debates are discussed freely and frequently, whereas others don't. What additional information could you provide, or differentiated material, to ensure there is equity in terms of how your pupils can access and analyse your chosen non-fiction texts?

In term of analysing the language choices and potential effects in Activity 9.1, you might have decided to explore the use of pronouns and how they have been used to directly target different audiences. Vote Leave's choice of the second-person possessive pronoun 'your' could be said to reinforce the divide between Britain and the EU – almost as if pitting one side against the other – because the reader is at risk of losing something which belongs to them (money). In contrast, the Green Party takes a more inclusive approach through their use of the first-person plural pronoun 'we' (or in this instance the informal contraction of 'we are' to 'we're'). It could be argued that by using 'we', this poster is suggesting that everyone reading it is in this situation together – there is no them and us.

Taking a similar approach to the task above, have a go at analysing a longer extract of writing in Activity 9.2 and consider how the writer's linguistic choices can impact on how the reader constructs meaning from their chosen words.

Activity 9.2

Theme park blog

Look at the next non-fiction extract below which is taken from Alton Towers' blog introducing the launch of a brand-new ride. Write a paragraph explaining how the writer has crafted their writing to persuade the intended reader to go to the theme park. Pay particular attention to the writer's use of, language, grammar and structure and how these different elements have been shaped for a particular effect. Aim to include quotations from the extract to evidence your point and explain the intended impact on the reader:

Launching Galactica

> After two years in the making and months of preparation to get the ride ready for its official launch, Galactica is now open! Taking passengers into space from Staffordshire, the brand new ride experience features cutting edge virtual technology that creates an interstellar journey into the beyond. Soar into another dimension and fly above earth, all whilst hurtling through twist and turns on the Resort's iconic flying rollercoaster.
>
> www.altontowers.com/about-alton-towers/blog/launching-galactica/

Given that we have been considering the sociocultural view of writing in this chapter, it seems an apt time to briefly mention the importance of the role of talk and cooperative forms of learning. Rich classroom discussion can help bridge the contextual and linguistic gap which might exist between different cohorts of pupils. And whilst it is well recognised that talk is a vital tool for learning across all subject areas (Alexander, 2008a), it is particularly useful as a tool for supporting pupils' understanding of how language and grammar can be used for effect, something

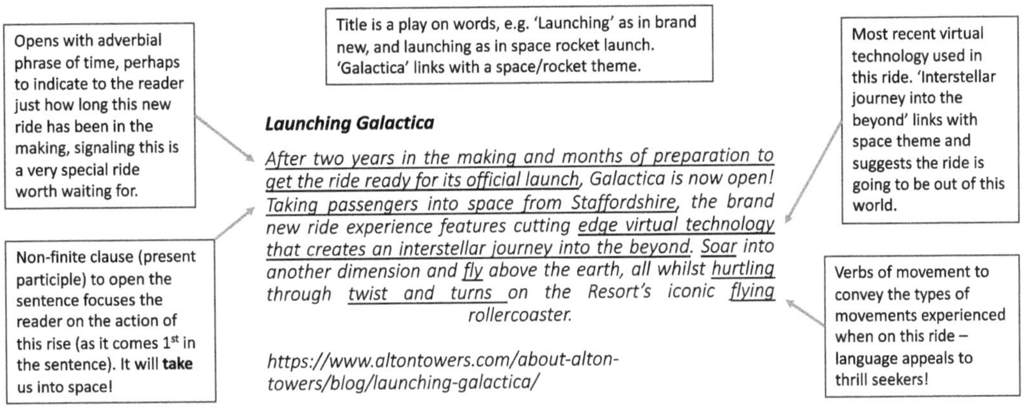

Opens with adverbial phrase of time, perhaps to indicate to the reader just how long this new ride has been in the making, signaling this is a very special ride worth waiting for.

Non-finite clause (present participle) to open the sentence focuses the reader on the action of this rise (as it comes 1st in the sentence). It will **take** us into space!

Title is a play on words, e.g. 'Launching' as in brand new, and launching as in space rocket launch. 'Galactica' links with a space/rocket theme.

Launching Galactica

After two years in the making and months of preparation to get the ride ready for its official launch, Galactica is now open! Taking passengers into space from Staffordshire, the brand new ride experience features cutting edge virtual technology that creates an interstellar journey into the beyond. Soar into another dimension and fly above the earth, all whilst hurtling through twist and turns on the Resort's iconic flying rollercoaster.

https://www.altontowers.com/about-alton-towers/blog/launching-galactica/

Most recent virtual technology used in this ride. 'Interstellar journey into the beyond' links with space theme and suggests the ride is going to be out of this world.

Verbs of movement to convey the types of movements experienced when on this ride – language appeals to thrill seekers!

Figure 9.1 Annotated blog indicating how language and grammar can shape meaning

pupils need to be able to confidently do when analysing non-fiction. So do take time during your lesson planning to build in opportunities for your pupils to discuss and share their thoughts about how writers use language to create a particular effect.

In the annotated example shown in Figure 9.1, I have used grammatical terms to support my analysis. From 2017 onwards in England, 16-year-olds have sat a revised General Certificate in Secondary Education (GCSE) in English which places more emphasis on spelling, punctuation and grammar than the legacy GCSE. Therefore, being able to explore the writer's use of language using specific references to 'grammatical features for effect' is really important (Watson and Newman, 2017; p.382; DfE, 2013b, p.6). What you might experience as a teacher is that some pupils find it challenging to link the use of grammar to effect and therefore you may need to bridge this gap by modelling not only the analysis (similar to Figure 9.1 by using an interactive whiteboard to annotate during whole-class discussion) but also how to talk about the writer's language and grammar choices and the effect they create. You can do this by being precise in how you talk about the writer's language, grammar and structural choices, but you should also aim to build in regular opportunities for your pupils to talk about and discuss how language is being used in a particular context, for example, the use of pronouns in political campaigns. See Chapter 7 for more information about grammar teaching, and Chapter 2 for the role of talk.

Activity 9.3: Travel writing

Let's turn our attention to another reading task, this time with a different genre, an online travel article, 'Tales of the Tiger: Searching for Big Cats in India's Wildest State', taken from the *National Geographic* website. Read the extract and answer the questions below. Remember to be as precise as possible and use evidence (quotations) from the extract to reinforce your answers.

> A cold winter dawn is breaking on Bandhavgarh: blood-red stains are seeping into the sky and, all around us, wildlife is stirring. Babblers begin the morning's symphony, white-bellied minivets adding their short, sharp burst to the tune. Soon the canopy's orchestra is in full swing, with quails cooing and rollers calling – Mother Nature conducting a wild jungle song.

This is India's untamed heartland, where the looming, pine-crested Satpura Range dissolves into Kanha's grasslands to the east and the dense forests of Bandhavgarh to the north. There are 11 national parks in Madhya Pradesh, more than any other Indian state, and these pockets of wilderness are fiercely protected, their flora and fauna wonderfully diverse.

We turn away from the watch-post and rattle up another rocky peak. Bamboo thickets become denser, and the eyes of unknown creatures follow us from the undergrowth before the track spits us out at an ancient stone ruin. Piece by piece, nature is devouring the structure, the once-mighty columns cracked and crumbling, the floor subsiding and slick with moss.

1. How does the writer describe the location of Bandhavgarh? What impression do we get of this place? Remember to provide evidence from the extract in your answer.
2. What effect is created through the writer's use of noun phrases in the first paragraph?
3. What can we infer about the location through the writer's choice of verbs underlined in the examples below:
   - dawn <u>is breaking</u>
   - wildlife <u>is stirring</u>
   - blood-red stains <u>are seeping</u>
   - pine-crested Satpura Range <u>dissolves</u>
   - [We] <u>rattle up</u> another rocky peak
   - the track <u>spits us out</u>
   - nature <u>is devouring</u> the structure
4. The writer uses a range of vivid images to convey how magnificent this place is, but there is also an underlying tone of danger. Write a paragraph comparing and contrasting how the writer uses language, grammar and structure to convey different meaning regarding Bandhavgarh.
5. You have been asked to write a short blog for your school website describing a local area of beauty during two different times of the year. You can revisit the extract from the *National Geographic* website and review the writer's language and grammar choices to help you make some decisions regarding the crafting of your own blog. Remember, the purpose for this piece of writing is to describe.

WRITING NON-FICTION AND MODEL TEXTS

Building on the section above which highlights the importance of genre, audience and purpose as a pedagogical approach to teaching pupils how to read non-fiction texts, this section focuses on how the analysis of non-fiction texts also has the potential to scaffold pupils' writing (Vygotsky, 1991; Myhill et al., 2018), as it can make what was previously unfamiliar, familiar. This is particularly useful when it comes to writing, which is often considered to be cognitively demanding (Myhill, 2011; Sharples, 1999). One of the ways of alleviating some of the strain placed onto the working memory during the writing process, is to 'write within a familiar style and structure' (Sharples, 1999, p.92). When pupils analyse non-fiction sources and examine how a writer's choice of linguistic features have been chosen to create a particular effect on the reader, this in-depth analytical process also signals (either consciously or unconsciously) to pupils possible ways of creating their own texts

(Pareskeva, 2006, p.68; Watson and Newman, 2017; Myhill et al., 2020). This process also provides pupils with the necessary tools to critically reflect on their own language choices as a writer. Myhill et al. (2020, p.3) see this 'inter-relationship of reading and writing' where pupils develop their ability 'to monitor their own creation of meanings' as an important one. Likewise, Paraskevas (2006, pp.65–6) refers to the process of using model texts as an 'apprenticeship' and believes that these texts provide opportunities for pupils to imitate writing patterns, which she considers to be 'the first step toward giving writers choices that reflect their stylistic and rhetorical competence'. Furthermore, Myhill et al. (2018, p.8) remind us that one of the central values associated with using model texts in your classrooms is that they have the potential to develop pupils' 'awareness of the repertoire of possibilities of language choices' and therefore subsequently enable pupils 'to make more conscious choices in crafting written text'.

Another benefit associated with using model texts to support writing-based knowledge is that these texts can also provide opportunities for pupils to consider the appropriateness of their own language choices. Whilst they aren't professional writers, gaining a sense of 'appropriateness' can be a challenge for some pupils. Rather than be tempted to issue your class 'writing recipes' or formulaic approaches to writing, your pupils might find it useful to analyse real texts (as we have done in the earlier tasks) before writing their own. Sharples (1999, p.41) states the benefit associated with the use of model texts is that they can help strengthen pupil understanding of the relationship between 'content and style' and the broader contextual factors, such as audience and purpose – which when combined together, should give them a firmer understanding of how to shape their writing for a particular effect. Myhill et al. (2020, p.1) echo this and state that it is fundamentally important to ensure that pupils understand the 'link between linguistic choice and rhetorical purpose so that young writers are inducted into the craft of writing and empowered to make their own authorial choices'.

However, whilst model texts provide pupils with a mental image of how to approach their own writing, transitioning into confident writers who are able to 'take on' new genres can be a challenge. It is worth bearing mind that your pupils' learning might not necessarily be evident at the point of teaching. In fact, Sharples (1999, p.30) suggests that we should take notice of what our pupils do 'differently' rather than 'better' because 'The implications for the teaching of writing are disturbing: help children to become more mature, reflective writers and the quality of their compositions may well go down' (1999, p.31). So, don't always expect to see a linearity of progress – learning can be messy, with lots of trials and errors along the way. Fostering a classroom climate where writing is 'playful, risk-taking and experimental' and one which allows pupils to have 'failed attempts because through those attempts, they have been pushing the boundaries of their own use of language' is important (Myhill and Cremin, 2012, p.24). Whilst we might be aware of formulaic teaching approaches which promote and privilege the use of writing recipes and checklists for writing in different genres, pushing and adapting the genre boundaries to suit different purposes and the various needs of the readers, is to understand why language is adapted to suit different contextual factors.

CONCLUSION

This chapter has provided an insight into a sociocultural view of reading and writing which privileges the meaning-making process of a shared language. In doing this we have viewed non-fiction reading and writing through a genre approach and also considered how other contextual factors, such as who the intended audience is, what the purpose of writing is, as well as prior contextual knowledge, might impact on the reader's response to a text. This chapter has also explored how model texts provide opportunities for pupils to analyse how real writers shape their writing in order to obtain a particular effect on the reader. Given the reciprocal relationship between reading and writing, we have also considered how model texts can function as a template in terms of scaffolding the writing process for pupils when presented with their own writing tasks.

SUMMARY AND KEY POINTS

- Through a sociocultural perspective, our shared understanding of genre and textual meaning is jointly constructed through the writer-reader relationship.
- Reading and writing is a reciprocal process where one supports the other.
- Writing is not solely about 'what to write', but also 'how' to write, and we therefore need to consider how to craft and shape our writing in order to convey meaning to our readers.
- Model texts can be used to support pupils' analysis of how meaning is conveyed in real texts, as well as to scaffold the writing process for pupils.

KEY RESOURCES

1. London School of Economics. The Brexit Collection. Available: https://digital.library.lse.ac.uk/collections/brexit. [Accessed 1 July 2020.] This resource is a digital library which holds campaign publications from the 1975 and 2017 EU referendum in the UK.
2. Hair Raiser Roller Coaster POV Ocean Park Hong Kong B&M Floorless On-Ride www.youtube.com/watch?v=0xfhspqJzZQ [Accessed 1 July 2020]. A point-of-view video for a roller coaster in Hong Kong. This is useful for planning to write a persuasive review of a roller coaster.
3. The *National Geographic* website: www.nationalgeographic.co.uk. The *National Geographic* website is a useful source for gathering a range of non-fiction texts.
4. Myhill, D.A., Lines, H. and Jones, S. M. (2018) Texts that teach: Examining the efficacy of using texts as models. Contribution to a special issue in honor of Gert Rijlaarsdam: Making Connections: Studies of Language and Literature Education. *L1-Educational Studies in Language and Literature*. 18. pp.1–24. https://doi.org/10.17239/L1ESLL-2018.18.03.07. The findings of this empirical research study highlight the link between writer's choices and rhetorical purpose.
5. Myhill, D., Lines, H. and Watson, A. (2011b) Making meaning with grammar: A repertoire of possibilities. *English in Australia*. 47 (3). pp.29–38.
6. Nystrand, M. (1989) A social-interactive model of writing. *Written Communication*. 6. pp.66–85. Outlines the social interactive model of writing and the reader-writer relationship and how they negotiate meaning. It also explores genre as a social construct.
7. Paraskevas, C. (2006) Grammar apprenticeship. *English Journal*. 95 (5). pp.65–9. This paper explores the role of model texts and how they can be used to support pupils.

Chapter 10 Shakespeare

SUSAN CHAPMAN

INTRODUCTION

If you were educated in the UK, you almost certainly had the experience of studying William Shakespeare at school. Perhaps you were involved in school productions as well as studying plays for examinations or coursework. You might have chosen to study modules on Shakespeare as part of your degree and have developed a habit of enjoying the plays in the theatre or in film adaptations. Whatever your own experience, as an English teacher, you are responsible for guiding the pupils in your classes to engage with Shakespeare's plays and to develop their own understanding and responses.

Working with Shakespeare's plays gives you opportunities to develop pupils' core skills and to broaden their experience of drama, theatre and media and to engage with the cultural significance of the texts. Their learning develops from the diverse knowledge, understanding and experience that your pupils bring to your lessons. The great majority, and it is tempting to say all, already know something about Shakespeare. To some, he may simply be a name, while others may have had direct experience of seeing a play or working with the texts in primary school. Others may be fans of *Upstart Crow* or have encountered *Manga Shakespeare*. While your job is not to ensure that they all love Shakespeare, your pupils should have the chance to make their judgement from a position of knowledge, experience and understanding.

At the end of this chapter you should be able to:

- reflect on the position of Shakespeare's work in culture, society and in the curriculum;
- plan for learning opportunities in oracy, reading and writing that arise from the study of Shakespeare;
- select, evaluate and develop a variety of approaches to and strategies for teaching and learning with Shakespeare's plays;
- recognise, use and evaluate some of the resources available to support learning.

DOI: 10.4324/9781003093060-11

SHAKESPEARE IN SOCIETY

Young people's initial response to a unit of work on Shakespeare is often 'why are we doing this?' As their teacher, you need to have a good answer to the question. As a starting point, reflect on what you might say to your pupils; you could think about classes you have taught or observed and consider how to answer that question for them.

Pupils' apprehensions about studying Shakespeare are often rooted in the view that the plays are centuries old and can have nothing to say to a young person in the twenty-first century. But Shakespeare is so closely woven into our culture, for example, in advertising, computer games, journalism and soap opera plots, that we do not always recognise his presence (Prescott, 2010). You and your pupils might also question the dominance of one British writer's work in the canon. It is worth bearing in mind, therefore, that Shakespeare's work has been translated and produced in many languages in many parts of the world since the middle of the eighteenth century – and possibly earlier – and that there are now texts in at least 80 languages (Bosman, 2010). Andrew Dickson, travelling in search of Shakespeare around the globe, has shown that theatre practitioners throughout the world take the plays and reshape them to reflect their own practice and the needs of their own audiences (Dickson, 2015). We may not be able to follow in Dickson's footsteps, but the MIT Global Shakespeares – Video and Performance Archive (https://globalshakespeares.mit.edu/) is a rich resource with videos of productions from around the world. As a cultural product Shakespeare no more belongs to the UK than the English language does. The four hundredth anniversary of his birth marked heightened interest with the publication of the British Council's report *All the World's* (British Council, 2016) surveying the extent of global engagement. In the same year, the UK government published a White Paper with a broader focus on culture, recognising the importance of Shakespeare to the economy as well as to education and well-being (Department of Culture, Media and Sport, 2016).

SHAKESPEARE, ENTITLEMENT AND 'CULTURAL CAPITAL'

Shakespeare's position in wider culture underpins the inclusion of his work in the curriculum to the extent that the study of Shakespeare's plays is a part of the entitlement of all young people and a key element in the development of cultural capital. The concept of entitlement was central to the National Curriculum from its inception (Coles, 2013), while the discussion of 'cultural capital' gained momentum in UK education after the term was included in the Office for Standards in Education's (Ofsted's) *School Inspection Handbook* (Ofsted, 2019). While there are complex social and educational debates to be had around both of these concepts which cannot be pursued here, it is important to place the study of Shakespeare in this context. There are questions about what pupils learn from their experience of studying Shakespeare (Coles, 2013) and these are placed into a wider context in Sarah Olive's comprehensive study of the teaching of Shakespeare at the turn of the twenty-first century (Olive, 2015). Ofsted define the term 'cultural capital' as:

> [T]he essential knowledge that pupils need to be educated citizens, introducing them to the best that has been thought and said and helping to engender an appreciation of human creativity and achievement.
>
> (Ofsted, 2019, p.43)

The definition is a reframing of the National Curriculum (2013e) view of the canon, as 'the best that has been thought and said', through the lens of 'cultural capital', a term originating with Bourdieu (1984) and signifying the passing of knowledge and experience through families rather than through education, analogous to the passing of inherited wealth. Both definitions (Ofsted and Bourdieu) refer to 'knowledge', so it is worth asking what that word means in the context of Shakespeare. Bear in mind that the reference to 'essential knowledge' is drawn from the National Curriculum for England, while the statutory requirements for Northern Ireland, Scotland and Wales frame their curricula in terms of 'knowledge understanding and skills', 'knowledge, skills and attributes' and 'experiences, knowledge and skills' respectively. It is worth exploring how the concept of 'knowledge' is framed in the curriculum that you are working with and what that means in relation to pupils' study and experience of Shakespeare.

SHAKESPEARE AND THE CURRICULUM

One reason for teaching Shakespeare is that it is a compulsory part of the curriculum in some parts of the UK. There is, however, more to the curriculum than statutory requirements, and teachers must reflect on the broader messages and models that schools promote (Kelly, 2009). English teachers are in a position of power in modelling enthusiasm for literature and excitement about the possibilities of language. The requirement to teach a play by Shakespeare in Key Stages 3 and 4 was introduced in the National Curriculum following the 1988 Education Reform Act. Devolution has changed the landscape and while the Key Stage 3 curriculum in England stipulates the study of a Shakespeare play, the curricula in Scotland and Northern Ireland do not, and from 2022 it will not be a requirement in Wales. General Certificate of Secondary Education (GCSE) English Literature specifications in Northern Ireland and Wales require the study of Shakespeare but the equivalent qualification in Scotland does not. The inclusion of Shakespeare in GCSE English Literature specifications is another reason why Shakespeare is taught in the lower secondary years, so that pupils do not encounter the plays for the first time in the context of external examinations. Activity 10.1 invites you to develop this aspect of your professional knowledge.

Activity 10.1

Research the GCSE and General Certificate of Education (GCE) A level specification (National Qualification in Scotland) taught in your school and reflect on the choice of plays and on nature of the tasks set for assessment. What opportunities for learning and teaching do the tasks offer?

Even before the Education Reform Act, Shakespeare was a staple of the curriculum (Olive, 2015), and, as early as 1909 C.T. Hunt argued that

> No child's education could be at all well balanced unless it included [...] the beautiful verse, the grand flowing lines, and the delightful songs that Shakespeare has given us.
>
> (p. 396)

A teacher in the twenty-first century might not express their enthusiasm in the same terms, but in 1909, Hunt saw a need to persuade teachers that children had an entitlement to experience Shakespeare. Notwithstanding the statutory requirements, however, the teaching of Shakespeare is valued by English teachers now. In their study of the teaching of Shakespeare's plays, Elliott and Olive (2019) found that 91% of the teachers surveyed believed that it was important, although fewer (74%) believed that it should be compulsory.

LEARNING WITH SHAKESPEARE

Pupils must have the opportunity to engage actively with Shakespeare's writing, and teachers must plan opportunities for pupils to take responsibility for their own learning and to explore and interact with the texts (Capel, Leask and Younie, 2019). Pupils can be encouraged to see their exploration in the same light as that of actors and directors who have worked with the material over the centuries, exploiting the plays' potential for interpretation. In a popular and scholarly work on Shakespeare, Emma Smith (2019) identifies the gaps in Shakespeare's plays and the questions that they ask rather than the answers that they give, as reasons for their continued life in production. And if this is true in the theatre, it is also true in the classroom, making Shakespeare a rich source of opportunities for active and creative learning.

Shakespeare's language is often seen as the main obstacle to pupils' engagement with the text (Olive, 2015; Yandell and Franks, 2019). So how can teachers support pupils to meet this challenge? There are broader debates in English about the pre-teaching of key words or difficult vocabulary (Bleiman, 2020), but one way is to create safe opportunities for pupils to use the language and to become actively engaged with it. This need not mean reading a scene around the class on the first encounter; other strategies may offer more support. Pupils can be given short pieces of script, even as little as one line, first to read silently and then to read aloud with a partner or to the class. All pupils in the class are given the chance to speak the words for themselves rather than simply listening to the more confident pupils. Pupils use the words, with Shakespeare's line breaks and metre acting as a scaffold, and can begin to inhabit the language and to own it for themselves. You could identify a short extract from a play you are planning to teach and consider how you could use it to build pupils' confidence and vocabulary. Another popular activity is to work with the rich resource of Shakespeare's insults, which gives pupils a chance to use the language expressively.

Some aspects of Shakespeare's language do require explanation because of their difference from modern English. But before you embark on preparatory activities, investigate your pupils' current linguistic knowledge. Pupils who speak a language other than English, one which uses the familiar or singular form of the second-person pronoun, are in a good position to understand its significance in Shakespeare's work.

WRITING: CHARACTER AND CONTEXT

Shakespeare has given us characters and plots that other artists have mined for inspiration since the seventeenth century and imaginative writing is often a useful way into a text. A simple example is to introduce the play by presenting a selection of characters' problems in the form of letters to agony aunts and asking pupils to write a response; see Table 10.1.

Table 10.1 Agony aunt

Agony Aunt: *Romeo and Juliet*	
Character	Problem
Mercutio	My best mate spends all his time thinking about a girl and won't come out with us any more.
Romeo	I'm in love with a girl but don't have the courage to tell her.
Juliet	My parents want me to marry the man they have chosen for me but I don't feel ready.

The activity creates an opportunity to explore familiar issues and experiences through the characters of Mercutio and Romeo and to discuss the question of Juliet's marriage at the age of 14.

Examination specifications require pupils to demonstrate an understanding of the context of production and reception of the plays. There is more to an appreciation of context than an awareness of the economic and social conditions underpinning early modern theatre, interesting as this may be for pupils. There is a debate, however, about how and when pupils engage most effectively with context (Bleiman, 2020). There are potential benefits to exploring aspects of context before embarking on a play, for example, discussing the practice of boy actors playing female roles in preparation for the gender complexities of *Twelfth Night.* Alternatively, the exploration of context as integral to the study of a play can minimise the risk of historical detail appearing as an afterthought to a piece of written work. Study the schemes of work and resources that your school uses for teaching Shakespeare plays and reflect on the approach to exploring context.

Within the plays, Shakespeare writes in different ways and his characters have different purposes. It is possible to use extracts from the plays as writing models for more than writing drama, for example, writing to persuade or describe. In *Richard III*, 1.2, for example, Richard persuades Anne to be his wife, and in the Prologue to *Henry V*, Chorus persuades the audience that they will see 'the vasty fields of France'. Pupils can analyse the strategies and use them as a model in their own writing. Shakespeare's theatre had limited scenic effects so included description to guide the audience. Pupils can analyse the strategies Shakespeare uses to create visual effects, for example, in Clarence's speech in *Richard III*, (1.4 ll. 9–33) or Titania's speech which begins 'These are the forgeries of jealousy' from *A Midsummer Night's Dream* (2.1 ll. 81–117). These speeches can serve as models for their own writing.

PERFORMANCE: PARTICIPATION AND ANALYSIS

Pedagogical advice on teaching Shakespeare emphasises the importance of performance (Gibson, 1998; Olive, 2015; Purewal, 2017); pupils should have opportunities both to perform for themselves and to analyse performance. It has never been easier for pupils to experience Shakespeare in performance on video even if their geographical location makes theatre trips an expensive luxury. Without compromising the centrality of the language, a simple production image can provide a rich focus for discussion of a character, supporting a detailed analysis of the play. Short video extracts demonstrate to pupils how the text becomes performance, and any differences between the lines spoken and the text on the page present opportunities for exploring interpretation. You can find many production images and extracts available online. Consider how you might use them to develop understanding of character, plot and productions. Ensure that you respect image usage rights.

Performance is a practical solution to the problem of covering the whole text in a relatively short time. A common pedagogical choice is to focus in detail on extracts from the play and to provide pupils with an overview of the plot to support their understanding of their detailed study. Video is one way to provide this overview, but there are others such as dramatic storytelling as suggested by Gibson (1998). Pupils are given characters to perform, an outline of the plot and some key lines to speak while the teacher tells the story collaboratively with the pupils. One value of this approach is that the story becomes memorable because they have participated themselves and associate roles with their friends who played them.

While the study of Shakespeare in Years 7, 8 and 9 is the opportunity to familiarise pupils with the language to enable them to read the lines comfortably, pupils need guidance on the rhythms and structure of lines, scenes and acts. Playing with the language to try out the metre, noticing where stresses lie (usually on content rather than function words), and exploring sense units all engage pupils actively with the language. Rehearsal activities such as reading a short extract and having each speaker point at the person being addressed helps pupils understand that the text is dynamic and interactive.

Shakespeare is currently a compulsory element at GCSE (although not in Scottish National 5), so the reading and study of the play must address the examination requirements. The assessment objectives require an 'informed personal response', which can only be developed through active engagement with the play. You can gain a better understanding of what examiners expect by reading the Chief Examiner's Report on the relevant paper of the GCSE specification that you are teaching. Reflect on the key messages and consider how they inform your approach.

PRACTICAL STRATEGIES FOR TEACHING SHAKESPEARE

As a student teacher you probably have limited control over which text and which edition you use, but it is nevertheless worth considering the various alternatives. The choice of play at GCSE and GCE A levels is limited to the range determined by awarding bodies and, in general, there is some degree of common ground among them. In England and Wales teachers choose a play from a list of between four and six plays including: *Macbeth*; *Romeo and Juliet*; *The Tempest*; *The Merchant of Venice*; *Much Ado About Nothing*; *Julius Caesar*; *Twelfth Night*. In Northern Ireland and Wales, Shakespeare is part of the non-examination assessment, giving teachers more choice of text. A wider range is generally available for study at GCE A level including, for example, *King Lear*, *Hamlet* and *The Taming of the Shrew*. In Years 7, 8 and 9, the choice is open to the teacher or department.

In addition to choosing the play, it is also important to think about the way that you present the text to the pupils. It is likely that you are limited to the school's current stock of books, but it is worth considering how the presentation of the text can support pupils' engagement and understanding. In some schools, especially if an abridged version is being taught, teachers create their own editions suited to their pupils and tasks.

Activity 10.2

Think about the classes you are teaching or observing and consider which play would suit their needs. Investigate the editions available (see publishers' websites) and consider what kind of content would be useful, for example, glossaries, activities, information about context, images, production histories. What would your priorities be in an edition of a Shakespeare play for a Year 7 class, a Year 10 class and a Year 12 class? How could you adapt existing resources to meet the needs of your pupils?

EXAMPLES OF PRACTICAL STRATEGIES

The following tasks enable pupils to explore the text as material for performance, either as an end itself or as preparation for analytical or imaginative writing. Use these strategies as templates for your own activities to meet the needs of your pupils and the opportunities presented by the play you are studying. You can find further guidance in Chapter 11, 'Teaching Plays', and Chapter 12, 'Drama in English'.

Activity 10.3: *Owning the language* (oracy activity)

A simple activity allowing all pupils to engage with Shakespeare's language.

- Choose a key speech from the play which can give clues to the plot and themes, for example, the opening soliloquy of *Richard III* (1.1, ll. 1–31) or Egeus' speech from *A Midsummer Night's Dream* (1.1, ll. 22–45), or a selection of shorter speeches.
- Distribute the lines around the class so that each pupil has one line and give them some time to try out reading it aloud.
- Ask each pupil to choose one word from the line. They have completely free choice and should feel no pressure to choose a challenging word.
- All pupils say their word aloud to the class in the order of the lines. Everyone in the class then has experience of speaking Shakespeare's language aloud.
- The single words are then the basis for a discussion on the speech and the play. What do the words suggest about plot, character or theme?
- The activity can then be developed with pupils working with the whole line.

Activity 10.4: *What is happening here?* (reading activity)

This is a strategy for introducing an unfamiliar text through recognition of familiar experiences. Working from what your pupils already know, you can choose a video clip from a play that resonates with them and builds their understanding of the play from their recognition of the relationships.

- Show pupils a short clip showing relationships between characters. Play the clip without sound at least twice.
- Ask the pupils to discuss the following questions:
  i. What is the relationship between the characters?
  ii. What are their feelings towards each other?
  iii. How do you know?

iv. Are there any other characters in the scene and what do they add?
v. What does the setting suggest?

- Pupils begin to develop an understanding of the scene before encountering the text.
- On studying the written text, pupils also note that Shakespeare gives us few stage directions, so directors are free to make staging decisions.
- An example of a clip that works well in this activity is from the BBC series *The Hollow Crown, Henry IV Part 1,* where Prince Hal is summoned to court by his father (3.2, ll. 36–93). Pupils recognise the family dynamic of the father reprimanding his son and of the other sons watching and observing. They might also consider that the presence of the other sons is the director's decision and what impact that has on the audience.

Note: all references to plays are to the Alexander Edition.

SUMMARY AND KEY POINTS

- Shakespeare's position in the literary and wider culture of the UK and beyond, justifies the inclusion of the plays in the curriculum as pupils are entitled to participate in that culture.
- The plays were written as texts for performance and should always be treated as such.
- An understanding of contexts is important and that includes not only the context of the plays' original composition but the many contexts of interpretation since then.
- Pupils should have the opportunity to speak and, if appropriate, perform Shakespeare's language as a means to understanding and ownership.

KEY RESOURCES

Theatre companies produce many resources for English teachers, drawing on drama rehearsal techniques to encourage active engagement. Regional or touring theatre companies may offer practical workshops to accompany productions and these are a good source of professional learning. In addition, the RSC and the Globe Theatre have excellent education departments and offer resources including lesson plans.

1. RSC Education: www.rsc.org.uk/education/teacher-resources
2. The Globe Theatre: www.shakespearesglobe.com/learn/
3. The Shakespeare Schools Festival is an excellent opportunity to participate in a production of an adapted and abridged play in a professional theatre. Workshops and training are available for pupils and teachers: www.shakespeareschools.org/workshops
4. MIT Global Shakespeares: videos of productions of Shakespeare or derived from Shakespeare across the globe. https://globalshakespeares.mit.edu/

Chapter 11 Teaching plays

JUDITH KNEEN

INTRODUCTION

Plays are part of the wonderful diversity of English literature. They have a rich history, rooted in ancient Greece and including mystery plays, Elizabethan theatre, restoration plays, theatre of the absurd and modern-day theatre. Plays have flourished in different forms throughout the world, including forms such as kabuki (dance-drama from Japan), and puppetry and masked theatre across both Africa and Asia. And yet, with the notable exception of William Shakespeare, playwrights can be easily overlooked in the English classroom. They are also given scant consideration in many books that provide guidance on English teaching. This is a great shame as plays offer a world of rich narratives and characters, of intriguing plots and contexts, of challenging ideas and themes, and in a format that encourages collaborative study.

At this point it is worth saying what this chapter is not. It is not about the study of *drama*, which is a much broader consideration, covering areas such as dramatic performance, acting, direction and production. Nor does this chapter focus solely on the richness of studying Shakespeare. (Both drama in English and Shakespeare are covered elsewhere in this volume.) Rather, this chapter considers why plays, as a form of literature, are eminently worth studying within the English classroom, and it also suggests some creative approaches that you might take. Hopefully you will discover that plays are not only enjoyable and accessible forms of literature for the classroom, but they also offer structure and room for improvisation and interpretation (Sawyer, 2011) which makes them a productive source for imaginative teaching strategies too.

At the end of this chapter you should be able to:

- appreciate the place and the value of plays as literature texts within the English classroom;
- establish what is distinctive in learning about plays;
- consider various strategies for learning with and about plays.

DOI: 10.4324/9781003093060-12

Activity 11.1: Getting to know plays

- Table 11.1 shows some of the plays commonly taught in secondary schools. Note those plays which you already know, and those which you need to get to know.
- Consider (a) why these plays are commonly taught in schools and (b) whether they offer suitable variety and diversity for study (e.g. consider the gender and ethnicity of the protagonist).
- Carry out an audit of the play texts taught in your department.
- Talk to colleagues about which plays work well in the classroom and why. In your discussion, try to establish which aspects need to be considered when choosing suitable play texts, for example, appropriate themes, accessibility, length etc.
- If you have a drama department, find out which plays they study. Discuss how they go about studying plays in drama, so that you can establish where the similarities and differences lie.

WHY STUDY PLAYS?

What do plays offer the English classroom? Let's start with Hamlet's well-known words: 'The play's the thing'. Hamlet, Shakespeare's eponymous protagonist, is set upon avenging the murder of his father. These words refer to a play he has arranged; it contains a scene that mimics the murder of his father. This play-within-a-play is designed to provoke a reaction from his uncle, the murderer. On seeing the scene, his uncle leaves the room abruptly, convincing Hamlet of his uncle's guilt. So Hamlet recognises a significant feature of plays: they speak directly to an audience. Plays allow for a shared, collective experience. This makes them a powerful and influential form of literature, which is evidenced by the long and rich history of plays within cultures across the world.

Within English, we can exploit the 'public' disposition of plays by arranging our study of this form of literature to be collaborative in nature. English teachers commonly manage the shared reading of a text, such as a novel, and this usually requires some consideration of how best to arrange the reading. A play has some distinct advantages in this situation. A playscript lends itself to be being read with others, with different parts that can be readily allocated to the pupils. The words are intended to be read aloud and to be spoken for a shared appreciation of the content, the language, the impact etc. Plays are designed for the benefit of a

Table 11.1 Plays commonly taught in secondary schools

Ages 11–14	Ages 15–16	Age 16+
• *A Midsummer Night's Dream* (Shakespeare) • *The Crucible* (Miller) • *Dracula* (Adapted by Calcutt) • *Frankenstein* (Adapted by Pullman) • *Much Ado About Nothing* (Shakespeare) • *Our Day Out* (Russell) • *Romeo and Juliet* (Shakespeare)	• *An Inspector Calls* (Priestley) • *Blood Brothers* (Russell) • *DNA* (Kelly) • *History Boys* (Bennett) • *Macbeth* (Shakespeare) • *My Mother Said I Never Should* (Keatley) • *The Merchant of Venice* (Shakespeare) • *The Tempest* (Shakespeare)	• *A Streetcar Named Desire* (Williams) • *All My Sons* (Miller) • *Hamlet* (Shakespeare) • *Journey's End* (Sherriff) • *King Lear* (Shakespeare) • *Top Girls* (Churchill) • *The Duchess of Malfi* (Webster) • *Translations* (Friel)

collective audience, whilst novels are generally designed for an individual reader. The difference between *audience* and *reader* may be subtle, and of course both elicit individual responses, but the notion of an *audience* encourages a shared response to the text, which potentially facilitates a widening appreciation and interpretation of ideas about the text.

When pupils read a play together in the classroom, they may also benefit from the following opportunities:

- developing confidence and competence in reading aloud
- reading with expression and appropriate tone
- listening skills
- developing interpretation skills
- prediction
- visualisation
- exploring characterisation
- exploring plot structures and twists
- acting and using drama strategies.

Another attractive feature of plays for the English teacher is that, with the notable exception of Shakespeare's plays, playscripts are often shorter texts that can be read and appreciated in their entirety.

But perhaps the main reason for studying plays is that pupils enjoy them. With the right choice of play and teaching strategies, you might find that 'teaching a play could be one of your pupils' most rewarding and eye-opening experience of literature' (Dymoke, 2009, p.123).

Activity 11.2: Exploring pupils' experiences

Choose one of your classes and find out about their experience with plays. Perhaps give them a short questionnaire. (If this is not possible, reflect on your own experience.) Questions might include:

- Have you seen a play performed?
- What plays have you seen?
- Where have you seen plays?
- Have you read any plays in school? If so, what and when?
- What do you like about reading plays?
- What don't you like about reading plays?

This information can help inform your choices of plays to study, as well as your planning. Pay particular attention, for example, to the needs of pupils who have not had experience of seeing a play. They may need some input on play/theatre features and conventions. One way of doing this is to show a play on video, and to ask pupils to identify the differences between TV/films and plays.

TEXT VERSUS PERFORMANCE

'There is something mysterious about the effect and impact of a good play, something that might originate in the intentions of an author, but which soon outstrips them' (Waters, 2011, p.1). Plays are designed to be performed. A justifiable question, therefore, is why we should read them in English. Wouldn't it be better just to watch them?

Of course, there is no real substitute for seeing drama on stage or screen. A performance helps to bring the characters to life, to show their interactions and their dialogue, as well as the physicality and visual impact of the drama. We can enhance this appreciation through literary study. Reading a playscript is bit like taking a look 'under the bonnet' in that it helps us better appreciate the impetus and workings of the play. It provides insight into the playwright's intentions.

The real joy of reading a play as a class, however, is that it creates its own performance. The pupils take on the parts and become the characters. It puts the words of characters into pupils' mouths, so they can become a part of the story. This is both a compelling and an exciting way to experience literature.

PLAYSCRIPT CONVENTIONS

Plays tell stories, but in a different way to novels, films, ballads etc. They have their own conventions and you need to share these conventions with your pupils as part of your introduction to the play.

Structure

Point out that plays have their own organisational structure, for example

- a list of the characters, or *dramatis personae;*
- plays are often divided into sections known as acts and scenes;
- there may also be line numbers, particularly in school versions of Shakespeare plays.

It is a good idea to give pupils practice at finding their way around a play. For example, give them an act/scene/line reference to a famous line or a significant phrase and ask them to look up the words.

Presentation

Playscripts are also set out in a conventional way, of course, and you can help pupils recognise these conventions by giving them a short section of playscript and asking them to mark up the presentational features of a playscript, such as the example in Figure 11.1. This example is taken from the start of Oscar Wilde's play *The Importance of Being Earnest*. The play is a farcical comedy involving love and relationships, in which Wilde pokes fun at Victorian manners, morals and hypocrisy. The tone is light-hearted and witty.

Stage directions

Stage directions can provide both helpful background and essential directions. They can tell us extra information about the following:

- where and when the scene takes place;
- who is on stage;
- characters' movements and actions;
- how words should be spoken;

- who is addressed;
- characters' feelings and reactions;
- what is on stage (e.g. scenery and props);
- sounds that can be heard.

Helpful contextual information is given at the start of the scene in Figure 11.1: the play is set in a real-life context (Half-Moon Street in Westminster, London), and the setting is chic and affluent. These details support understanding of the context but are not critical to the action. However, information essential to the action is also given: 'The sound of a piano is heard'. Playwrights usually make use of stage directions, to a greater or lesser extent, but it is worth pointing up for pupils which stage directions are important to the plot.

Props

As a starter to introduce a play (or scene, or character), extract some 'items' that might be associated with the play. The 'items' can be concrete things or intangible (e.g. music, emotion, weather); they can be introduced as words on a whiteboard, pictures on a PowerPoint slide, or even as props. Give pairs of pupils two minutes to discuss then share what the items might reveal. For example, in the case of the extract in Figure 11.1, you might choose pictures of a piano (or even listen to piano music), a cucumber sandwich and a silver salver. Other examples are shown in Table 11.2.

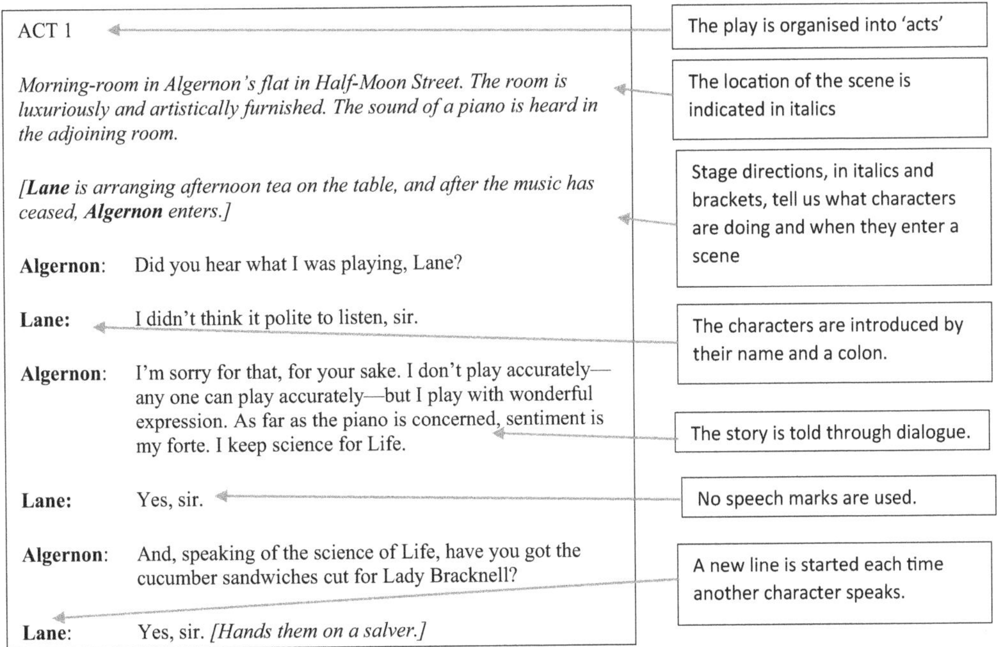
ACT 1

Morning-room in Algernon's flat in Half-Moon Street. The room is luxuriously and artistically furnished. The sound of a piano is heard in the adjoining room.

*[**Lane** is arranging afternoon tea on the table, and after the music has ceased, **Algernon** enters.]*

Algernon: Did you hear what I was playing, Lane?

Lane: I didn't think it polite to listen, sir.

Algernon: I'm sorry for that, for your sake. I don't play accurately—any one can play accurately—but I play with wonderful expression. As far as the piano is concerned, sentiment is my forte. I keep science for Life.

Lane: Yes, sir.

Algernon: And, speaking of the science of Life, have you got the cucumber sandwiches cut for Lady Bracknell?

Lane: Yes, sir. *[Hands them on a salver.]*

Figure 11.1 Annotation of the features of a playscript (*The Importance of Being Earnest*)

Table 11.2 Examples of props to introduce plays

Play	Examples of items
King Lear	Crown, map of Britain, the sound of a storm, jester/fool, family tree
Blood Brothers	Pram, pills, cardboard boxes, picture of DNA
An Inspector Calls	Bottle of port, engagement ring, bottle of disinfectant, picture of *Titanic*
Romeo and Juliet	Astrology symbols, party invitation, dagger, heart shape

Activity 11.3: Props to introduce plays

Think of one or two plays you know well. List the props that you might use to introduce them to a class. The aim should be to intrigue pupils, as well as to encourage thoughtful responses.

Plot and dialogue

With any story, it is important for pupils to understand the plot. The plot of a play is held within the dialogue, and pupils may need support in grasping the plot, particularly with a challenging playscript. You can achieve plot familiarity through a range of strategies.

i. *Revisiting the text* can help pupils understand the story. You can do this in several ways, for example:
   - Pupils read the scene in a small group, then you revisit it as a whole class.
   - Read a scene as a class, then watch a video version of the play.
   - Listen to an audio version of the play, before reading significant parts of the play as a class. (Audio versions have the advantage of allowing pupils to follow the reading, whilst visualising it in their minds, thereby creating their own interpretation.)
   - Reading the play as a class, before asking groups of pupils to make their own audio recording of a scene. (Different groups can take on different parts of the drama.)

ii. Another helpful strategy is to ask pupils to *quiz the text*. Provide them with a limited section of text, and prompt them to ask questions about what is happening. You can provide some questions as examples, and then encourage them to pose their own questions focusing, for example, on:
   - information retrieval,
   - understanding,
   - deduction,
   - inference,
   - analysis, and
   - prediction.

In the case of the script in Figure 11.1, the following questions might be posed:

1. Who is playing the piano?
2. Does he play the piano well? How do you know?
3. What is the relationship between the two people in the scene?
4. What sort of person do you think Algernon is?
5. How does the playwright introduce humour into this scene?
6. What do you think will happen next?

Pupils can *quiz the text* in pairs and offer their questions for another pair to answer, or put them to the teacher, or to the whole class.

iii. Another approach to reinforcing the plot is to *headline the action*. In Baz Luhrmann's modernised version of *Romeo and Juliet*, a television newscaster reads the prologue of the play and effectively headlines the action.

Capulets wow Verona

Verona's celebs dressed up in their latest finery, to celebrate the Capulets' traditional feast. All the Capulets were there, including Lord and Lady Capulet, their teenage daughter Juliet and the quick-tempered Tybalt. Wine was flowing, food was in abundance, and musicians played for the dancers.

Lord Capulet was in good spirits as he welcomed their guests to the masked ball. He proclaimed: 'Everyone must enjoy themselves at our feast. Nothing at all should spoil the party.' It is rumoured that love was in the air for some. Even young Juliet appeared to have found a young admirer.

Figure 11.2 A 100-word news article about *Romeo and Juliet*, Act 1, scene 5

Provide pupils with a scene from the play and ask them to provide the headlines of what is occurring. Alternatively, ask them to provide a 100-word news article, as in Figure 11.2.

Character notes and thoughts

Playwrights sometimes provide character notes. In *The Crucible*, Arthur Miller provides lengthy notes about some characters. This play is about a witch-hunt and is based on historical events. As Miller introduces characters, he tells about their place in history and their nature. His notes are designed for readers of the play and interrupt the dialogue to provide a sort of metanarrative of comment on the characters.

This is a technique that can be utilised by your pupils. They can provide detailed character notes, either at the entrance of a character in the play or at significant moments in the drama. These notes can relate their perceptions of the character, character relationships and the development of the character in the play.

Another way to focus on character is to consider their thoughts. Plays focus on a character's words, but we know that what we say does not always equate to what we think. This activity encourages pupils to think not only about what a character is saying, but also what they are thinking.

Give pupils a suitable key extract – perhaps only a few words. Allow small groups time to consider what the characters are thinking and to write out thought bubbles to accompany the words on big pieces of paper. Ask some pupils to read the characters' words whilst others hold up the thought bubbles. Compare the ideas of different groups.

READING ALOUD

Reading a play together as a class or in groups provides a ready opportunity for reading aloud – both the teacher and the pupils. Reading aloud has been recognised as an effective strategy for developing literacy skills at primary and middle schools (Albright and Ariail, 2005; Merga, 2017), but it is less frequently used with older pupils (Cliff Hodges, 2011). However, there is evidence that reading challenging literature aloud can be a very valuable experience for weaker secondary school readers as it helps reposition '"poorer readers" as "good" readers' (Westbrook et al., 2019, p.60).

Managing the reading of a play does require preparation. Table 11.3 indicates some of the aspects to consider.

Table 11.3 Aspects to consider when reading a play with a class

Aspect	Considerations
Allocating parts to pupils (Should the teacher choose, or should you invite volunteers?)	Aim for fluency – to keep everyone interested and engaged. Asking for volunteers tends to elicit responses from the same pupils. So it is a good idea for the teacher to allocate the parts, particularly at first, so that you can change the pupils who are reading if necessary. Importantly, it also allows you to include/encourage as much pupil involvement as possible, in particular, those who may be more reticent or shy. Allocating parts according to the competence and confidence of the pupils helps maintain reading momentum.
Responding to pupils who do not want to read	Some pupils may not want to read a part. It is unwise to force a pupil to read, but you can provide them with another role in the lesson, e.g. noting down what they learn about a character so they can share this later in the lesson. Talk to reluctant readers privately, to ascertain the reason, and see if they are willing to read a short part on another occasion.
How to deal with stage directions	The stage directions can be helpful but they can also interrupt the flow of the story, so judge how best to use them. Stage directions indicating how words are spoken can be noted by the reader but not read aloud. However, the directions which indicate entrances, exits and other actions are important to flag up. It can be helpful for the teacher to read these out. This also gives you the opportunity to sum up the action and check understanding as you go.
How much to read	• Plan your reading to include an interesting or complete episode, so that pupils feel they are making good progress through the story. • If possible, leave your reading on a cliffhanger, so that your pupils are keen to come back to it. • Avoid interrupting the story too much by pausing and explaining every incident. However, do stop and check understanding regularly.

Activity 11.4: Preparing to teach

Preparing to support your pupils' encounters with a play text is important. As noted earlier in this chapter, you may need to consider the format, the conventions, the ideas, the vocabulary etc. Figure 11.3 provides an extract from *She Stoops to Conquer*. This is an eighteenth-century comedy which involves matchmaking, mishaps and misunderstandings. In this scene, Tony is wanting to go to the pub, but his mother (Mrs Hardcastle) tries to dissuade him. Imagine you are introducing the play to older pupils. How might you support a reading of this extract? Some areas you might want to consider are:

- *Historical setting* (the eighteenth century is shown through the setting, the language, the relationships etc.)
- *Vocabulary and pronunciation* (reading a play aloud can put pressure on pupils, so anticipate unfamiliar vocabulary and guide them on how to say the words)
- *Social and cultural conventions* (you need to help pupils understand social expectations, e.g. obedience to parents)
- *Humour* (comedy can come from different sources, e.g. dialogue, physical slapstick, which are both present in this scene)

SCENE—Mr and Mrs Hardcastle in a Chamber in an old-fashioned House.

Enter Tony, crossing the stage.

Mrs Hardcastle:	Tony, where are you going, my charmer? Won't you give papa and I a little of your company, lovee?
Tony:	I'm in haste, mother; I cannot stay.
Mrs Hardcastle:	You shan't venture out this raw evening, my dear; you look most shockingly.
Tony:	I can't stay, I tell you. The Three Pigeons expects me down every moment. There's some fun going forward.
Hardcastle:	Ay; the alehouse, the old place: I thought so.
Mrs Hardcastle:	A low, paltry set of fellows.
Tony:	Not so low, neither. There's Dick Muggins the exciseman, Jack Slang the horse doctor, Little Aminadab that grinds the music box, and Tom Twist that spins the pewter platter.
Mrs Hardcastle:	Pray, my dear, disappoint them for one night at least.
Tony:	As for disappointing them, I should not so much mind; but I can't abide to disappoint myself.
Mrs Hardcastle:	*(detaining him.)* You shan't go.
Tony:	I will, I tell you.
Mrs Hardcastle:	I say you shan't.
Tony:	We'll see which is strongest, you or I. *(Exit, hauling her out.)*

Figure 11.3 Extract from *She Stoops to Conquer* by Oliver Goldsmith

Florinda:	What an impertinent thing is a young Girl bred in a Nunnery! How full of Questions! Prithee no more, Hellena; I have told thee more than thou understand'st already.
Hellena:	The more's my Grief; I wou'd fain know as much as you, which makes me so inquisitive; nor is't enough to know you're a Lover, unless you tell me too, who 'tis you sigh for.

Figure 11.4 The opening lines of *The Rover* by Aphra Behn

INTERPRETATION

Interpretation is a key skill in script reading. How the characters' words should be spoken may be indicated in stage directions, but it is often open to interpretation. This interpretation is what gives the lines impact. It is also what helps bring the characters to life. You can give pupils practice in developing this skill by asking them to 'direct' some of the lines in a play.

For example, look at the opening lines from Aphra Behn's play *The Rover* (Figure 11.4). Behn lived in the seventeenth century and is notable for being one of the first women in England to earn her living through writing. *The Rover* is a comedy about love, amorous adventures and unwelcome matches. The play opens with two Spanish sisters, Florinda and Hellena, discussing love.

How these lines are spoken indicates something of the relationship between these two sisters. Which words are emphasised indicates important themes in the play. For example, are Florinda's words spoken in anger, with humour, with fatigue, or perhaps with condescension? Does Hellena reply sadly? wistfully? angrily? petulantly? Which words might be emphasised and given significance? How the lines are spoken also reveals their personalities and what is important to them.

Give pupils experience and practice in directing the reading of short passages. This helps them both understand the play and develop their skills of deduction, inference and interpretation. Use photographs of different productions to help them see differences of interpretation so that they can develop their own interpretations.

SUMMARY AND KEY POINTS

- With their rich literary heritage, plays offer valuable opportunities for literature study throughout secondary school.
- Plays are designed to be shared and seen by an audience, which makes them ideal for the classroom.
- Watching a play is the ideal way to appreciate a play; engaging with a playscript helps pupils join in the performance and helps them better understand a playwright's intentions.
- When studying plays, pupils can develop confidence and competence in a range of areas including reading aloud, listening skills and the ability to interpret text.
- Plays use particular literary conventions, and these need to be taught.
- Introducing a playscript can be a fun and very enjoyable form of literature to study and share in the English classroom.

KEY RESOURCES

1. **BBC Bitesize** has a range of helpful resources for both younger and older secondary pupils, including helpful video clips of performances.
   www.bbc.co.uk/bitesize
2. **The British Library** has a wealth of teaching resources on literature, including twentieth-century drama, deception drama and global Shakespeare.
   www.bl.uk/teaching-resources?teachingsubjects=english-literature
3. **The Royal Shakespeare Company** has an excellent education section on their website that includes teacher resources and a learning zone for pupils.
   www.rsc.org.uk/
4. **The V&A:** The story of theatre provides a journey through the history of theatre in England.
   www.vam.ac.uk/articles/the-story-of-theatre

Chapter 12 Drama in English

HELENA THOMAS

INTRODUCTION

Drama and English are 'twin traditions' (Bunyan and Moore, 2005) united in many aspects of content and purpose; divergent in areas that have the potential to be mutually enriching. Their status in compulsory education, however, differs considerably: English takes centre stage while drama watches from the wings – undermined, some argue, by the close relationship between the two (Fleming, 2017). Certainly, in England, since the non-inclusion of drama in the English Baccalaureate (leading to the removal of Drama General Certificate of Secondary Education (GCSE) courses in many schools), the subject has found itself more vulnerable than ever. This chapter acknowledges drama is a complex and challenging area of study, separate from English, but argues that drama pedagogies can enliven, enrich and deepen teaching of all areas of the English curriculum. The English classroom is generally a more static, desk-bound space than the drama workshop. The aim of this chapter is to convince you that this need not be the case.

Before reading on, take a moment to reflect: how do you feel about using drama pedagogies in the English classroom? Perhaps you have significant expertise in drama – for example, at A Level or degree – and need little persuading; perhaps, on the other hand, you deliberately avoided drama and balk, now, at the thought of embracing it in your teaching. Whatever your level of expertise, this chapter aims to provide you with the inspiration and confidence to give it a try. It begins with a brief history of drama and English in secondary education, followed by a theoretical overview of the benefits of drama pedagogies in all aspects of the English curriculum – oracy, reading and writing. Throughout, I include examples of practical activities using drama, including case studies provided by members of my own cohort of English Postgraduate Certificate of Education (PGCE) students at Bath Spa University, showing that, no matter your career stage or level of expertise, it is possible to give drama a go!

At the end of this chapter, you should be able to:

- understand key arguments in support of drama pedagogies in English;
- apply your understanding of drama pedagogies in a classroom context;
- evaluate your practice in terms of pupils' progress and development.

DOI: 10.4324/9781003093060-13

ENGLISH AND DRAMA: A BRIEF HISTORY

English and drama could be described as disciplinary siblings, such are the overlaps between them. In terms of the school curriculum, however, the relationship is not straightforward. In England, drama has only ever existed in written policy documents as an aspect of English, with varying degrees of emphasis (resulting in a mixed offer from schools, with some preferring to teach drama as part of English and some offering the subject separately, often within the 'arts'). Scotland, Wales and Northern Ireland, on the other hand, give drama official credence with its own curricular framework as part of the Expressive Arts, which, in theory, ensures a more reliable provision for pupils in those countries. By contrast, the curriculum offer for English is quite a different story. English is enshrined in hefty, written curricula across all countries and has been since the first National Curriculum in 1989: if English and drama are siblings, then English is undoubtedly the favoured child.

Despite the differences in curricular history, English and drama both share a troubled history with their own identity as school subjects. According to Fleming and Stevens (2015), drama has suffered from a lack of firm definition: it means 'different things to different people' (p.156). Part of the confusion comes down to a distinction between 'theatre', which centres on content, and 'dramatic play', which focuses on creative self-expression: learning *about* or learning *through* drama. Likewise, there is no consensus on what English is or should be. In fact, the slippery nature of the discipline is one of its defining features; it is 'a quicksilver among metals – mobile, living and elusive' (Dixon, 1975, p.1). This elusiveness can be exciting, but also divisive, and the history of English as a school subject is strewn with the debris of dissent and disagreement: it might be dynamic but it is also a 'sack of snakes' (Wilson, 1964).

To come full circle, one of these 'snakes' is drama and drama's place in English. Whilst it is generally understood that learning *about* drama, in the form of studying playtexts, is central to English, the idea that we can and should learn *through* drama is not so universally accepted. Nevertheless, there are clear arguments for the use of drama pedagogies in all three components of English – oracy, reading and writing – and I take each in turn to make this case.

Activity 12.1

Use the internet to explore the approaches to drama taken in all four corners of the United Kingdom. How does each country define drama? What conclusions do you draw from the differing emphases? For each, what aspects, if any, do you think have relevance and value to English?

DRAMA AND ORACY

Like drama, oracy is a contested area of English, as Ruth Newman explores in Chapter 2, pointing out both its unstable nomenclature and its variable status in curricula over time. The first National Curriculum in 1989 foregrounded 'Speaking and Listening', deliberately listing it before 'Reading' and 'Writing' in recognition of its crucial role in language acquisition and development. Since, almost all English curricular frameworks across the United Kingdom have followed suit, with the notable exception of the current English Programmes of Study in England, in which 'Speaking and Listening' is replaced with 'Spoken Language', positioned last rather than first. This arguably represents a downgrading of oracy in England, especially when considered alongside the removal of the oral component of the English Language GCSE grade. By demoting oracy, there is an attendant risk that drama pedagogies disappear from the English classroom, as there is a straightforward link between the two.

Why is oracy important? The most obvious answer relates to employability: employers value good oral skills, which accounts for the Confederation of British Industry's objection to the removal of the Speaking and Listening assessment at GCSE and the evidence that multinational corporations prize oracy highly (Mercer, 2015). However this, according to the English-Speaking Union, is but one of the key benefits of teaching oracy; they claim a range of wider gains for pupils, including confidence, resilience and empathy, as well as protection against behavioural or psychological issues. Certainly, if you consider the impact of your own advanced oral skills, you are likely to conclude that they have been instrumental in, for example, your success in presenting a convincing and impressive case when it mattered most (not least when securing a place on your teacher-training programme!) or in forging strong relationships with those who mean the most.

How do we define good oral skills? A number of frameworks exist but I have chosen to include O'Toole and Stinson's helpful checklist (see Table 12.1). Use this now as a frame for your reflections on your own oracy development. How often have you used good listening or turn-taking skills to work collaboratively? Can you think of examples where you have adapted your oral language to inform, control or imagine? Can you recall times when your ability to draw on a wide vocabulary and appropriate register impressed an audience? Perhaps this was aided by your verbal expression and use of silence? The deft use of a combination of these skills forms the basis of the kind of eloquence and articulacy that it is the English teacher's job to promote.

This checklist is useful, also, for considering the benefits of using drama to teach oracy. Reflect on what skills pupils develop when they, for example, devise a role play in a group, assigning roles between them, cooperating in rehearsal and choosing the language appropriate for each invented character. Studies show that well-executed drama pedagogies significantly develop pupils' abilities to: cooperate and negotiate with each other in preparation for a dramatic outcome; consciously choose and reflect on language, extending vocabulary as well as understanding of register (including formal registers); use verbal and non-verbal emphasis for effect; and develop active listening skills (O'Toole and Stinson, 2013). Moreover, O'Toole

Table 12.1 O'Toole and Stinson's (2013) checklist of oracy skills

Functional	**Dialogical**
Informing	Listening
Controlling	Responding
Negotiating	Turn-taking
Feeling	Leading
Imagining	Narrative
Linguistic	**Paralinguistic**
Diction	Vocal expression
Vocabulary	Non-verbal and gestural
Grammar and syntax	Proxemics
Register	Energy
Colour	Silence
Public address	

and Stinson's (2013) research found that using drama – specifically, a series of group role-play activities – impacted on levels of *engagement* across all pupils, particularly (and possibly counter-intuitively) reluctant or shy pupils, one of whom commented, 'Like … when I am myself I am not very confident … but when I was in role it was easier' (p.174). This suggests that drama can be a powerful way to 'adapt teaching to respond to the strengths and needs of all pupils'.

Activity 12.2

Case study: *PGCE student Sophie Maxted experiments with a mock court trial for* Macbeth

A **mock court trial** *involves acting out an imagined trial of characters from any text. In the classroom, it can be used to help pupils draw on evidence to make judgements and, therefore, develop interpretations of character and plot.*

Sophie says:

> Pupils were assigned roles in groups of three to four. The groups represented the prosecution and defence for Macbeth, Lady Macbeth and the witches. There were also six members of the jury who deliberated following the trial to decide who was truly responsible.
>
> The pupils had to come up with three arguments supporting their side and be prepared to present these during the trial. They also had to prepare for questions from the jury. During the preparation lesson, the jury had to consider questions they could ask and come up with criteria for the 'winning' team. In limiting the time they were able to speak during the trial, the pupils had to concisely summarise their arguments and choose their strongest points (skills that are central to planning essay answers). They also had to choose quotations from the play that supported their arguments. Providing a worksheet for them to complete helped them structure their arguments effectively. In terms of skills development, the pupils had to utilise teamwork skills in deciding what to argue, in addition to working on their speaking and listening skills.
>
> The pupils really engaged with the trial and enjoyed taking on the role of lawyers. I hope, and think, it was a memorable experience for them.
>
> In terms of practicalities, I had to rearrange the classroom to replicate a courtroom. The only issue with behaviour was pupils talking over one another, but as the 'judge', I was able to limit this. It was great to see how passionate and engaged the pupils were.
>
> In terms of resources, I created worksheets for the preparation lesson. When assigning 'roles', each team was given the opportunity to come to the front and pick a piece of paper out of an envelope to decide which character/s they would be defending/prosecuting. Some pupils decided to make props (e.g. a copy of fingerprints on the dagger) so spare paper was necessary. I also had a prize for the winning team.

Reflect on the case study using the following prompts:

- How might you decide which pupils should sit on the 'jury'? What might you need to consider as part of this decision?

- How important do you think the preparation time and resources were to the success of this activity?
- How does this activity support the development of the oral skills tabled above?

DRAMA AND READING

Reading at secondary school encompasses a wide range of texts, from non-fiction to film to canonical literature. For the purposes of this chapter, we focus on the particular benefits of drama and the teaching of literature, although that is not to say that drama cannot be valuable for other forms of reading: in fact, drama can encourage pupils to interact with a range of texts in fresh and exploratory ways (see Franks and Bryer, 2014). Nevertheless, the case for using drama pedagogies to explore literary texts is strong. To make this case it is necessary to briefly explore the nature of reading itself, particularly literary reading.

As student English teachers, you are all expert readers, but have you ever considered what this involves? Take a moment to reflect on it now. When you read, do you read continuously, or do you pause to think, to question, to look back at another part of the text? Do you accept a text's meaning at face value, or do you actively search for possible alternative meanings? When you read, do you see just the words, or do the words provoke images? Does reading ever register in your body: fast-beating heart or sinking stomach? Does reading stop when you put down the book? When you talk about the text with others, and listen to their ideas and experiences of the text, how does it affect your reading? When you reach a conclusion about a text, is it final, fixed forever, or is it subject to change? If you read a book at 20 and again at 40, is it the same experience?

These questions should prompt you to challenge the notion that reading is somehow static; quite the opposite, reading is active and dynamic, particularly in the case of challenging literary texts – those that leave the most interesting interpretative gaps for the reader. Those gaps are addressed in what Rosenblatt (1970/1995) called the 'aesthetic mode' of reading, in which 'readers are fully engaged as a whole person seeking out the significance of the textual experience and establishing a meaning' (Goodwyn, 2011, p.133). Rosenblatt's transactional theory is one of the reader-response theories that transformed English studies in the twentieth century, placing the reader at the heart of the process: 'A novel or poem or play remains merely inkspots on paper until a reader transforms them into a set of meaningful symbols' (p.24). This spotlights the creative, dynamic and intellectual job of the reader and demonstrates that reading is not neutral: any reading of a text is influenced by the experiences, values and predispositions of the reader. This understanding has, according to Eaglestone (2017), come to define how we 'do' English, which might be best described as *entering a conversation* (Eaglestone, 2017; Bleiman, 2020), one that is altered and extended by each contribution, rather than internalising a stable body of knowledge.

This has significant implications for teaching, for *your* teaching in secondary schools. If by 'doing' English we mean empowering pupils to make valuable and robust contributions to an intellectual conversation, and providing them with a meaningful literary *experience*, then this impacts on how we teach. Approaches designed to build knowledge, such as 'low-stakes' quizzes or 'knowledge organisers' (which are widely used in England as a consequence of the Office for Standards in Education's (Ofsted's) current focus on 'knowledge-rich' curricula), are, alone, insufficient to fully include pupils in the 'conversation' about literature.

They might well be useful for recalling facts about plot, character or context, but do not fully recognise that in English: 'knowledge is *made* through the experience of reading and can't simply be "poured into you" as if it were water and you were a bucket'. (Eaglestone, 2017, p.5, my italics).

How does this relate to drama? Firstly, drama pedagogies have the power to enhance 'aesthetic' reading by providing opportunities for pupils to *experience* the text in an active and embodied way. The potentially immersive nature of this experience has the benefit of giving pupils *time* with a text, resisting the rush to a definitive interpretation (duly cemented in a point/evidence/explain (PEE) paragraph), which is, in many ways, the antithesis of literary reading. By spending time with a text (quality time, if you like!), pupils are likely to generate ideas that will, ultimately, improve their analytical writing, making it a clear method to 'promote pupils' progress', although it is not always recognised as such.

In addition, drama pedagogies encourage pupils to *collaborate*. This is crucial because collaboration allows pupils to explore, evaluate, reject and refine ideas about a text: the all-important *conversation* about literature which promotes thoughtful speculation rather than bland regurgitation of someone else's ideas and/or tangential facts about the text.[1] It is important to remember, too, that dramatic pedagogies are *engaging*, helping pupils build bridges between their experience and the writers', forging that transaction that makes meaning. The issue of engagement is not a trivial one: when reading William Wordsworth's *The Prelude*, for example, or Robert Louis Stevenson's *The Strange Case of Dr Jekyll and Mr Hyde*, teenagers do not necessarily make immediate connections, the language, ideas and context presenting potential barriers to the meaning-making process. Drama can provide a way to overcome these barriers without resorting to language glossaries, contextual fact sheets or teacher-led interpretations. These authentic readings are more likely to result in good quality analytical writing.

Activity 12.3

Choral reading – *Romeo and Juliet: Act 3, Scene 5*

Its roots in Greek theatre, **choral reading** *involves reading in unison and can be not only a powerful dramatic method but also a supportive way of encouraging pupils to engage in drama in the classroom.*

Divide your class into groups of five or six. Nominate a 'Juliet' in each group and then, if possible, send them to a separate room or a part of the room. They do not have to prepare anything but should read the scene and discuss Juliet's dilemma and emotions. The remaining pupils are 'Capulet' and are going to prepare a choral reading of his words in the scene.

First, pupils should go through the scene and decide which of Capulet's words, phrases and images are most aggressive/impactful, highlighting them as they go. Once they have made their selection, and agreed on it as a group, they can begin to play around with this, deciding on an order in which to say the words and whether or not to repeat any words or phrases. At this stage, they might also discuss how they will perform his words: which they will shout or whisper; which they will say in chorus, which individually; whether they will stay still or move as they perform etc. Once done, pupils can begin to rehearse until they are satisfied with their performance.

At this point, bring the 'Juliets' back and ask them to sit on a chair with their eyes closed, where they will stay for the remainder of the performance.

The 'Capulets' then present their choral reading in a circle around 'Juliet', who, eyes closed, feels the full force of his traumatic words. The 'Juliets' should then explore their experience in discussion with the group, drawing out new insight into the impact of this scene at this point of the play.

In terms of resources, you need scripts for all 'Capulets' to write on. Space is advantageous – this activity is unlikely to work in a small classroom.

To scaffold this, you might provide pupils with a 'script' of Capulet's words, removing the requirement to choose his language themselves.

Reflect on this using the following prompts:

- To what extent does it support the 'aesthetic mode' of reading?
- What might you need to do before and after the activity to maximise its impact in terms of pupils learning and progress?

Activity 12.4

Case study: *PGCE student Amy Keeble experiments with a hot-seating exercise with the play version of* A Curious Incident of the Dog in the Night-Time

Hot-seating *is an exercise used in rehearsal rooms to help actors inhabit their characters as fully as possible. In role, they answer questions from peers and these questions often encourage them to consider aspects of their character (and the play) that they may not have considered before. In the classroom, it can be used in a similar way. One pupil sits in the 'hot seat' in role as a key character and answers questions from their classmates. This can work across a range of genres, not just plays. Sometimes, pupils can benefit from being in role as an author, poet or playwright, too.*

Amy says: 'Students were eager to do this task long before we used it. Through generating and responding to questions, they gained a developed understanding of key characters in the text, including the motivations of each character. The exercise also helped them to find key information in the play; they needed to refer to specific events, actions and words in order to form and respond to the questions. This helped to prepare them for GCSE as well as bringing a sense of fun and enjoyment to the lesson.

'The practical considerations were few; the activity is a quick and easy set-up, with only chairs at the front of the room needed. I found it important to pick a particular scene or event to provide a focus for questions, and I also set clear ground rules about asking and responding to questions, for example: hands up to ask questions; characters choose the questioner; all the audience members should show they are listening; questions must be relevant to the text and must be possible to answer with reference to the text (no "what's your favourite ice-cream flavour" questions!)'.

Reflect on this using the following prompts:

- How might you choose the pupils who answer the questions? Volunteers? Confidence or ability level? What are the implications of this?
- As not all questions can be asked, how might you ensure that all 'audience' members are fully engaged during the activity?

Activity 12.5

Tableau – *Of Mice and Men, chapter 4*

A tableau *is technique used by actors to explore characters through purely physical representation. By freezing in poses in a key moment of a play, actors can tease out important relational aspects like power dynamics, motivations or emotional reactions. In the classroom, this can work well for a variety of texts and purposes.*

Put pupils in groups of four and ask them to create a tableau of the moment that Curley's wife threatens Crooks. They should be encouraged to think about who has the most power in this moment, and how this might be shown; they should also be encouraged to think about how the onlookers – Lennie and Candy – might react in the moment and what this says about the characters and the context, in terms of prejudice of all forms.

To extend the activity, you could ask pupils to prepare a short 'inner-thoughts' line for each character (sometimes called '**thought-tracking'**), which they deliver on your prompting when presenting their tableau to the class. An alternative to this activity would be to ask pupils to write 'director's notes' for the scene, in which they would consider the same ideas but individually and in writing.

Reflect on this using the following prompts:

- What kind of practical reorganisation of your classroom might be necessary for this activity to work?
- Should pupils follow this with written work? If so, what might you set and why?

DRAMA AND WRITING

Ted Hughes once said that children should be taught not so much 'how to write' but 'how to try to say what you really mean' (Hughes, 1967, p.12). The distinction is hugely important, making a vital link between language and *meaning* that is sometimes lost in schooling. In English classrooms currently, there is much focus on linguistic features as signifiers of success in pupils' writing. A descriptive piece, for example, might be judged on how many devices – simile, metaphor etc. – are inserted rather than its composition or content (Anderson, 2013). This is arguably a consequence of the genre approach to writing, which advocates explicit teaching of the distinct linguistic features required by the differing purposes, audiences and forms of a written text (sometimes referred to as PAF). This means that pupils often write according to a checklist of these features, commonly acronymised (look out for AFOREST when in schools, for example). Whilst this approach has merit, there is, nevertheless, a danger that it weakens the all-important connection between writing and meaning, leaving pupils with 'little voice or choice when it comes to writing' (Dobson and Stephenson, 2020, p.246). When pupils have something to *say*, it can act as a driver to express it in the most impactful way, which in turn motivates pupils to learn and draw on relevant linguistic tools to do this. With so many pupils, mainly boys, struggling to undertake extended writing in schools, the importance of this drive cannot be underestimated.

As any classroom teacher will tell you, however, there is one potential problem with framing writing around the expression of pupils' *meaning*, and that is a lack of ideas. What happens when pupils feel they do not have anything meaningful to say or to write about? How can teachers overcome this hurdle and provide pupils with the confidence (for it is more likely lack of confidence than ideas) to express themselves in writing? As Dunn, Harden and Marino (2013) show in their review of the research on drama and writing, studies demonstrate that drama pedagogies offer a way of circumventing this problem. In fact, the studies are remarkably consistent in their findings, showing that drama pedagogies: help pupils generate rich and interesting ideas to use in their writing; *motivate* pupils to write, securing pupils' engagement in the process; enrich pupils' use of vocabulary and syntax; and develop pupils' understanding of elements of authorship when writing creatively – like narrative voice, character portrayal and dialogue.

How does drama make this kind of difference? Firstly, drama can provide pupils with a direct, often immersive, sometimes emotional, experience that can form the basis of the content of their writing. Secondly, the *time* spent on the drama activity allows for the incubation of their ideas, so that they are fully developed by the time pen is put to paper. The studies suggest, too, that pupils' motivation can be enhanced by a sense of tension and urgency created by the drama, which, in one study, led pupils to believe that 'what they were writing about mattered and would be important to the person reading it' (Dunn, Harden and Marino, 2013, p.251). Oral rehearsal is another significant benefit of drama: by playing with word choice and sentence structure verbally, pupils build a kind of language 'bank' that transfers into their writing, resulting in more advanced vocabulary and syntax. Likewise, imaginative writing can be enlivened through role play, which encourages pupils to take different perspectives, sharpening their understanding of narrative voice, as well as helping them write more convincing characters and dialogue.

Activity 12.6

The story of this object

Oral storytelling *is one of the most primal and foundational forms of drama. Its accessibility can make it a powerful tool in the classroom for a range of purposes.*

Gather a range of unusual objects from your home (in the past, my collection has included a red squirrel nutcracker, a Buzz Lightyear toy, a brass candlestick and a rusty lock). Put pupils into groups and give each group an object, keeping one for yourself.

Pupils should be encouraged to first pass around their object, talking about what it looks and feels, perhaps even smells, like. Then pupils should begin to invent a story for their object: where has it lived, for how long, and with whom? Who has cared for it and what has it seen? Has it been involved in significant historical events or lived a steady, domestic life? At some point, you should pause the activity to show pupils your object and to tell the class its tale – an intervention which both prompts or develops their ideas as well as models the performance aspects of oral storytelling which they will later use.

Once their stories are settled, pupils should prepare an oral retelling of their object's tale ready for showing to the rest of the class. On completing this, pupils are then free to pick the object, and story, which has most inspired them and write this as a piece of creative writing using the object as narrator.

Reflect on the activity using the following prompts:

- What specific classroom management strategies might you need to use to ensure the activity works smoothly?
- What extra support might struggling writers require?
- How does the activity differ from writing creatively using a checklist of features and/or 'success criteria'? What is lost and what is gained through use of either approach?

PRACTICAL CONSIDERATIONS FOR DRAMA PEDAGOGIES IN AN ENGLISH CLASSROOM

Rarely are English classrooms spaces that can accommodate drama pedagogies without taking the time and effort to reorganise the room, which is something that you must factor into your planning. A messy start to a drama-based lesson can add behaviour management challenges that might undermine your confidence as you begin to experiment with these approaches. Whilst not all activities require a big central space, most do, and therefore you need to think about whether you have the capacity to undertake this before the start of the lesson. You might only attempt a drama-based lesson when you have break or lunchtime before the lesson so that you can set up the room in plenty of time.

Once you have organised your room appropriately, you need to think about how you manage pupils as they enter. A change in environment tends to suggest to pupils that usual rules and routines do not apply! Speak to your colleagues in the drama department and find out by what means they communicate to pupils that they require silence; often, it is as simple as a raised hand. Your pupils will be used to responding to this in their Drama lessons, so it is likely to be more effective than trying your usual methods, which may not work in the altered classroom. Similarly, once you have pupils' attention, you want to use this to set clear expectations for the lesson; without this, you might find that pupils test the boundaries, even if they are usually well behaved in your lessons. With this kind of preparation and forethought, there is nothing to stop you enjoying a fun, lively and valuable lesson using drama pedagogies with your pupils.

FINAL THOUGHTS

> You don't unearth meaning, you construct it through an interchange.
>
> (Greene, 2014, p.126)

> The way to develop one's mastery over English is to live within a rich context of its lively use.
>
> (Holbrook, 1967, p.23)

Perhaps more than almost any other subject, English is not so much about what pupils *recall* about a body of content but about what *meaning they make* from it. Although this is most obviously true of the study of literature, where pupils must develop convincing and articulate interpretations, it also applies to oracy and writing. This is not to unduly denigrate the place of knowledge – pupils must draw on a wide range of vocabulary and knowledge of grammar, for example, to achieve the eloquence required to be successful in any aspect of English – but it is to remind you that, alone, knowledge is not enough. In fact, it is probably better to think of knowledge in English as 'knowledge-in-action', as Applebee did (Bleiman, 2020, p.56): it must be used in the service of interpretation and communication in order for pupils to succeed. It is the equivalent of the Science student being assessed on what use they make of their scientific knowledge in experiments, rather than on their scientific knowledge alone. Success in English is about application and advancement of the knowledge base, not reproduction of it.

Given this, and given the confidence required to achieve it, drama pedagogies are amongst the most effective and appropriate ways to promote pupils' progress in English. They have the potential to nurture a learning environment that *engages* pupils in the process of developing their linguistic dexterity and expertise, providing that 'rich context' of 'lively use' prized by Holbrook.

SUMMARY AND KEY POINTS

- Drama and English are siblings, overlapping in content, purpose and, potentially, approach.
- Drama pedagogies have the potential to enrich the English classroom, supporting your pupils' development and progress immeasurably.
- Drama pedagogies can inspire confidence, motivation, resilience and pleasure in learning.

RESOURCES AND FURTHER READING

1. For a thorough grounding in dramatic pedagogies as well as drama's identity as a school subject, Fleming, M. (2017) *Starting Drama Teaching* (4th ed.), Abingdon, Oxon: Routledge, is an excellent read. Likewise, the chapters on drama in Fleming, M. and Stevens, D. (2015) *English Teaching in the Secondary School* (4h ed.), Abingdon, Oxon, Routledge, and Davison, J. and Daly, C. (2014) *Learning to Teach English in the Secondary School* (4th ed.), London: Routledge, are superb introductions to the opportunities drama can provide in the English classroom.
2. Extensive online material, including a range of multimedia resources and plenty of teaching ideas, can be found on The Royal Shakespeare Company's website (www.rsc.org.uk/education), The Globe Theatre's website (www.shakespearesglobe.com/learn/) and the National Theatre's website (www.nationaltheatre.org.uk/learning). Excellent materials on the process of creating theatre can be found on Kneehigh's website (https://kneehighcookbook.co.uk/cookbook/).

NOTE

1. This point has been raised again and again in GCSE examiners' reports, which review the quality of responses in each year's GCSE papers. Both the 2017 and 2018 AQA reports, for example, make much of the 'distraction' of pupils identifying word classes or literary techniques or the 'bolted-on, extraneous context' (2018) which does not add value to the argument. These are inadvertently encouraged when we stress 'recall' in English instead of focusing on the important and challenging process of meaning-making.

Chapter 13 Storytelling, myths and legends

JOAN FOLEY

INTRODUCTION

Mary Beard has captured the significance of mythology, the fact that 'Myths are a framework for how we think about who we are' (2008). This chapter invites you, as a new English teacher, to consider the place of myths and legends in the twenty-first-century English classroom and, at the same time, to consider further the discussion about spoken language as a medium for teaching and learning from Chapter 3. The chapter invites consideration of the skill of storytelling – connected, of course, with myth-sharing in the past – as an aspect of the repertoire of talk in English and its affordances for both teacher and pupil. In drawing on some features perhaps usually associated with primary classroom practice the chapter highlights the rich possibilities for Key Stages 3 and 4, and even the possibilities in General Certificate of Education A level teaching. In primary phase classrooms the sharing of classical myths, for example, might find its place in cross-curricular or thematic approaches to learning as part of the KS2 History and English requirements (Lister, 2007). Storytelling, too, is a significant skill in the early years/primary teachers' repertoire. So, what do approaches used in primary schools have to offer learning in the secondary phase? In particular, how might *listening* help pupils engage with stories of complexity and challenge? And what are the stories, the myths and legends we choose to share with pupils? Whose legends and why?

The chapter looks briefly at: how myths and legends have figured in the various iterations of the National Curriculum (NC) for English since 1989; how they might contribute to learning in English across Key Stage and ability up to, and including, A level, for example, through literary allusion; how storytelling and listening are framed in the current curriculum documents for the UK and how storytelling might promote inclusive practice in today's English classroom.

The chapter asks you to explore sources of independent study material online but also encourages you to work through tasks with your peers both in pairs and in small groups through discussion and rehearsal.

You are encouraged to share these – and other – oral texts with your pupils.

DOI: 10.4324/9781003093060-14

At the end of the chapter you should be able to:

- understand how myths and legends from classical and Western repertoires and, importantly, from other cultures, might contribute to the English curriculum;
- understand further the relationship between talking, listening and learning, and the curriculum expectations for spoken language;
- explore strategies for developing oracy using storytelling pedagogy in English;
- explore how to develop confidence in teacher voice through storytelling.

But …

Let's start at the beginning with the stories themselves … why should we tell ancient tales in our classrooms?

MYTHS AND LEGENDS

Activity 13.1

Consider the dictionary definitions for key terms used in this chapter taken from both the Oxford and Cambridge online dictionaries – *myth; legend; epic*. What do you notice about the differences in the definitions? Why might these elements be useful in teaching English to 11–14 year olds? 14–18 year olds?

OED online www.oed.com/

Cambridge Dictionary online https://dictionary.cambridge.org/dictionary/english/

Throughout your teaching career you will make important decisions about the texts you choose to share with your pupils. Some decisions are determined by NC or examination specification demands; some, simply, by the resources you have available to you in your department. Ideally, however, your choices are also prompted by what you feel *your* pupils in *your school* need at their current point of development and progress. Which poems, plays and prose speak to them now? Why? What do they have to say?

Certainly, I would argue that myths and legends, as seminal oral texts, as seminal stories, can speak to pupils at different points in their secondary school development. The significance of myths and legends from the different corners of the UK, and from the different cultures represented in our schools, should not be ignored but celebrated. Tales from the King Arthur cycle such as *Gawain and the Green Knight*, from Anglo-Saxon stories such as *Beowulf* and the Welsh *Mabinogion*, from Scottish, Irish and Celtic traditions, from the Norse world to those from beyond Europe to tales from the *Gilgamesh* and *Ramayana* epics, to Egypt, Hindu and Yoruba myths can be shared. To list some of the possibilities would be to exclude and, as Railton (2015) points out in her article which describes her work with a Year 10 group on sharing the myths and stories from their home cultures, it is incumbent upon the teacher to draw on what the child (of any age) brings to the classroom. Forty years ago the Bullock Report, so central to the history of the development of our subject discipline, promised that 'No child should be expected to cast off the language and culture of the home as he crosses the school threshold' (DES, 1975, p.286). Railton believes this promise has been forgotten.

This chapter focuses on classical myths and the wealth of resources available to the English teacher, but there are connections with other mythologies and legend cycles that could be explored. In order to uphold the promise made by Bullock, English departments might well choose to audit the mythologies and legends of their pupils and look at how those connections might be explored.

Classical myths, epics and stories have lasted for a very long time! Their significance for early audiences fuelled the desire to capture the oral into the written form. These tales are 'accessible, relevant and inclusive' (Lister, 2009, p.1). Secondary pupils are often already familiar with the classics from the primary curriculum and from the 'morphed' versions in popular culture in film and television; they inform the stories that pupils know, watch and read such as the *Percy Jackson* series and, of course, *Harry Potter* (Gerson, 2011; Haynes, 2016).

The stories are rich in themselves; their themes and moral dilemmas reflect not only the concerns of their time but also have resonance for today – it's no wonder that poets such as Carol Ann Duffy (*The World's Wife*), Kate Tempest (*Brand New Ancients*) and Inua Ellams (*The Half God of Rainfall*) take stories such as the Icarus myth into modern settings to explore the challenges faced by teenagers on the cusp of adulthood, and that novelists such as Adele Géras and Natalie Haynes in young adult (YA) fiction, and Margaret Atwood, Pat Barker, Madeline Miller, Natalie Haynes (again) and Kamila Shamsie take the stories from the epics of the *Iliad* and *Odyssey* of the war with Troy and show them to us from the alternative perspectives and interests of the twenty-first century. So, classical myths can provide ways into understanding other stories, into understanding how texts talk to each other across time. Beyer's (2013) article about her work with first-year undergraduates in English notes the significance of studying what she terms 'foundational texts' as they 'remind[s] us of the essence of storytelling' (p.401). Our pupils are entitled to meet – and enjoy! – these in the secondary phase.

THE IMPORTANCE OF SPEAKING AND LISTENING – REVISITED

The earlier chapter on speaking and listening as a tool for learning cited key thinking in this area from Vygotsky (1978) through to Mercer (2007). Here I would like to build on that discussion and emphasise not only Alexander's work on talk in the classroom (2003 and 2012) which makes clear claim about its centrality in all pupils' academic attainment but also Littleton and Mercer's later work in 2013 where their term 'interthinking' encompasses productive collaboration and creativity through talk. They focus on its potential to not only help groups problem-solve but also its capacity to help humans make sense of the world. In his online introduction to Ovid for the British Library, Andy Armitage cites Ted Hughes' suggestion that the stories are 'units of imagination' that unconsciously combine with other stories, and experiences, to help us to make sense of our inner and outer realities (Armitage, 2016). It would seem, then, that there is synergy here.

STORYTELLING IN EDUCATION – IS THERE A DEFINITION?

It is significant that any search about oral storytelling in education rarely leads to research papers on storytelling in the secondary phase. Refine the search to 'oral storytelling primary school' then 'oral storytelling secondary school' and you will probably find that there are half as many about secondary. You will also see that of the papers you do find for secondary, the majority are written in the USA not the UK. In her work about creative English teaching Cremin (2009b) highlights the fact that storytelling as a pedagogy resides predominantly in the early years phase; the use of a potentially rich art form decreases as we move through the school stages. This is, no doubt, linked to the various iterations of national curriculum-led programmes of study where, currently, for example, in England, the place of speaking and listening has been devalued in General Certificate of Secondary Education specification requirements. See **Storytelling in the Curriculum**.

We need to look to the USA for a definition of storytelling in education. The National Council of Teachers of English (NCTE, 1992) provided a position statement that describes oral storytelling as

> relating a tale to one or more listeners through voice and gesture [...] Each listener, as well as each teller, actually composes a unique set of story images derived from meanings associated with words, gestures, and sounds. The experience can be profound, exercising the thinking and touching the emotions of both teller and listener.

It's worth reading the position statement in its entirety – see ***Key Resources***. Hibbin (2016) develops the definition further in her article where she advocates the 'non-instrumental' use of talk in the primary classroom, that is, the importance of talk for talk's sake, not talk as necessarily a precursor to writing, and suggests that oral storytelling is complex and that its use in the classroom requires reciprocity between teller and tale, that the tale is improvised and 'dynamic' and that the spoken word's physicality is acknowledged. What, then, are the potential challenges and affordances of this pedagogy in your secondary classroom?

Unlike the formal presentation, perhaps, there is a real demand for active listening in oral storytelling – how does this figure in current curriculum demands?

STORYTELLING IN THE CURRICULUM

The chapter on speaking and listening asked you to consider the differences in how oracy/spoken language is framed in the current Key Stage 3 curriculum for England and Wales and suggested that there might be a difference in emphasis on presentational talk and interactive talk.

Activity 13.2

Look at the charts in Chapter 3 again and, with a partner, highlight the statements which you think are concerned with storytelling in the classroom in these two versions. What place does it have in the current curriculum? Are there any potential constraints or possibilities?

Compare your findings now with the current Scottish Curriculum for Excellence material on speaking and listening:

https://education.gov.scot/Documents/literacy-english-eo.pdf
https://education.gov.scot/nih/Documents/lit10-group-discussion-skills-diagram.pdf
https://education.gov.scot/improvement/learning-resources/group-discussion-professional-learning-resource

Where are the opportunities for storytelling in these documents?

What's striking is the omission of storytelling from the English NC but the explicit address of it in the Welsh framework. Where there is a notion of performance in the English document, it fails to embrace storytelling explicitly but, rather, focuses on the performance of a *written* text. The English framework mentions 'speak confidently and effectively'; the Welsh framework pays attention to audience and listening, to 'dynamic texts', a more fertile ground for storytelling.

MYTHS AND LEGENDS IN THE CURRICULUM

> storytelling is one of the most important, most humane, most liberating and most democratic things that human beings can do, and it should have a central place in every classroom.
>
> (Philip Pullman, in Lister 2007, p.1)

Surprisingly, stories and storytelling have not always had a secure place in the national curriculum. In its first iteration in 1989 there were over 50 references to 'story' covering the key skills in English – speaking, listening, reading and writing. Story is valued explicitly in Cox's statement that 'children construct the world through story' (Cox, 1989a, p.94), and the document makes direct reference to classical texts, 'Learners should be alerted [...] to [...] relevant translated works, including classical stories from Greece and Rome', and this was offered as a way of introducing pupils to 'forms of discourse which were powerful in the past and from which our own culture has developed' (Cox, 1989a, p.95). However, the 1999 version sees the demise of 'story', while requiring pupils to read 'myths, legends and traditional stories' (DfEE, 1999, p.26) as part of their Literature entitlement and to consider their appeal and influence over time, the references to 'story' are reduced significantly, and are concerned only with the reading and writing of them, not the telling of them or listening to them. In 2004, the revision of this curriculum states in its introduction to the English orders that pupils 'learn to become enthusiastic and critical *readers* of stories, poetry and drama' (DfES, 2004, p.43) (my italics). (This phrase remains in the 2007 version.) But, although pupils are again expected to learn about 'the influence of Greek myths' (DfES, 2004, p.48), there is no encouragement to use storytelling per se. By 2007, they are perhaps mentioned only by implication in the reading requirements (DCSF/QCA, 2007a, p.70):

> 3.2 The texts chosen should be:
> 3.2a [...] of high quality, among the best of their type, that will encourage pupils to appreciate their characteristics and how, in some cases, they have influenced culture and thinking.

In the current version of the NC, classic myths find their place in the primary Department for Education (2013c) History curriculum:

> They [pupils] should understand how our knowledge of the past is constructed from a range of sources.
>
> Pupils should be taught about:
>
> Ancient Greece – a study of Greek life and achievements and their influence on the western world.
>
> (DfE, 2013c)

For secondary English, there is no mention at all of the classics or myths, and almost all reference to 'story' in English has been lost. At KS3, pupils are required to read 'a wide range of fiction and non-fiction including, in particular, whole books, short stories, poems and plays with a wide coverage of genres, historical periods, forms and authors' (DfE, 2014b, p.15). However, the requirement that 'The range will include high-quality works from [...] seminal world literature' might offer some opportunity to include these tales. In KS4, 'story' and 'stories' disappear altogether. A student should simply read 'a wide range of high-quality, challenging, classic literature and extended literary non-fiction, such as essays, reviews and journalism. This writing should include whole texts' (DfE, 2014b, p.19). These 'challenging' texts might well include Simon Armitage's *The Last Days of Troy* (2014) or Margaret Atwood's *The Penelopiad* (2006), but given the time constraints on the curriculum this will probably be unlikely.

A NOTE ON 'CULTURAL CAPITAL'

'Cultural capital'

> 178. As part of making the judgement about the quality of education, inspectors will consider the extent to which schools are equipping pupils with the knowledge and cultural capital they need to succeed in life. Our understanding of 'knowledge and cultural capital' is derived from the following wording in the national curriculum: 72 'It is the essential knowledge that pupils need to be educated citizens, introducing them to the *best that has been thought and said* and helping to engender an appreciation of human creativity and achievement'.
>
> (Ofsted, 2019, p.43)

Since the inception of the current national curriculum in 2014, there have been debates about the content of one of its key aims – see my italics – and about how 'the best' is identified. The *Ofsted School Inspection Handbook* from 2019 introduced a term in its descriptors of quality of education which also suggests a 'best' and draws on both Pierre Bourdieu (1986) and E D Hirsch (1988): 'cultural capital'. Bourdieu suggests that social assets in terms of education (knowledge and intellectual skill) lead to advantage in reaching higher status in society; Hirsch focuses on the importance of 'cultural literacy' for pupils to thrive in the modern world. There is much debate about these somewhat loaded terms. After all, who decides what significant cultural capital is? Numerous educational blogs at the time of the new Office for Standards in Education (Ofsted) framework's publication certainly signalled acceptance of the notion that a person's level of cultural capital (How do you measure it?) is an indicator of academic success (How do they know?). Concerns, though, were also raised by some educationalists that 'cultural capital' implies that certain cultures are objectively more valuable than others. Barbara Bleiman's blog is useful here (see Key Resources at the end of the chapter).

Consider this in relation to the next activity.

WHICH STORIES DO YOU KNOW ALREADY?

Activity 13.3

Individual:

- Take five minutes to list all the myths and legends you know.
- Which ones do you know well? Which ones do you know less well? Why might this be?

Pair/share:

- With a peer, compare your lists – similarities/differences? – and then categorise these stories in ways that are meaningful to you both
  - For example:
    - theme
    - character
    - where they are from
- What conclusions do you draw from this initial categorisation? (Note: This is also a useful task to use with pupils when eliciting understanding of genre, for example).

Pairs to fours:

- Share your categories with another pair.
- What do you notice? Commonalities? Surprises?
- Can you make links between these stories and stories that you have encountered recently in your subject knowledge development/preparation for school placement?
- What might this say about an 'unconscious canon' of shared stories? Why these stories?

TEACHERS AS STORYTELLERS

Case study – PGCE English University of West of England, Bristol (UWE, Bristol)

Since 2012, an element of UWE Bristol's Postgraduate Certificate of Education Secondary English induction programme is the opportunity to take tales from Ovid's *Metamorphoses* into local schools to share with mixed-ability Year 7 pupils. Following an interactive workshop on teaching myths at the university with Bob Lister, student teachers use his excellent materials from Cambridge Classic Tales (https://classictales.co.uk/) to help them plan an early teaching episode using storytelling pedagogy.

How might storytelling help the beginning teacher?

In exploring storytelling as a key part of practice and pedagogy, student teachers develop:

- their subject knowledge per se. As foundational myths, the original stories of Achilles, Odysseus and of *Metamorphoses* are often yet to be discovered by the majority of student teachers;
- their subject pedagogy. Storytelling and teaching through narrative and analogy is part of experienced teachers' repertoire. New teachers need the opportunity to practise the skill of weaving a story, for hooking pupils into texts both spoken and written;
- their teacher voice in the early stages of their training.

How might storytelling help the pupils?

The project allows pupils to:

- have access to rich stories through *listening* to the teacher storytellers so that the literacy demands of the word on the page do not exclude those in a mixed-ability classroom with literacy difficulties;
- expand their knowledge of classic tales to help inform their reading of other texts;
- have opportunities to explore the complex moral dilemmas faced by characters in these tales;
- develop their own storytelling skill and practise active listening.

The story begins …

The online materials from Cambridge Classic Tales provide rich, powerful telling of tales from Greek and Roman mythology by professional storytellers Daniel Morden and Hugh Lupton, supported by excellent teaching resources and transcripts of the stories. To prepare for the storytelling event student teachers are invited to spend an afternoon in a 'picture book wallow' – where they read and share stories from a myths and legends book box in which wonderfully illustrated picture books, mostly intended for primary classrooms, are the source material for exploring Ovid and Homer. Student teachers practise reading aloud to each other from various versions written by Anthony Horowitz, Robin Lister, Rosemary Sutcliffe and others noting recurring motifs and patterns of suspense and climax. Importantly, however, they then listen to the retellings online by Morden and Lupton, firstly to enjoy but on subsequent hearings to note the storytellers' art of breaking the stories down into what Daniel Morden calls, 'pictures of the mind' – an almost cinematic/storyboarding technique to track the story's arc. In listening pairs and trios they identify the techniques deployed by the storyteller – so that metatalk informs their own practice. They annotate the transcripts to identify how the teller uses emphasis, dynamics, pause, rhythm, rhyme and repetition, accent, pitch, inflection and tempo, and then consider how, in their own live retelling they might use non-verbal language of the body (glance, gesture, pause and physical expression) to aid their listeners' understanding. Traditional epithets, for example, 'swift-footed Achilles', 'grey-eyed Athene', are used as mnemonic aids for the teller and help bring characters to the listener's mind's eye. From this, student teachers rehearse their own retellings of the tales ready to share with Year 7 who are, in turn, asked to tell the story back. Key here is that the teacher storytellers are encouraged to avoid keeping to a fixed script but instead to storyboard the tale as a visual prompt in the early stages of the process.

To support their pupils in their storytelling, the student teachers develop ideas for visual/physical prompts to capture plot details. In the past they have worked with pupils to make character puppets from paper plates/wooden spoons; have used outlines of giant Greek vases to capture scenes using synoptic storytelling (i.e. a representation of the stages of the story captured in one image); have collected plot prop boxes filled with crowns, swords and bottles and, on one occasion, a 'mythtery' bag (!) was created to take into school.

Student teachers tell their versions of *Metamorphoses* – for example, Arachne, Echo and Narcissus, Icarus and King Midas and there is always what Kuyvenhoven (in Phillips (2013, p.ii)) describes as the 'listener's hush'.

Pupils then retell their versions using the plot prompts made by the student teachers and their own alternative props, pictures and puppets.

The story continues …

The significance of the project is clear in testimony later in the course. Student teachers feel that they understand the power of storytelling in classrooms and that it gives them confidence in their emerging teacher voice and a way into sharing other stories later in their training. Some go on to develop schemes of work on Greek myths in their schools, and some design schemes of learning which encompass myths from different cultures. Student teachers describe this as 'empowering' in their growth as teachers.

The next section of the chapter takes just one story from Ovid's *Metamorphoses* and the storytelling materials from Cambridge Classic Tales and suggests links to other texts – written and visual – to suggest how the story might be shared and how classical texts can 'talk to' other texts.

LET ME TELL YOU A STORY: ICARUS

The story of Icarus is one that 'talks' to pupils from 11–19. It is the story of a young man who, seeing the chance for freedom – for flight – refuses to heed his father's advice. It's part of a bigger story about the father, Daedalus, the inventor of the Labyrinth built to imprison the Minotaur, and his imprisonment with his son in Crete for aiding Ariadne and Theseus. Already you see that the story links to other famous stories …

What is significant about this tale for secondary pupils is that it is about what it means to be a young adult. What does it mean to be a young man? What are the rights and responsibilities? Perhaps the story warns against his complacency and hubris …

Let's look at some versions. The tasks which follow could be part of your planning for a sequence of learning with pupils as appropriate to their age and ability but can also serve as a way of developing your own subject knowledge for teaching.

CONTEXT

The Open University has free online courses, one of which is Icarus: Entering the World of Myth: www.open.edu/openlearn/history-the-arts/icarus-entering-the-world-myth/content-section-0?active-tab=description-tab. You could start your preparation with this, or visit the material in *Further Resources*.

Start with the version by Ovid in ***Metamorphoses***, Book 8, 183, available from Perseus Digital Library, Tufts University, a free online repository of classical texts in translation (see Key Resources).

Activity 13.4

If you were to use the storyboarding technique from the case study, how would you deal with this version of the text? What are the pictures in your mind? What is the story's arc?

Cambridge Classic Tales

Now listen to the audio version told by Daniel Morden linked in the Key Resources (8 mins 25 secs). With a peer, identify what has been kept in and what has been removed. Why has the storyteller done this? Consider the way in which Daniel speaks, the way he tells the tale. What is the meta-talk you might elicit from your pupils if you were sharing this version with them?

What do we understand about Icarus from this telling?

Read the transcript of Daniel's version. Text mark this to identify similarities and differences with Ovid. What do you notice now?

TEXTS TALK TO TEXTS – PERSPECTIVES

The Cambridge Classic Tales website also directs the teacher to other representations of the story in both art and poetry which could be introduced to pupils in an arts-based approach to the text.

The link in the Key Resources leads to the Bruegel picture *Landscape with the Fall of Icarus* and to poems about the picture, ekphrastic texts: *'Musée des Beaux Arts'* by W H Auden and 'Landscape with the Fall of Icarus' by William Carlos Williams. Discussion of these visual texts could usefully lead onto discussion of perspective.

Other depictions of the story in art from Bruegel to present day to share with pupils might include:

- Joos de Momper (1500s) *Fall of Icarus*
- Frederick Leighton (1800s) *Icarus and Daedalus*
- Henri Matisse (1940s) *Icarus*
- John Armstrong (1940s) *Icarus*
- Chris Burden (1970s) *Icarus, April 13, 1973*
- Andrew Denman (2000s) *Fallen Icarus*.

CONTEMPORARY WRITING

The story of Icarus speaks to writers today. Kate Tempest's *Icarus* deserves to be heard (see Key Resources). Listening to her telling, think:

How is Icarus presented here? Which lines are the most significant and why?

A more recent text imbued with references and allusions to Icarus is *The Half God of Rainfall* by Inua Ellams, a poem in which the Olympian gods and the 2012 Olympics collide. Listen to the author reading the opening here and note the fusion of Greek and Nigerian Yoruba mythologies (see Key Resources). Note that the Icarus figure, a basketball player (Demi – half-god himself), is protected by his **mother** from the fickle gods.

And for a sharp, comic comment on hubris in the story, read Carol Ann Duffy's 'Mrs Icarus', part of her collection *The World's Wife* where she writes from the view-point of the women caught up in the stories from myth, legend, the Bible, fairy stories and history and offers an alternative perspective.

FINAL THOUGHTS

Classical myths and legends inspire and inform the texts we teach in English from William Shakespeare to Mary Shelley's *Frankenstein* to *Harry Potter* to Kate Tempest's *Brand New Ancients*:

we're the same beings that began,
still living,
in all of our fury and foulness and friction.
Everyday odysseys.
Dreams vs decisions.
The stories are there if you listen.

In a rich curriculum the sharing of these tales through the medium of oral storytelling has the potential to bring them alive for all pupils.

SUMMARY

- The sharing of stories in the English classroom is a key experience for all pupils.
- The significance of sharing seminal world stories in English classrooms deserves the attention of new and practising teachers.
- Storytelling pedagogy provides gateways for pupils of all abilities to rich, satisfying texts and to make deep connections between these and other story texts written and visual.
- Talking, listening and learning are key communal experiences in English for teachers and pupils alike.

KEY RESOURCES

Approaches to sharing classical myths are drawn from the inspirational work of Bob Lister and the excellent free resources on the Classic Tales website which include tales from Ovid and Homer. For more detailed discussion of how student teachers have used these materials, see resources 5 and 6.

1. Barbara Bleiman's blog at the English & Media Centre is always insightful. This entry discusses the problem of how 'cultural capital' is understood: www.englishandmedia.co.uk/blog/whose-cultural-capital
2. Online resources for exploring the story of Icarus, as introduced earlier in this chapter:
   - Perseus Digital Library, Tufts University, free repository: www.perseus.tufts.edu/hopper/text?doc=Perseus%3Atext%3A1999.020028%3Abook%3D8%3Acard%3D183
   - The Cambridge Classic Tales Website
     - Daniel Morden video: https://classictales.co.uk/metamorphoses/daedalus-and-icarus
     - Daniel Morden transcript: https://classictales.co.uk/sites/default/files/transcriptdaedalusandicarus.pdf
   - Kate Tempest video: www.youtube.com/watch?v=yv5fggapRwQ&feature=youtu.be
   - Inua Ellams video: www.youtube.com/watch?v=hXK8LpAOe-A
3. Lister, B. (2007) *Changing Classics in Schools.* Cambridge: Cambridge University Press.
4. Lister, B. (2012) Telling tales. *English, Drama and Media.* 22. pp.16–22.
5. Foley, J. (2015) The trainee teachers' tale. *Teaching English.* 8. pp.64–6.

6. Smith, L. and Foley, J. (2015) Talking together, learning together: The story of English PGCE student teachers' adventures in classics. *Changing English: Studies in Culture and Education*. 22 (1). pp.60–71, https://doi.org/10.1080/1358684X.2014.992212
7. NCTE (1992) *Teaching Storytelling A Position Statement from the Committee on Storytelling*, 1 June 1992 https://ncte.org/statement/teachingstorytelling/.

Chapter 14 Media in English

RACHEL ROBERTS

INTRODUCTION

In Marshall McLuhan's famous words: 'the medium is the message' (McLuhan, 1964). That is to say, the meaning of a text is inextricably linked to the form in which it is presented. English is principally about the process of meaning-making in the reading and creation of texts (Roberts, 2020). It is a *conversation* (Eaglestone, 2017) between texts and between pupils and texts, over time. Often conversations about media as a school subject divide it into the study of 'high-brow' literature and popular culture (that is 'low-brow') media. This notion should be challenged as it is highly reductive and diminishes English as a subject.

This chapter argues for a broader understanding of the subject English and suggests a greater range of texts for analysis and invention to use in the classroom. It considers the meaning of 'media' in the English classroom and makes a case for its inclusion in day-to-day teaching, exploring a range of teaching approaches, treating media texts both as a tool of analysis and as distinct and worthy in themselves.

The chapter explores the relationship between text, media and English and media's place in the curriculum. It then pinpoints key pedagogical approaches to teaching media in English and shares some examples of media in English in practice.

At the end of this chapter you should be able to:

- consider what we mean by 'media' in English and why it should feature in the teaching of English;
- understand how to use a range of approaches to the teaching of aspects of English using media and multimodal texts, as tools of analysis and as texts themselves.

WHAT IS MEDIA?

The dictionary definition of 'media' seems straightforward: 'the main means of mass communication (broadcasting, publishing, and the Internet) regarded collectively' (www.lexico.com/definition/media). This communication takes place

DOI: 10.4324/9781003093060-15

through *texts.* Before reading any further, it's worth unpacking what is meant by 'text' and its relationship to media and English.

WHAT IS A TEXT?

Activity 14.1

Begin by making a list of texts – perhaps everything that you've engaged with in the last 24 hours. Now group them, using any criteria that you like (for example: Tweets, Facebook posts, WhatsApp messages could go under 'social media').

What did you notice about the connections between the texts doing this exercise? Write down what criteria you used; could you regroup the texts? Were there some texts that belonged to more than one category?

You might, for example, create the following groups:

- **Social Media**: Tweets, Facebook posts, WhatsApp messages
- **News**: Sky News bulletin, *The Times* newspaper, the local BBC news website
- **Books**: *The Testaments* by Margaret Atwood, *Media and Society* by Curran and Hesmondhalgh, *The Gruffalo* by Julia Donaldson

It might be possible to recategorise them as follows:

- **Personal information**: WhatsApp messages, local BBC news website
- **Public information (for work)**: *Media and Society* by Curran and Hesmondhalgh, Sky News bulletin, *The Times* newspaper
- **For pleasure**: *The Testaments* by Margaret Atwood
- **For someone else's pleasure!**: *The Gruffalo* by Julia Donaldson

In the first set of groups I used *format* as a way of categorising texts; in the second *use* or *purpose*. This might be further considered in terms of *how* the texts were read (on a smartphone, laptop, paper), and there are various other criteria we might use, including means of production, genre, ephemerality etc. Why might consideration of the nature of texts be important for teaching English?

Another helpful way to think about texts and how we categorise them is to use a 'washing line' of degrees of functionality (Figure 14.1). If you were to put your original list of texts in a line from the poetic to transactional (getting things done), what order would they go in and why? Where would you put a signpost or one of Keats' odes? This can also be a useful activity to use with pupils when thinking about the nature of texts.

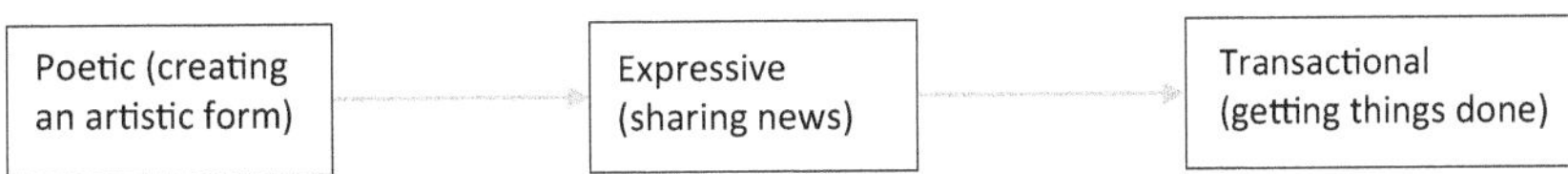

Figure 14.1 Degrees of text functionality
Source: Adapted from Dymoke (2009) and Beard (2000).

The notion of *text* is diverse and complex and is a concept that pupils may not have encountered before beyond that of an everyday meaning of messaging. 'Text' as a noun originates from Latin, meaning something that is woven or fabricated (Etymonline.com, 2020), and it is in this latter sense that we might develop our understanding of *texts* not just as things that are created but *mediated.*

The term 'media' originated in the word *medium*, which

> has had the sense of an intervening or intermediate agency or substance [...] Media became widely used when broadcasting as well as the press had become important in communications; it was then the necessary general word, MASS media [...] there has probably been a convergence of three senses: (i) the old general sense of an intervening or intermediate agency or substance; (ii) the conscious technical sense, as in the distinction between print and sound and vision as media; (iii) the specialised capitalist sense, in which a newspaper or broadcasting service – something that already exists or can be planned – is seen as a medium for something else, such as advertising.
>
> (Williams, 2015, p.153)

This origin might suggest that media is primarily a way of transmitting a message and implies a power dynamic of the creator of the media text over the consumer of the media text. It also suggests that there is meaning 'hidden' within the media text that an audience must decode. This is quite a simplistic view of media texts and what we do when we consume them and, from this perspective, there are implications regarding how analysis of media texts is taught, which we explore in the next section.

MEDIA AND ENGLISH

English and media: a familial history

English, media, drama and creative writing are all distinctive subjects at higher education institution (HEI) level, yet at secondary level their boundaries are blurred under an English subject umbrella. Although media and drama both have discrete qualifications at Key Stage (KS) 4, English can encompass aspects of all of them. We might consider them siblings (Eaglestone, 2017), 'kissing cousins' (Burn, 2011, p.117) or a three- (or four-)legged stool (Franks et al., 2006).

The complexity of this relationship lies in the origins of the subjects: English grew out of classics and philology, and was established in school teaching in England 1904 (Davison and Daly, 2014). The earliest HEI course on moving image was available in America in 1915, not long after the birth of cinema itself (Polan, 2007), although the academic study of film was (arguably) not properly established until the 1950s with the development of critical frameworks such as auteur theory (Benyahia and Mortimer, 2013).

Media Studies grew, inauspiciously, out of the denunciation of the decline of literary standards (Leavis, 1932); from the negative influence of Hollywood cinema (Leavis, 1930) to the evils of advertising (Thompson, 1943), the study of media in the first part of the twentieth century is largely critical and pessimistic.

Cast in a negative light, the study of texts that were 'popular' and associated with the dangers of mass communication is connected to the ideas of cultural hierarchy espoused by the Leavis school of thought. Media Studies, the younger sibling of English and Film Studies, was first taught in England at undergraduate level in 1975 at a London polytechnic (Golding, 2019). Conceivably, since its birth was non-establishment, it continues to suffer from being considered a 'lesser' subject than English, seen as lacking in intellectual rigour. Ironically, as a so-called Mickey Mouse subject (BBC News, 2003), it has suffered from sustained attacks from the media itself. Though often criticized for lacking academic rigor *and* not being vocational enough (Buckingham, 2019), this is not actually the case in undergraduate studies (Curran, 2013).

Culture and status

English (literature in particular) has historically had a higher status than media. Until 2019 (Whittaker, 2019), the Russell Group (a group of 'elite' universities), published a list of 'facilitating' Certificate of Secondary Education (CSE) A level subjects which they described as being 'the subjects most commonly required or preferred by universities to get on to a range of degree courses' (Successatschool.org, n.d.). English literature features, along with history, modern and classical languages, maths, the natural sciences and geography. English language and media do not.

This hierarchy is reflected in the National Curriculum (NC) in England, the stated intention of which is to introduce 'pupils to the best that has been thought and said' (DfE, 2014a, p.5), begging the question of *who decides* what is 'the best that has been thought and said'. The NC's paraphrasing of Matthew Arnold's concept of culture from *Culture and Anarchy* (1869) invokes an understanding of culture as *capital*. This notion, from Pierre Bourdieu (Bourdieu and Passeron, 1977), argues that identifiers of class enable or hinder social progression. In relation to education, this has been used to push a 'knowledge-rich' curriculum, influenced by American educationalist E.D. Hirsch (Gibb, 2015). This perception of the curriculum and what it should do adheres to the 'great tradition' of English advocated by F.R. Leavis (1948), which argues for the importance of studying canonical texts.

Activity 14.2: Culture and text value

What do you understand by 'high' and 'low' cultural texts? Are there any texts that, in your view, *should* be taught (or should not)? How have you made these judgements about the quality or value of texts? How are moving image or other media texts judged in terms of cultural value?

Mark Reid of the British Film Institute, argues that being literate should mean 'being able fully to participate in a culture' (Reid, 2015, p.85), which, in the twenty-first century, would need grounding in media, given the proliferation of media texts in modern life. Do you agree? What implications does this have for the English curriculum?

The question becomes, then, how we choose which texts to teach. If we agree that language and media should be features of secondary school English teaching, the way in which the English curriculum is perceived in policy and assessed through examinations will have implications for practice in classrooms. We might, for instance, challenge the notion of the canon (or at least that the curriculum should focus *entirely* on a select number of 'classics'), particularly if the kinds of knowledge that we explore in English and media are different from other disciplines such as maths and science. English and media 'involve fluid notions of cultural value, canonicity and personal and public subjectivities' (Burn and Connolly,

2020, p.37). As English teachers, perhaps we need to be comfortable with this uncertainty.

For a good overview of the Media Studies' history, see Golding (2019) and for a rebuttal of criticisms of Media Studies, see Curran (2013). See also Barbara Bleiman's critique of the use of cultural capital in the teaching of English (Bleiman, 2020).

The English and media overlap

To become comfortable in moving between analysis and creation of different kinds of texts, it is worth understanding how much similarity there is in the English and Media Studies disciplines. The Quality Assurance Agency for Higher Education (QAA) subject benchmarks for guiding higher education courses in the UK also indicate the similarities of the subjects. Compare the opening statements in Table 14.1.

Goddard (2012) argues that English and media cover the same ground in terms of:

- The nature and scope of the subject: how discourses represent the world around us.
- Course coverage: approaches to analysing text and discourse.
- Analytical techniques: evaluate texts in relation to their purposes and uses, including literary, communicative, sociological, and ideological evaluations. (Goddard, 2012, p.50)

Similarly Graham and Green (2011) argue that there are concepts and approaches that apply to both English and media texts:

- Literacy covers all kinds of texts (regardless of format).
- Texts are polysemic (they have more than one possible meaning).
- All texts are constructs (they are *mediated*).
- To become fully literate, pupils need to become both readers and writers in the widest range of modes and text types.
- Media analysis is founded on concepts and is akin to reading.

Table 14.1 Benchmark statements

English subject benchmark statement	Communication, Media, Film and Cultural Studies benchmark statement
'English is a core academic subject encompassing study of the structure, history and usage of the English language, critical analysis of literature written in English, and the practice of creative writing. Students of English engage with multiple forms of communication, study past and present cultures, and use language and literature to reflect critically and imaginatively on their own learning and thinking. English is relevant to contemporary society as its focus on the production, interpretation and negotiation of meaning develops the capacity to understand the world from a variety of perspectives' (QAA, 2019, p.3).	'Social life depends upon the constant development and varied use of modes of communication and upon shared and contested understandings of the world. Consequently, it requires the systematic study of communication, media, film and culture in national, transnational and global contexts. Degree courses in communication, media, film and cultural studies seek to understand the role of symbolic structures in societies, and the means by which they are produced, distributed and consumed' (QAA, 2019, p.3).

What seems clear is the focus on communication through texts to *understand* and make meaning.

Activity 14.3

English and Media: Overlapping Skills, Concepts and Knowledge

Consider the following lists of skills, concepts and areas of knowledge and decide which are exclusive to either English or Media, and which are common to both (note: this is not an exhaustive list!).

Skills	Concepts	Knowledge
Speaking	Convention	Audiences
Listening	Construction/deconstruction	Forms/formats/ platforms
Reading	Stereotyping	Economics of production
Writing	Ownership/control	Production technologies
Framing	Narrative	Conditions of reception
Collaborate group work	Fact/fiction/bias	Genres
Planning/drafting	Ideology	Institutions
Problem-solving	Genre	Familiarity with 'classics' or the canon
Critical analysis	Representation	
Scripting/storyboarding	Language	
	Authorship/agency	

You should find that there is more in common with media and English than is exclusive to one or the other. If English and media are principally about textual analysis and creation (where 'text' is not necessarily limited to the written word), then the *aim* of both is the same. Where there may be differences is in the nature of the texts, the terminology used to describe and analyse texts, and possibly the technology that might be used to create texts.

MEDIA IN THE CURRICULUM

The official position of media within the curriculum is problematic and varies considerably across the British Isles. This section considers the role of media in relation to English in the UK and briefly look at the discrete subjects of media and film at KS4 and CSE A Level.

In the current National Curriculum for England there is no explicit mention of media in the English KS3 or 4 documents (DfE, 2014b), and no separate curriculum for media, although there are specifications for General Certificate of Secondary Education (GCSE) Media and Film Studies (which is distinct from English Literature and Language GCSE). The KS3 English curriculum's focus is on literature and language (including grammar), where reading encompasses:

> a wide range of fiction and non-fiction, including in particular whole books, short stories, poems and plays with a wide coverage of genres, historical periods, forms and authors. The range will include high-quality works from:
>
> - English literature, both pre-1914 and contemporary, including prose, poetry and drama

- Shakespeare (two plays)
- seminal world literature.

(DfE, 2013d, p.4)

The teaching of writing refers to 'stories, scripts, poetry and other imaginative writing [...] notes and polished scripts for talks and presentations [...] a range of other narrative and non-narrative texts, including arguments, and personal and formal letters' (DfE, 2013d, p.5). Whilst previous versions of the NC have included the requirement to study 'multimodal' texts (QCA, 2007b, p.65), this does not feature in current provisions. Reference to 'a wide range of fiction and non-fiction' and 'other imaginative writing [...] range of other narrative and non-narrative texts' suggests that we find *media* texts in the gaps around those outlined here: 'We have always had to work creatively around the spaces left by the official curriculum' (Graham, 2018, p.37). Compared to previous iterations of the NC, the current version is slim and (except for William Shakespeare) no mention is made of specific texts or authors. With the increased interest in the curriculum, our job as curriculum designers is particularly important. If the explicit teaching of media texts is an important aspect of English, then teachers of English must plan for it to feature in their classrooms. This would be a dynamic English curriculum that reacts to the changing world around us (Potter, 2020).

Media's role as a distinct subject and as part of an English curriculum varies across the UK. You, of course, need to consider the context in which you teach, including statutory education policies, school curriculum and departmental expertise and facilities (see website for further details).

MEDIA PEDAGOGIES

So why *should* we study media and why it should feature as a part of English? The first question seems self-evident: we are saturated in media; it is 'like the air we breathe' (Buckingham, 2019, p.8). Accordingly, to function in modern society pupils need to be able to engage with, understand and respond to media texts. As an aim, this is not fundamentally different to English, as discussed below. In addition, teaching aspects of media and media texts enriches other aspects of English, such as examining different interpretations of literary texts.

Burn (2013) suggests a number of reasons for including media arts in the curriculum:

- Popular culture is important and should not be ignored due to spurious arguments about quality.
- It provides a format to explore cultural history through and between texts, such as video games of *Beowulf.*
- It enables analysis of the modern use of rhetoric: *ethos* (knowledge), *logos* (words), and *pathos* (emotion) are similar to media's consideration of institution, language and audience.
- Media texts have an aesthetic dimension, and these should be acknowledged and explored.
- Media lends itself to working across the curriculum and across the arts in its multimodality and potential for embracing cultural change.

These arguments do not seek to replace study of traditionally canonical texts such as Shakespeare, rather to broaden the diet of an English curriculum.

Historically, pedagogical approaches to teaching media have tended to be either 'protectionist' or 'celebratory' (Buckingham, 2019). The former attempts to inoculate pupils against false messages and potential dangers (such as various moral panics around the links between media and violence (Springhall, 1999)); the latter, based on the benefits of 'Web 2.0' of user-created content, lacks criticality. What is needed, Buckingham (2019) argues, is critical literacy and cultural analysis.

A media education that does more than just warn pupils about the evils of media or to use technology so that they are able to become 'well-informed, discriminating media users [...] active citizens and [...] skilled, creative workers' (Buckingham, 2019, p.30), must develop critical literacy. For media texts, this means understanding that format, mode or platform is more than technology, it is a

> cultural form, which provides meaning and pleasure In the same way, a service like Facebook or Twitter or Instagram is not merely a means of delivering content: it is also a cultural form, which shapes that content, and our relationship with it, in particular ways.
>
> (Buckingham, 2019, p.14)

The medium is the message!

KEY CONCEPTS IN MEDIA AND ENGLISH

As discussed above, there is significant overlap in knowledge, concepts and skills in English and media. In media teaching, the following key concepts have been developed and are central to understanding how to approach the teaching of media texts:

- *Media language*: including how the text is constructed to convey meaning, including codes and conventions, narrative, genre, structure and specific techniques related to the particular form, such as camera angles in moving image texts
- *Media audiences*: including how texts are aimed at target audiences; how audiences use texts and respond to them, such as moral panics and active/passive use of media
- *Media institutions*: including who owns and constructs texts, such as global corporations
- *Media representations*: who is represented (or absent) in the text and how they are represented, including gender, stereotyping, depictions of reality (Buckingham, 2003).

These concepts are also used to structure the GCSE and CSE A level qualifications. There are many textbooks that offer comprehensive guidance for you to find out more about key concepts, often endorsed by the exam boards; search the exam board websites for further information.

Understanding these key concepts enables you to link analysis and creation of texts in English and enhance your existing subject knowledge. A good way to make use of these concepts is to frame your approach to teaching texts through using key questions, not dissimilar to Kress' (1994) suggestion of five questions to ask of any text when constructing a written text. When we read and analyse texts, we are effectively asking questions of it. These questions might focus on textual 'levels' such as word, sentence or text level (Dean, 2003), focusing on word choice, sentence construction and whole-text effect and context respectively.

Drawing from discourse analysis, Kress (1994) suggests five questions to ask of any text:

1. What is at issue in this text?
2. What are the crucial characteristics of the social situation in which the text has been, is being made?
3. Where does this way of writing or talking about the topic at issue come from?
4. Are the makers of the text more interested in coming to (seemingly unproblematic) resolution, or are they more interested in keeping the discussion open?
5. What material circumstances are there which produce limits on the size or scope of the text? (Kress, 1994, p.222).

By revisiting these concepts, through different kinds of texts at different points and with increasingly levels of sophistication, the concepts can be joined up in a 'spiral' curriculum (Graham and Green, 2011).

Whilst the media key concepts may go into more depth than we might need for some aspects of English study, they can be useful for developing pupils' understanding of texts and contexts. Essentially, the overlap between English and media literacy can be summarized as:

- reading (textual analysis);
- writing (creative production);
- contextual analysis (setting texts in a broader social context).

(Buckingham, 2019, p.69)

Principles for teaching media in English

To embed aspects of media in English, you can:

- Consider where in the curriculum aspects of media might be taught, such as considering what constitutes 'fake news' as part of a study of non-fiction texts.
- Use different productions of literary texts to explore a range of interpretations, such as comparing the opening scenes from Franco Zeffirelli's 1968 and Baz Luhrmann's 1996 versions of *Romeo and Juliet*.
- Use multimodal texts to transform or transpose one medium to another, such as creating a script version of Oliver asking for more when studying *Oliver Twist*.

These are just some ideas. The aim is to enable pupils to engage with texts ('ways in') and to learn more about them and the process of text construction. This is also a creative endeavour; pupils learn about writers' choices through a process of reading and writing themselves – whatever kind of text they are creating.

Some principles that might be used in media education would be:

1. Begin from what the pupils already know (Buckingham, 2019).
2. Be aware that, though they may be 'digital natives', there is much about media production and use that they do not know (Thomas, 2011).
3. Use creative tasks to allow pupils to demonstrate their understanding of how texts are constructed and to 'test' media theories (Buckingham, 2019).

Table 14.2 Links between English, media and creativity

Aspect of English	Aspect of media	Creativity
Reading and contextual analysis	Textual analysis and setting texts in a broader social context	Reading is active and dynamic (Rosenblatt, 1970); critical reading involves emotion and affect as well as 'objective' deconstruction
Writing	Creative production	All kinds of textual creation, not limited to 'creative writing'
Spoken language	Creative production and collaborative work	Thinking and dialogue

ENGLISH, MEDIA AND CREATIVITY

The criterion of creativity is where harmony between English and media becomes possible. The creative production of media texts has always been a central element of Media Studies, whether it is a mock-up of a tabloid newspaper front page or a short film, the connection between 'knowing' about media texts and 'doing' them has always been strong, as reflected in the coursework requirements for Media and Film Studies at both GCSE and CSE A Level. The role of creativity can be connected with Vygotsky's (1998) understanding of play in learning. There is a clear link between the conceptual (such as a pupil indicating a camera angle on a storyboard) and the technical (where a pupil then uses a camera to capture a series of camera angles for an intended effect) (Burn, 2018).

Drawing on social constructivism, McCallum (2012) persuasively argues for a broader understanding of creativity that 'brings new meaning into being. Learning brings new meaning into being. Creativity is learning. Learning is creativity' (p.5). He argues that learning and creativity are effectively one and the same thing. This is quite a different way of thinking about what we do in English; often 'creativity' can be seen just in terms of writing a story or a poem. However, we can see all aspects of English learning as creative and this coheres with key concepts of media, as seen in Table 14.2.

The example lesson in Activity 14.4 demonstrates how you can bring aspects of media into your everyday teaching of English while retaining the essential purpose of learning in English. These are activities that you can use directly in the classroom or adapt to whatever you are teaching.

Activity 14.4

Lesson Example: The Simulation – Being a Reporter

Analysing newspapers or news websites provides an opportunity to explore the linguistic and presentational features that are used in non-fiction news writing. This analysis can use media critical concepts of production, representation and audience and cover reading, writing and oracy.

'Fake news' is a very current concern, although the skill of being able to distinguish fact from fiction has regularly featured in GCSE English Language papers. If you are teaching an aspect of news coverage/reportage, it is a good opportunity to explore the linguistic and presentational aspects of non-fiction reporting. David Buckingham's blog provides an excellent overview of the 'fake news' phenomenon (see: https://davidbuckingham.net/2017/01/12/fake-news-is-media-literacy-the-answer/). He argues that engaging with 'fake news' in the classroom requires considering the wider context, acknowledging that: 'media are inevitably selective and partial [...] we need to be identifying the forms of bias that are present in *all* sources of information' (Buckingham, 2019, p.43, italics in original).

Because the writing of news reports (whatever the format) is reliant on writing about real-life events, using a 'simulation' activity (Graham, 2018) can be an excellent way to introduce this to pupils and has cross-curricular possibilities, such as with Personal, Social and Health Education.

The lesson could be a longer project or linked directly to the BBC Young Reporter Competition; see: www.bbc.co.uk/academy/en/collections/youngreporter. Prior to using a simulation activity, spend some time analysing different news outlets (compare *The Times* and the *Daily Mail* or BBC News and Fox News, for example), how news stories are constructed and how they are influenced by the institutions that make them. *The Guardian* provides some useful resources: www.theguardian.com/gnmeducationcentre/2017/aug/11/news-literacy-teaching-ideas-for-secondary-schools

Objective: To understand how news reports are constructed and experiment with the form

1. Assign small groups a named news outlet, ensuring a range within the class (broadsheet, tabloid, local, print, website). Provide examples of news stories that their outlet has produced and ask the pupils to decide if they have particular slant or styles of reporting.
2. Invent a story (such as a tiger escaping from a zoo) and provide some 'facts' for it using the five Ws (who, what, when, where, why).
3. Ask them to write their story, in the style of their given news outlet (this could utilize technology if they wanted to do a television news report) and could include presentational devices.
4. Share their results with each other, explaining how they've tailored the story.
5. Introduce the concept of 'fake news' (use some of Buckingham's resources); ask if they have seen any examples. Share the BBC's suggestions for spotting fake news (see: www.bbc.co.uk/newsround/38906931 and the podcast 'Seriously ... How to cure viral misinformation' (2020) www.bbc.co.uk/programmes/m000hh0d).
6. Ask the pupils to rewrite their news story to *show* that it is fake (which it is!).
7. Discuss what this exercise suggests about the nature of news reporting and some of the wider context around fake news, such as *why* individuals might want to spread disinformation.

SUMMARY AND KEY POINTS

- The aim of English is to analyse, explore and create texts; media has the same aim.
- 'Text' can mean all kinds of texts, including moving image.
- We live in a media-saturated world and the study of media texts should be a part of the English curriculum.
- There are key concepts and principles that can be used to think about teaching media in English as a creative endeavour and these can bring together reading, writing and oracy.

- Studying and creating media texts in their own right and as 'ways in' to teaching other aspects of English enriches the English classroom.

KEY RESOURCES

1. David Buckingham, Emeritus Professor of Media and Communication, is a world expert in media education. In addition to writing numerous books and articles, his blog is regularly updated and contains a wealth of resources, ideas and material: https://davidbuckingham.net/
2. The English & Media Centre provides excellent continuing professional development and they publish the quarterly *Media Magazine*, aimed at those studying CSE A level Film and Media: www.englishandmedia.co.uk/media-magazine/.
3. The National Association for the Teaching of English (NATE) provides a wealth of materials and ideas. The website contains a searchable archive of the quarterly magazine *Teaching English* and an entire scheme of work on media advertising 'Creative Persuasion' aimed at KS3 in the members' area: www.nate.org.uk/creative-persuasion/
4. *Media Literacy in Schools: Practice, Production and Progression* by James Durran and Andrew Burn (London: SAGE, 2007) is an excellent handbook providing both critical perspectives and practical ideas for the teaching of media.
5. The British Film Institute (BFI) is the best place to look for information, history and resources for anything film related: www.bfi.org.uk/
6. *The Media Teacher's Handbook* (London: Routledge, 2012), edited by E. Scarratt and J. Davison, is a sound guide to the theoretical, practical and professional aspects of teaching media from KS3 English to A level Media Studies.
7. Andrew McCallum's 2012 book *Creativity and Learning in Secondary English* (Abingdon, Oxon: Routledge) is an excellent guide to thinking about English creatively and provides lots of classroom activities that utlise multimodal texts.
8. Bordwell and Thompson's classic text *Film Art* (New York: McGraw-Hill, 2019) is now in its twelfth edition. This is a facinating handbook and is probably the best introduction to moving image analysis.
9. The *Media Education Research Journal* (MERJ) is a peer-reviewed academic journal publishing research in media education and well-worth exploring: http://merj.info/
10. To continue to develop your subject knowledge, mass open online course provider Future Learn (www.futurelearn.com/) is always worth checking out for relevant courses.

Chapter 15 Digital and multimodal writing

ANDREW MCCALLUM

INTRODUCTION

Digital writing is any writing that is composed and read on a computer or other digital device. It can take on many forms, from the replication of long-established paper-bound practices (note taking, letter writing, essays, poetry etc.), to computer code that is indecipherable to all but a few experts. It can also relate to the conventions of particular digital platforms, such as Twitter, Facebook, Instagram or blog sites. Digital writing has opened up, in previously unimaginable ways, possibilities for drawing easily on different modes of communication. Sometimes written and spoken language might be bypassed altogether in favour of images or sound, in processes that can be seen as, themselves, a form of writing. Other times, image and sound can be combined with words. Combining different modes in this way is called multimodality.

Digital technologies have transformed ecologies of writing. New possibilities for production, consumption and distribution now both complement and challenge traditional forms of publishing. You can, for example, make your writing available to the whole world at the press of a button; you can also select your reading material instantly from a multitude of sources. Such transformations mean that you can get your news from an established, regulated source, or you can take at face value the words of total strangers posting on social media. You can buy the latest book by your favourite author, or you can read alternative versions of their work on fan fiction websites.

The ubiquity of digital devices in the lives of pupils means that, in one way or another, they are likely to be reading and writing more than any previous generation.[1] It would seem to make sense, then, to teach them in ways that help them understand and draw on digital writing as well as produce their own. There are three simple arguments as to why this makes educational sense. First, it involves pupils in learning about forms that they are actively involved with and will continue to be involved with in adult life. Second, it provides them with multiple ways to express their thoughts and ideas, a process that has been shown to increase all kinds of learning (Brown et al., 2014). Third, it allows them to develop strategies to navigate the astonishing proliferation of texts they meet on a daily basis, including the critical literacy skills needed to recognise authenticity and bias.

DOI: 10.4324/9781003093060-16

Statutory requirements to study digital texts and multimodality vary across the UK and change over time. In England, for example, the requirement to study and produce multimodal texts was embedded in the 2007 National Curriculum (QCDA, 2007). It is entirely missing from the 2014 version (DfE, 2014a), as is mention of any digital form of writing. You might like to consider why this is. What political motives exist to deny pupils engagement with digital writing and multimodality? Are they deemed a threat to traditional forms of authority, and so to be held at arm's length? Or do they take away from the rigour of established ways of reading and writing in the classroom?

This chapter is written in a spirit that recognises the importance of digital writing, even as it is not always codified in official policy. It does so in the surety that, regardless of the to-ing and fro-ing of various policymakers, it offers fascinating and pedagogically valuable insights into the functions of language and literature in general, and has much to add to pupils' experience of English.

At the end of this chapter you should be able to:

- understand how you and your pupils can draw on the internet as a language resource;
- recognise how digital and multimodal forms can develop your pupils' language awareness;
- reflect on how digital and multimodal writing complement the broader aims of a mainstream English curricula.

THE INTERNET AS A LANGUAGE RESOURCE

The internet offers a vast free language resource. Learning to navigate it is fundamental to becoming adept in modern forms of reading and writing. Indeed, there are some contemporary writers who argue that the internet has transformed the very notion of writing itself. Prominent among them is poet/artist/academic Kenneth Goldsmith, whose *Uncreative Writing* (2011), stands as a manifesto for this kind of work. He doesn't dismiss the merits of traditional forms of writing, but for his own work argues that:

> faced with an unprecedented amount of available text, the problem is not needing to write more of it; instead, we must learn to negotiate the vast quantity that exists. How I make my way through this thicket of information – how I manage it, how I parse it, how I organise and distribute it – is what distinguishes my writing from yours.
>
> (p.1)

In practice, Goldsmith has published work that, initially, seems outlandish and pointless. *Seven Deaths and Disasters* (2013), for example, offers transcripts of live radio broadcasts of seminal moments in American history. However, recontextualised in book form, these transcripts take on a raw, poetic force. This, for example, is from a live broadcast at the assassination of Senator Robert Kennedy:

> Unbelievable situation. They're clearing the halls. One man has blood on himself. We're walking down the corridors here. Repetition in my speech. I have no alternative. The shock is so great. My mouth is dry. I can only say that here in the kitchen of the Ambassador Hotel, the back entrance, from the podium, in the press room, the senator walked out the back. I was directly behind him. You heard a balloon go off and a shot. You didn't realise that the shot was a shot.

> And yet a scream went up. Two men were on the ground, both bleeding profusely. At this moment we are stunned, we are shaking, as is everyone else in this kitchen corridor at the Ambassador Hotel in Los Angeles. They're blocking off the entrance now, supposedly to make room for the ambulance. That's all we can report at the moment. I do not know if the senator is dead or if he is alive.
>
> (p.45)

Writers used such techniques in the past, particularly the modernists. James Joyce's *Ulysses*, for example, contains several passages where the language was 'found' in other sources. But in the predigital age this involved laboriously transcribing text by hand. Goldsmith, in contrast, could produce his work relatively effortlessly, using digital technology that scoops up language and places it somewhere else; in other words, that relies on the humble cut-and-paste function. Cutting and pasting is, one could argue, a significant form of contemporary writing in its own right. It has already resulted in some extraordinary work. Jonathan Lethem's 'The Ecstasy of Influence: A Plagiarism' (2013) is a brilliant essay about plagiarism. At the end of the work, Lethem reveals that it has been lifted entirely from different sources found on the internet in a process known as 'patchworking'. Does this make the work fraudulent? Or is Lethem demonstrating what Marjorie Perloff (2012) has termed 'unoriginal genius' by recontextualising found language?

Activity 15.1 invites you to select from four different ways to use language 'found' on the internet to help your pupils write poetry. Take one of the tasks and try it out with your pupils. Think carefully about what you want them to learn about the process – both in terms of language choices and in terms of concepts of ownership and authenticity. After you've taught the sessions, evaluate how pupils responded, as well as what they learned.

Activity 15.1: Found language poetry

Redaction poetry

Pupils cut and paste a text into a Word document (they can find one themselves, or work on something that has been studied in the classroom). They redact (black out) large chunks of the text so that they are left with a kind of poem. Focusing on the words left and the ones rejected helps them think about the language contained within the original.

Found poetry

A variation on the redaction task, here pupils cut and paste key words and phrases from a text and reformulate them into a poem. They can be flexible in their approach, for example, using some phrases more than once. Again, the resultant poem can shed light on the language of the original. In fact, this can be a specific direction when setting this task: craft a poem from the text using the cut-and-paste function that highlights in some way the language of the original.

Search engine poetry

Pupils search a term of their choice, or one given to them by the teacher. They cut and paste interesting words and phrases from the results and work on these to produce a poem as detailed in the stages below.

a. *Finding language*: pupils cut interesting words and phrases from their search results and paste them into a Word document.
b. *Writing a basic poem*: pupils manipulate the words and phrases on-screen so that the order makes some kind of sense (See Stage (b)).
c. *Crafting a final poem*: pupils craft their basic poem into one of their own, drawing on the found language, but making their own interventions too (See Stage (c)).

Stages (b) and (c) are illustrated below. You can see that just relying on the found language does not produce a particularly effective poem, but that it plays a decisive role in the production of the final version.

Stage (b)

Oxbow lake

a U-shaped body of water
stagnant alongside a winding river
shaped like an old fashioned 'U' shaped yoke
formed when a wide meander is cut off
flood waters fall
material is deposited
because of soil erosion
the old meander is sealed off
Since the river now flows straight
it has more energy
a 'dead river' is the transition stage between a river and an oxbow lake
a portion of the river becomes 'dead'
when the current no longer runs through it
eventually, the river moves away from the dead river and an oxbow lake
is formed
In Australia, *an oxbow lake is* called a billabong

Stage (c)

The oxbow lake

The river once lived in gentler times
meandered through the landscape
with a yawn's sense of direction
now with no time to pause
it flows straight

a devotee to energy and current
the old river is sealed off
a dead river
a billabong

Poems in translation

Translation engines, such as Google Translate, have all kinds of uses. At their most basic they can help English as an additional language pupils with understanding. Copy the English version of what you're reading into one box and it magically appears translated in another. Google Translate isn't perfect and is more effective in some languages than others, but it's more accurate than is often thought and, if computer scientists are to be believed, will be incredibly accurate within the next decade or so.

It can also be used to bring different languages into the classroom by enabling pupils to write bilingual or multilingual poems. How might this version of Hamlet's famous soliloquy, with some French translation, compare to and throw light on the original?

To be, or not to be: *telle est la question*
Whether 'tis nobler *dans l'esprit* to suffer
Les frondes et les flèches d'outrageous fortune
Or to take arms against *une mer de troubles*
And by opposing end them. To die, to sleep –
Pas plus – and by a sleep to say we end
Le chagrin d'amour, and *les mille chocs naturels*
That flesh is heir to.

BLOGGING

Teacher Richard Long has been using blogs with his pupils for several years.[2] Pupils are required to provide responses to their area of study in a secure, shared blog, set up for just that purpose. The example below comes from a Year 7 pupil working on poetry. She is writing about one poem that she chose from a small selection.[3]

> Hey everybody! It's Naomi-lee here! Today I will be discussing my favourite poem called 'this poem …'. This poem is so interesting and also very puzzling. I like this poem because it is funny and it is kind of like washing up detergent adverts because one of the lines of the poem is 'it should not be left within the reach of children, even adults'. It is very comedic and made me laugh the first time I read it.
>
> The thing that puzzles me about the poem is actually what another pupil, Kaiden, said which was 'is this really a poem?' this made me wonder a little bit. Is it? This made me think in to my knowledge of poems and I came to the conclusion that I am in fact not sure and would like to hear another pupil's ideas to help decide mine. I like the end line 'words can seriously harm your heart'. I like this because in a way it is true Poems do have an effect on your emotions which is one of the things I love about poems. They can take you away from society and the real world.
>
> Thank you for reading my response!

The tone is recognisably different to that found in pupils' exercise books. Most striking is the informality linked to the direct form of address (*'Hey everybody! It's Naomi-lee here!'*). Naomi-lee is excited to be part of a shared endeavour. With this excitement comes the chance to offer a genuinely personal response where she is working out and sharing what she thinks. In doing so, she moves from thinking about a particular poem to thinking about poetry in general. You can see her actively puzzling over meaning and reflecting on how a shared reading might help her understand it better.

The response is obviously incomplete, limited in some ways and lacking attention to punctuation and grammar. As teachers, though, we need to ask if this really matters here, as well as being clear about exactly what digital responses like this can offer that standard ones in books cannot. The technical errors can, in this instance, be ignored. This is not writing for assessment, but instead a forum for getting down and sharing ideas. In some ways it is, like other forms of digital writing, a hybrid between spoken and written language, with informality part of the form itself. It privileges what pupils says over how they say it. Consequently, it frees them up to make statements they might not otherwise make, such as Naomi-Lee's comment about wanting to hear other ideas. It is also a brilliant formative tool for teachers. In this case, Richard Long was able to comment on the blog entries with a similar level of informality and enthusiasm, with an absolute focus on the poetry rather than the writing. He could see how pupils were able to develop their initial thinking about poems, and recognise where they needed to do more work, particularly close-detail analytical work, to move their thinking on further.

Limitations of space mean it is not possible to show further blog entries from this class, but it is important to conceive of the writing by the whole class as a single piece. Another important aspect of digital writing is that it is easily shared. Pupils in the class did, voluntarily, read each other's work, and often commented positively. The blog thus became a forum for the safe sharing and development of ideas, much like Naomi-Lee's desired model. This also suggests that blogging is a form that pupils are comfortable with in ways they are perhaps not when writing in exercise books. In the latter, their audience is only the teacher. They are more likely to be required to write in a formal register, leading to anxiety about how to write rather than what to write. As a teacher, it's important to recognise that where the focus is on reading, it is often important not to demand forms of response that can discourage the free expression of ideas. Research suggests that where pupils are given more freedom to display their knowledge in a form with which they feel comfortable, they do so more effectively than when required to write within particular constraints (English, 2011). This would seem to be an excellent example: digital writing to encourage the development of ideas and shared thinking, so providing a useful stepping stone to the more formal, analytical requirements of the subject that can be developed at other points.

EMOJIS AND MULTIMODALITY

Different modes of communication are absolutely part of the digital landscape. When posting on, for example, Twitter, Facebook or Instagram, we are free to use images only (both still and moving), or to combine them with text. The image can exemplify what's in the text, but it can also add to or change its meaning.

With no official place for multimodality in many curricula, teachers must choose whether or not they give it classroom time. If the subject's priority is to provide pupils with a full understanding of the contemporary communicative landscape, then multimodality would seem to deserve a prominent place. However, if the priority is to develop linguistic awareness, in terms of the production and consumption of written texts, in whatever form, then it would seem to be of lesser importance. This isn't to avoid the importance of multimodality, but to recognise the difficult decisions that must be made about what can be squeezed into limited curriculum space. One compromise is to draw on different modes to shed light on how spoken and written texts work, so giving pupils experience of and access to contemporary communication forms while simultaneously recognising the ongoing centrality of speaking and writing (McCallum, 2012, pp.37–53).

A straightforward way to do this is to use visual texts to stimulate writing. In the transference of meaning from one mode to another, pupils can reflect on the specific requirements of verbal communication, for example, how it needs to spend considerable time providing detail and context in a way that images can often do in an instant. A fabulous text to use for this kind of activity is Shaun Tan's (2007) wordless novel, *The Arrival*. Almost any image on any page can be drawn on to stimulate writing. In doing so, pupils can reflect on the interplay between thought and language: how thinking about an image in a particular way generates ideas about – but also beyond – the image itself.

A second way to bring different modes into the classroom, is to create a short sequence of lessons around emojis. The suggestion that emojis could have a place in the classroom often generates a fierce negative reaction. Surely this is dumbing down? How can William Shakespeare's beautiful language be reduced to a single smiley face? Such a response, though, fails to recognise an established tenet of the discipline of English, particularly language study: that part of its very purpose is to explore and seek to understand how meaning is generated, no matter the mode or form used. Activity 15.2 uses emojis to help pupils understand how language itself works. The ideas come from my colleague Barbara Bleiman, and are included in the English & Media Centre's book *The KS3 Language Laboratory* (2018).

Try the sequence in Activity 15.2 with your pupils. Think carefully about what you want them to learn – both in terms of the communicative properties of emojis and in terms how this throws light on how written and spoken language works. After you've taught the sessions, evaluate how pupils responded, as well as what they learned.

Activity 15.2: Working with emojis

Can emojis take the place of words?

Give pupils five to six well-known emojis and asked them to 'translate' them into words or phrases. They compare their responses with classmates to see if they have come up with similar translations. Finally, they reflect on what emojis offer that words do not. This should include a discussion of when and why emojis might sometimes be more effective than words, or communicate things that words cannot.

Are emojis a form of punctuation?

Pupils discuss statements that apply to standard punctuation and assess whether or not they also apply to emojis. For example:

It can change the meaning of a sentence.
It indicates pauses and new lines of thought.
It indicates tone or mood.
It gives choice to the writer, who can use punctuation to stamp their own individual identity on their writing.

Do emojis have their own syntax?

Pupils explore whether emojis appear in a particular order in text communications and, if so, how it affects meaning. Figure 15.1 illustrates how emojis might be 'correctly' or 'incorrectly' presented.

Bringing it all together

Pupils read a series of articles about emojis (ones for or against their use; about their history; about why they are interesting to linguists). Based on their reading and their previous discussions, they complete the following task:

> *Imagine that General Certificate of Secondary Education awarding bodies have decided to include emojis in the English Language exam. Write a blog outlining your thoughts about why this is or is not a welcome development.*

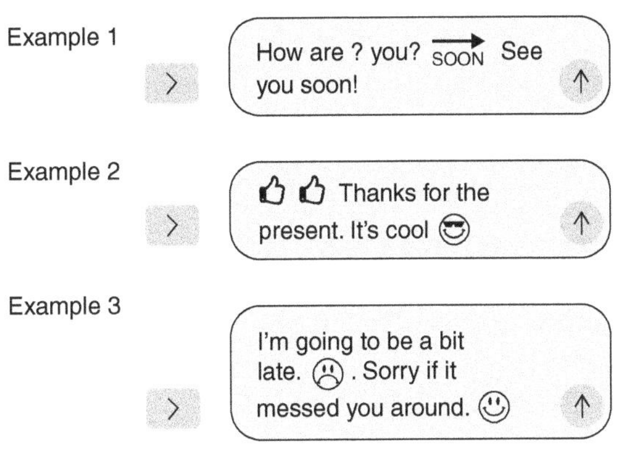

Figure 15.1 Emoji examples

SUMMARY AND KEY POINTS

- Digital technologies have transformed ecologies of writing and so require careful consideration about how they complement and enhance established forms of English practice.
- Digital writing and multimodality are not yet fully accounted for in most statutory policy documents, but nonetheless offer opportunities to enhance pupils' understanding and experience of language learning.
- The internet is a vast language resource with lots of potential for pupils to draw on it.
- Understanding digital forms is integral to the development of critical literacy skills.

KEY RESOURCES

1. Goldsmith, K. (2011) *Uncreative Writing: Managing Language in the Digital Age.* New York: Columbia University Press. A highly readable overview of conceptual writing that draws on the internet as a vast language resource.
2. Lethem, J. (2013) The Ecstasy of Influence. In Lethem, Jonathan. *The Ecstasy of Influence: NonFictions etc.* London: Vintage Books. A 'patchwork' masterpiece that allows you to question the very nature of creativity and originality.
3. English & Media Centre (2013) *KS3 Language Laboratory*. London: English & Media Centre. Unit 4, 'Evolving Language' allows you to explore the place of emojis in the language landscape.
4. English & Media Centre (2013) *KS3 Poetry Plus*. London: English & Media Centre. The unit 'Lost in Translation' contains ideas about how to draw on the internet to help your pupils create and transform poems.
5. Richard Long, 'To blog or not to blog, there is no question' at www.englishandmedia.co.uk/blog/to-blog-or-not-to-blog-there-is-no-question. An inspirational look at how blogging helps develop pupils' understanding of poetry.

NOTES

1. This doesn't apply to reading books. Surveys consistently point to young people reading fewer books that previous generations. See National Literacy Trust (2020). *Children and Young People's Reading in 2019*, accessed on 1 July 2020 at https://literacytrust.org.uk/research-services/research-reports/children-and-young-peoples-reading-in-2019/
2. Richard Long has written about the experience of using blogs with his pupils on the English & Media Centre website. See 'To blog or not to blog, there is no question' at www.englishandmedia.co.uk/blog/to-blog-or-not-to-blog-there-is-no-question, accessed on 1 July 2020.
3. You can read further thoughts on Naomi-Lee's work on the English & Media Centre's website. Bleiman, B. 2019. Big Picture English – Beyond the Brushstrokes, accessed on 1 July 2020 at https://www.englishandmedia.co.uk/blog/big-picture-english-beyond-the-brushstrokes

Chapter 16 Post-16 literature

BARBARA BLEIMAN

INTRODUCTION

The chapter focuses on core principles and underlying ideas about the teaching of advanced-level literature, with an emphasis on teaching students how to think as an English student does, to 'perform' the subject discipline. It is your role to introduce students to the conceptual understandings and ways of talking and writing that constitute academic study in English and allow them to participate in the conversations that are the lifeblood of the subject. The chapter is based on the idea that success in the subject involves students both thinking hard and thinking for themselves, developing their own authentic responses, rather than having someone else's ideas handed down to them. Students are examined in final examinations, whether they be General Certificate of Education (GCE) A level, International Baccalaureate, Highers or other advanced-level qualifications and, of course, they want to succeed in these examinations. However, the education they receive from you should go beyond the narrow confines of examination preparation. Rich, stimulating and challenging work that has inherent educational value and justifies itself beyond the search for a grade also itself helps students attain high grades. The principles upon which good post-16 literature teaching should be founded are explained and exemplified with classroom approaches that can be adapted for any text or specification.

At the end of this chapter you should be able to:

- build on your own experiences of the subject to offer something challenging and enjoyable for students;
- understand more about what's special about English Literature as a subject;
- consider what important literary ideas students should be introduced to, as they read individual texts;
- think about what is characteristic and significant about individual texts you might teach and decide what to focus on with students;
- know something about the kinds of classroom experiences that develop students' thinking and understanding about literature in general, as well as individual texts;
- recognise the relationship between reading and writing, the critical and the creative.

DOI: 10.4324/9781003093060-17

There are significant challenges for today's teacher of English at advanced level. For many decades teachers have complained that students of literature don't show evidence of enjoying literature and don't read enough. In a world where so much is available in other forms, digitally and online, this concern has been growing. Challenges also arise from the way the subject has come to be taught at 11–16. Students may arrive in your classroom with ideas about English Literature that are neither in keeping with your own view of the subject nor with that of either advanced-level examiners or academics teaching the subject at university. Some of the misapprehensions and misunderstandings include: the idea that literary study is about writing to a formula; the belief that you have to learn innumerable 'key' quotations off by heart; the notion that writing well involves ticking off responses to individual assessment objectives one by one; the idea that you are expected to write at great length about contextual issues of the period in which the text was set; the idea that there are 'correct' answers to be learnt off pat, rather than multiple, complex responses and interpretations of texts.

As a teacher of English Literature, you yourself may have experienced a complex mix of styles, approaches and messages in your own learning from school through university and into your training year. Your role as a teacher is to establish a classroom culture that allows the best practices of the subject to thrive. This may involve unpicking some of the misunderstandings that students bring to advanced-level English. A good starting point therefore might be autobiographical, to think back to what kinds of texts, experiences of literary study and engagement with others in reflecting on texts made you want to both study the subject further and then go on to teach it. (You might want to draw on the reading river you created in Chapter 3 on shared reading, in order to do this.)

Activity 16.1

What made English come alive for you?

1. Think about your own learning of literature. Identify one text that stood out for you as being particularly enjoyable to study. What made it so? What did your teacher/lecturer do to make it particularly interesting? Identify the underlying characteristics (for instance, whether it involved challenge, whether it required you to think for yourself, whether it involved talk and if so of what kind).
2. Think about your other 'shared' experiences of literature – talking to friends about books, being a member of a book group, reading a book and then an online review, or other such experiences. List what kinds of things you gain or gained from discussion with others.
3. Think about how classroom approaches to texts might capitalise on the pleasure of 'shared experiences' of reading, for example, 'A chance to say what you really liked or didn't like'. Reflect on whether what you currently see in classrooms, or do in your own classroom, retains any elements of this.

It is important to pay attention to the experiences of learning that worked well for you, bearing them in mind in constructing experiences for your students. This allows bridges to be built between advanced-level study and the subject discipline as a whole, in university English as well as in school.

READING LITERATURE IN A LITERARY KIND OF WAY

Your teaching also needs to draw on what we know about what's special about literary study, as compared for instance with science or maths or geography. Reading and responding to literary texts brings 'affective' as well as critical faculties into play – in other words one's emotions, beliefs, experiences and reactions. As Professor Robert Eaglestone says, in his book *Literature: Why It Matters* (2019, p.11),

> knowing about literature means something different from just knowing facts about say, the dates of the author, what happens in chapter 3 or reading the Wikipedia summary. Knowing about a work of literature is about experiencing it as a process, not – although it can sometimes feel like this – as a collection of answers for a quiz or exam: literature's the walk not the map. Knowing the chemical make-up of water is not the same as knowing what it's like to get soaked in a sudden summer storm.

This means that students' own responses have to be an essential part of the process. Exploratory talk and thinking, as well as exploratory writing, allow students to develop their ideas and sustain lines of inquiry, rather than rushing too quickly into polished critical writing. Asking students to write (thinking aloud on paper), for instance, before group or whole-class discussion, gives value to their initial responses and encourages them to make use of these in coming to more considered critical positions, fuelled by your additional knowledge and expertise.

Equally, reading in a literary way requires an intense focus on text – this is why we call so much of what is done in English classes 'close reading'. The writer and critic Francine Prose says in an interview (Moo, 2006):

> Too often students are being taught to read as if literature were some kind of ethics class or civics class – or worse, some kind of self-help manual. In fact, the important thing is the way the writer uses the language.

However, this is much more than just working through lists of language features, labelling and feature spotting. It is a process by which the reader develops multiple understandings about how texts work and then learns how to draw on these to shape a coherent reading. Shortcuts like searches for a metaphor or a bit of alliteration will not take your students very far down the road of becoming good readers, in a literary sense, where they can use what they know about how texts work to generate interpretations based on their authentic responses to the detail they see before them.

Andrew Dubois, in an essay introducing *Close Reading: The Reader* (ed. Frank Lentricchia and Andrew Dubois, Duke University Press, 2003) says this:

> Paying attention: almost anyone can do it; and it's not requisite for reading, but for reading well? At any rate, attention, properly paid, will, over time, with personally productive tendencies or habits of focus or repetitions of thought remembered into generally applicable patterns, beget method.
>
> (p.2)

This is an interesting and important idea: that methods emerge from developing practices rather than from you teaching a method that becomes their practice. It's an important corrective to the teaching of formulae for approaching texts or for writing about them, that students might have encountered in their studies at 11–16 and one that is worth bearing in mind at GCE A level.

LITERARY KNOWLEDGE – WHAT ADVANCED-LEVEL STUDENTS NEED TO KNOW

Texts are at the heart of all literary study and it is important that students immerse themselves in the particular texts you are teaching, exploring what makes them particularly interesting and enjoyable to read, learning how they are constructed. Response to the text is central to everything we do as teachers of literature. However, there is a balance to be struck between the shorter-term knowledge of and pleasure in an individual text and the longer-term understanding of concepts and ideas that students can carry with them from one text to the next, the common features of texts, the development of conventions and traditions over time, the way texts work within genres.

The American educationalist Arthur Applebee puts this very well in his book *Curriculum as Conversation*, where he talks about the relationships between texts and the kinds of links and conversations that a well-planned curriculum can foster. He argues that any English curriculum should be one long conversation and suggests that that conversation should be between texts as much as between students and teachers. At every level of English the kinds of conversations should be recognisable ones in the tradition of the subject discipline. A GCE A level student should essentially be talking in similar ways (if at a less sophisticated level or on different texts) to a PhD student. Applebee also makes a strong case for texts from different cultures and traditions not only speaking to the different identities of students in different classrooms but also enriching understanding of the mainstream literary traditions themselves. So in choosing texts, it is important to look for opportunities to develop cross-cultural conversations.

English is at its heart an intertextual subject; you cannot read one text without reference to others in the same genre, or without considering what the text draws on in terms of established conventions across time and place. The single sonnet can mean a lot to a student encountering it for the first time but so much more when seen in the light of other sonnets, other poems, poems as compared with prose and so on, providing an important literary context. Reading E.E. Cummings' '[i carry your heart with me(i carry it in]' or a contemporary love sonnet such as 'Wedding' by Alice Oswald is much richer for knowing how both have drawn on and subverted the conventions of what came before, in Thomas Wyatt, William Shakespeare or John Keats. So, an advanced-level curriculum should be looking to make rich textual links. It should offer two sides of the same coin: what is special about a particular text and what one can say about it in relation to other texts and wider reading that can illuminate it.

Activity 16.2

What's special about a single text in relation to other texts?

1. Choose a text you yourself studied either at school or at university.
2. Think about what its special characteristics are – what makes it unique. To do this, think about other texts in the same genre, or of the same type and use these as a foil to identify the special qualities of the one you've

chosen. Generate five to ten bullet points that identify its particular qualities in the light of other texts that you know. If read in combination, these should identify the text to anyone who has read it, without it ever being named.

Here's an example. Who might this writer be? Can they be identified by this combination of bullet points?

A poet

- Deceptively simple. The poems sound like children's rhymes but there's much more to them.
- Draws on religious images and symbols but subverts them and makes them his own.
- The imagery runs across poems, so that one can read one poem in the light of another and they build up meaning in the world of his poetry.
- A structure of binaries and oppositions, which are often broken down.
- Is preoccupied with issues around freedom, control, repression and the stifling of human joy and creativity.
- Unconventional uses of form and language make his poems ambiguous and open to many interpretations.
- Often uses the conventional form of hymns but disturbs the patterns (for instance by the use of half-rhymes or unexpected shifts), to unsettle the reader.

If you know the work of William Blake, these bullet points should have made it clear that that's whom I have been describing.

3. Reflect on what your bullet point list tells you about which aspects of your chosen text might be most important and interesting for students to have thought about by the end of studying it with you. These should be literary ideas that they can take forward into their future learning and allow them to identify and explore similar ideas in new texts. (So, for instance you might focus on the complex use of a third-person narrative voice, fluctuating between a distanced omniscient voice and free indirect style. This would allow students to explore another third-person narrative and bring to bear their knowledge of this one, drawing out similarities and differences and extending their understanding of the concept 'third-person narrative voice'.)
4. Choose one of these significant aspects of your chosen text and think about it in more detail, perhaps mapping out a lesson, early on in your teaching, in which you introduce something important about how it works.

THE ISSUE OF CONTEXT – ENGLISH NOT HISTORY

In English Literature GCE A Level, as well other advanced-level qualifications, students are expected to bring to bear knowledge beyond the text. However, all too often that can turn into the unhelpful regurgitation of historical facts and background information that does little to enhance critical analysis of the text itself. Literary context, the understanding of traditions and intertextual links, which is genuinely helpful, is often underplayed or even ignored in favour of facts about the period and the society.

Texts often provide much of their own context, and one reads them with pleasure partly because of what they themselves teach you about their worlds. So, for instance, you don't need to know a great deal about the workhouse or Victorian London to read *Oliver Twist*. Charles Dickens wrote the novel, in part, to inform people about the conditions for the poor in Victorian London. More helpful to know, when reading any novel by Dickens is that they were serialised in instalments and mainly read aloud. This understanding can give students genuine insight into the structure and design of his books – the use of episodes, cliffhangers, dialogue and naming, even perhaps the highly distinctive, memorable characters.

Front-loading a lot of context before reading texts can be both off-putting and distort the 'normal' reading experience. Obviously, some things may be essential for students to know, to avoid serious misunderstanding and to give them a steer before reading, but this should be carefully judged.

Even when something is helpful for students to know in the course of their reading, it doesn't necessarily mean that it is always be worth writing about in an essay. They need to make a judgement about what is genuinely illuminating, in relation to a whole text, or part of a text, or to a specific essay question. Knowing something about the Jazz Age, for instance, might be useful broad contextual background reading to contextualise a first reading of *The Great Gatsby*, but may not offer much of value in an essay question on the use of time in the novel or on Nick Carraway as a first-person narrator. It's important to distinguish between context for reading and context for interpretation and written analysis.

Professor Peter Barry is very helpful on this. His book *Literature in Contexts* (2012) makes a distinction between 'deep' and 'broad' contexts, arguing that broad contexts, often of an historical nature, tend to offer little genuine insight into texts – they are more like English masquerading as history. In an article for the English & Media Centre's (EMC's) magazine for GCE A level students, *emagazine* (2004), he uses two other terms that give us a way of judging the usefulness of contextual information – 'adjacent' and 'remote'.

> If we emphasise context too exclusively [...] then we will soon be doing History rather than English, in all but name. [...] Knowing about the context isn't much use unless it illuminates the [text]. So can we suggest any guidelines which will help us to keep some sense of proportion about context?
>
> We can do so if we distinguish between 'adjacent context' and 'remote context'. The former is explicit in some way in the text – it's mentioned or alluded to – indeed, we could say that it's the kind of context which is really content. Remote context, on the other hand has no such unambiguous warrant in the text.

Activity 16.3

Contextual Information: what is illuminating and relevant?

You could try this activity with students, having done it yourself, to demonstrate how contextual information is of variable use, depending on the text or essay question.

1. Read this extract from *The Rime of the Ancient Mariner* by Samuel Taylor Coleridge.

And now the STORM-BLAST came, and he
Was tyrannous and strong:
He struck with his o'ertaking wings,
And chased us south along.

With sloping masts and dipping prow,
As who pursued with yell and blow
Still treads the shadow of his foe,
And forward bends his head,
The ship drove fast, loud roared the blast,
And southward aye we fled.

And now there came both mist and snow,
And it grew wondrous cold:
And ice, mast-high, came floating by,
As green as emerald.

And through the drifts the snowy clifts
Did send a dismal sheen:
Nor shapes of men nor beasts we ken –
The ice was all between.

The ice was here, the ice was there,
The ice was all around:
It cracked and growled, and roared and howled,
Like noises in a swound!

At length did cross an Albatross,
Thorough the fog it came;
As if it had been a Christian soul,
We hailed it in God's name.

It ate the food it ne'er had eat,
And round and round it flew.
The ice did split with a thunder-fit;
The helmsman steered us through!

And a good south wind sprung up behind;
The Albatross did follow,
And every day, for food or play,
Came to the mariner's hollo!

In mist or cloud, on mast or shroud,
It perched for vespers nine;
Whiles all the night, through fog-smoke white,
Glimmered the white Moon-shine.

'God save thee, ancient Mariner!
From the fiends, that plague thee thus! –
Why look'st thou so?' – With my cross-bow
I shot the ALBATROSS.

2. Read these pieces of contextual information. All might throw light on some Romantic writers and poems. However, not all are significant and illuminating in relation to this extract from this poem. Decide which two or three genuinely throw light on the text.
   a. In 1789, the French Revolution began with the call for Liberty, Equality and Fraternity.
   b. Romantic poets and writers often used language which was deliberately old-fashioned and archaic to give an otherworldly flavour to their writings. They used elements of language that harked back to the medieval period.
   c. The sublime – a quality of greatness or grandeur that inspires awe, fear and wonder, especially in relation to nature. Ideas about the sublime influenced Romantic artists and poets.
   d. The ballad is one of the most basic, ancient forms of storytelling, enacting extraordinary events in the lives of ordinary people.
   e. During the second half of the eighteenth century there emerged in the middle classes a radical new political movement, led by activists such as Tom Paine, Mary Wollstonecraft and William Godwin, who argued for social justice, human rights and equality for all men and women.
   f. The eighteenth-century Enlightenment saw nature as something to be dominated, tamed and regularised. The Romantics rejected this view.
   g. The Romantics were troubled by the dramatic effects of industrialisation, its impact on the natural world, the growth of urbanisation, the pollution of the cities and the wider changes to people's lives and to the structure of society.
3. Does your decision change if you read this poem by another Romantic poet instead?

Sonnet XXIV
The world is too much with us; late and soon,
Getting and spending, we lay waste our powers:
Little we see in Nature that is ours;
We have given our hearts away, a sordid boon!
This Sea that bares her bosom to the moon;
The Winds that will be howling at all hours
And are up-gathered now like sleeping flowers;
For this, for every thing, we are out of tune;
It moves us not. – Great God! I'd rather be
A Pagan suckled in a creed outworn;
So might I, standing on this pleasant lea,
Have glimpses that would make me less forlorn;
Have sight of Proteus coming from the sea;
Or hear old Triton blow his wreathed horn.
(William Wordsworth)

With the extract from *The Rime of the Ancient Mariner*, understanding of the sublime, the Romantics' stance on the natural world, ballads and archaisms could all be more fruitful than knowing about the French Revolution and the wider social and political movements of the time. For Wordsworth's poem, the balance shifts somewhat. Industrialisation and its impact on the natural world, in a political system that values wealth over deeper values, is of greater interest than some of the other contexts.

This activity demonstrates how contextual material needs to be used selectively and judiciously, in order to enrich textual analysis.

THE RELATIONSHIP BETWEEN THE CREATIVE AND THE CRITICAL

Most people think of English Literature at advanced level as being only about critical analysis. However there has always been a strand of thinking that says that creative writing can enhance critical understanding of texts. It provides opportunities for students to experience writers' choices and literary styles in action. One important strand of this is textual interventions and transformations, as advocated by Rob Pope in *Textual Intervention: Critical and Creative Strategies for Literary Studies* and Ben Knights and Chris Thurgar-Dawson in *Active Reading: Transformative Writing in Literary Studies*. By intervening in texts, perhaps changing the voice in a novel from third to first person, or removing the retrospective point of view, you can discover more about the impact of the writer's own decisions. Equally illuminating is the approach which asks students to write in the style of a writer. This imitative practice requires close exploration of the key aspects of a writer's style and can therefore be excellent for crystallising what is both important and characteristic.

Creative writing activities do not need to be lengthy and time-consuming (though in some examinations there are opportunities to be assessed on creative/critical writing based on a text). They can be quick experiments, more important for what they reveal than for the quality of the final product. Activity 16.4 demonstrates this for you.

Activity 16.4

Textual interventions in a poem

1. Choose a short poem that especially appeals to you. (It doesn't necessarily need to be one that you know very well.)
2. Experiment with making a small change to it. It could be:
   - Changing the voice
   - Changing the tense
   - Changing line or stanza breaks
   - Removing adjectives or adverbs
   - Replacing polysyllabic with monosyllabic words or vice versa

In choosing what to do, consider what will make a significant difference to the poem. The act of choosing what to change itself flags up key aspects of the poem and how it works.

3. Read your reworked poem and reflect on what difference your change has made. Use these insights to reflect back on the original poem.
4. Think about how you might do this activity with a poem that you are teaching. What insights might your students gain from working in this way?

SUMMARY AND KEY POINTS

- A student's own response needs to be integral to everything they do in English at advanced level.
- Big ideas, broad literary concepts and ways of thinking should be developed through the study of individual texts.
- The choice of texts and ways of working with them should make links and connections, so that the course as a whole is one long 'conversation' about literature.
- Contextual information should be at the service of interpretation, not included for its own sake.
- The creative and the critical are interconnected and mutually supportive; students should be writing creatively in order to enhance their critical understanding.

KEY RESOURCES

1. *emagazine* (published by EMC and available from www.englishandmedia.co.uk) This print magazine and subscription website is for advanced-level students of Literature, Language and Language and Literature. It includes short articles by academics, writers, teachers and students written specifically for this audience. The website has a searchable archive of over 2,000 articles and videoclips on a wide range of texts and topics.
2. Atherton, C., Green, A. and Snapper, G. (2013) *Teaching English Literature 16–19*. Abingdon, Oxon: Routledge. This is an excellent practical guide to English Literature teaching at this level but it also offers underpinning principles and explanations that span the big issues of advanced-level teaching and the detail of how to teach different genres.
3. Eaglestone, R. (2009) *Doing English*. New York: Routledge. An overview of the key ideas and practices involved in the study of English, this book, intended for undergraduates and advanced-level students, is equally useful for teachers wanting to think about what literary study entails.
4. The British Library (2020) Learning. [online] Available at: <www.bl.uk/learning> [Accessed 11 March 2020]. The British Library website has many articles and original sources that are invaluable for GCE A level study.
5. Webster, L. (ed.) (2019) *The Literature Reader*. London: English & Media Centre. This collection of essays, intended for GCE A level students, ranges across genres and spans major issues and traditions in English Literature. The chapters are written mainly by academics who are experts in their fields, from Nathan Waddell and Chris Power to Peter Barry and Leila Kamali.

Chapter 17 Post-16 language

ANGELA GODDARD

INTRODUCTION

English Language at General Certificate of Education (GCE) AS/A Level is not simply a continuation of General Certificate of Secondary Education (GCSE) English Language, studied in greater depth and detail. In many ways it is a new departure. Although GCSE and AS/A level English Language share some common ground in that they both involve students developing their communication skills, the main focus of study at AS/A Level is of English language as a topic. English language is the content, not just a vehicle for expressing ideas.

You may be wondering what it means for English language to be the subject of study. But if you think about questions such as where English has come from, how and why it changes, how children learn it, and how it varies both socially and geographically, you are already viewing English language as a topic. These questions may look abstract, but they are all relevant to our everyday lives. For example, if you move from one area of the UK to another, you may well find yourself being addressed differently (love, mate, pet); needing new words for bread rolls (cob, barm, stottie); and puzzling over what kind of meal you've been invited to (is a midday meal lunch or dinner, and an evening meal dinner or tea? And what is supper?). These variants are all examples of English regional dialect vocabulary.

As well as using language, we all have attitudes towards it. For example, ask someone for a list of their favourite and least liked accents, and they will readily oblige. Our attitudes show that language is more than just a neutral medium; it is part of our social identities and it can act as a badge of group membership. To study language, then, is to study human behaviour.

By the end of this chapter you should be able to:

- understand the nature of the AS/A level English Language subject content;
- plan some accessible starting points for students of all abilities and backgrounds;
- see how there are some recurring aspects of language that have relevance to all texts, topics and theories;

DOI: 10.4324/9781003093060-18

- identify some resources and activities that can offer insights into the way language works;
- devise ways to give students opportunities to do independent language research.

SUBJECT CONTENT

English Language AS/A Levels share some of the concepts and theories that are taught on university Linguistics courses. But school-based specifications aren't simply Linguistics in another guise. If your own degree studies have not included Language, you shouldn't feel that you are embarking on an entirely new subject. AS/A level English Language is interdisciplinary, drawing on the Social Sciences and also having many connections with Arts and Humanities courses, particularly English Literature and Media/Communication Studies: for example, how meanings are created by writers and readers/speakers and listeners; the importance of context; and how language choices construct representations of things, people, places and experiences. However, while students of English Literature focus solely on literary texts, students of English Language embrace texts of all kinds, from written advertising to political speeches, and from text messages to conversations at the bus stop. For English Language study, all texts are seen as having patterns of one kind or another that can be analysed; and all uses of communication are seen as valid for study.

The Department for Education (DfE) sets out the content for AS/A level curricula in England, and all Awarding Bodies (ABs) have to comply with these requirements in devising their specifications. Because education is devolved in Scotland, Wales and Northern Ireland, those countries have their own versions of subject content that their respective ABs have to follow.

The DfE (2014d) describes the aims and objectives for English Language AS/A level specifications offered in England as follows:

Specifications should develop students' interest in and enjoyment of English Language as they:

- develop and apply their understanding of the concepts and methods appropriate for the analysis and study of language;
- explore data and examples of language in use;
- engage creatively and critically with a varied programme for the study of English Language;
- develop their skills as producers and interpreters of language.

> In addition, A Level specifications must encourage students to develop their interest in and enjoyment of English Language as they independently investigate language in use.
>
> (DfE, 2014d, p.1)

In terms of knowledge and understanding, students are expected to learn about 'language levels', which represent a traditional way of categorising language for purposes of study. The idea of levels was first proposed in the early twentieth century by Ferdinand de Saussure, a Swiss linguist who is often regarded as the founder of modern Linguistics in Europe. The levels set for study are explained as follows:

- phonetics, phonology and prosodics – how speech sounds and effects are articulated and analysed

- lexis and semantics – the vocabulary of English, including social and historical variation
- grammar including morphology – the structural patterns and shapes of English at sentence, clause, phrase and word level
- pragmatics – the contextual aspects of language use
- discourse – extended stretches of communication occurring in different genres, modes and contexts.

The levels don't simply constitute knowledge in their own right: they are tools that can be applied to different contexts. AS level students are expected to show how the language levels can be applied to texts and discourses; A level students are expected to work at greater depth, applying them to historical, geographical, social and individual varieties of English, as well as to aspects of language and identity. A level specifications must enable students to understand how the applied areas (i.e. geographical, historical, social and individual contexts) are connected.

To see how this interconnectedness works, think about the examples given earlier – of address terms, labels for bread rolls and the names of meals. These items are part of the vocabulary system of (British) English, so they sit within the 'lexis and semantics' level, above. They are part of regional dialects (geographical), which have been losing their distinctive vocabulary over time (historical). Some of these terms also appear to vary according to gender: a man might be called 'mate' by strangers, but would he be called 'love' or 'pet'? (social). Also, terms for meals are thought to be connected historically with occupation, where heavy labour required a more substantial meal at midday – 'dinner' as opposed to 'lunch' (social and historical). Any one individual sits in a nexus of all these connections between geography, history and social group membership.

Individuals also have idiolects – ways of using language that are uniquely their own, a bit like a set of linguistic fingerprints. This is illustrated by the work done by forensic linguists, who are sometimes employed in court cases to identify speakers or the authorship of written texts. There are also highly individual instances of language use that are particular to families. You should already be able to see that it is possible to cover a lot of ground, both in terms of the 'language levels' and in terms of the various social factors, by focusing on language items that are well within students' everyday experience.

A LANGUAGE AUDIT

Our personal experience of language is a helpful starting point. However, this same quality also has a downside. A sense of familiarity can mean that we don't see what's under our noses, including our expertise in negotiating everyday linguistic encounters. As well as showing students that they already know a lot about language, the task for any teacher of AS/A level English Language is also to defamiliarise aspects of language and help students notice language afresh, seeing it for the amazing phenomenon that it is.

You can start immediately on this process by getting students to think about their own language resources, in the form of an 'audit'. This initial activity has multiple functions: helping students stand back from their own language enables them to see that they have lots of personal resources they can draw on, which develops their confidence; it enables them (and you) to see how those resources could provide the basis for their independent research; and it shows how much material you and the group could assemble as part of a language research community. It is no accident therefore that many textbooks begin by suggesting this kind of activity (e.g. Carter and Goddard 2016, p.7). Activity 17.1 illustrates how a language audit works.

Activity 17.1: A language audit

Think about the following headings and list any material that you could collect. When you have finished, think about how you could adapt this audit for students. For example, are there further categories that could be added?

- You as a young child. Many parents or carers keep examples of children's early language. Children themselves are also great collectors, so you might have saved scrapbooks and comics, diaries, early reading books, pieces of digital communication, schoolwork, reports, fanzines.
- You now. Do you belong to an interest- or work-based group involving a certain type of language? Do you read, write or collect particular types of material? What communication systems do you engage with and what kind of language is used there? Do you have friends who use language in an interesting way?
- You within your wider family. Do you and/or anyone in the wider family use a regional accent or dialect? Does anyone speak an additional language? Do any family members use occupational language? Does anyone have specific language impairments, or disabilities that involve language use?
- Loves and hates. Everyone has aspects of language that they enjoy, and that interest them enough to want to know more. Equally, there are things that hold no interest value, or that grate and jar. What are your loves and hates?

BUILDING A CLASSROOM RESEARCH COMMUNITY

So far, language has been seen as a common resource, and the teacher's role as enabling students to view that resource in a more analytical way. But this doesn't mean that the teacher is expected to have all the answers. Teachers of English Language often report that they learn a lot from their students, especially in areas such as bilingualism, or new technologies, where the teachers might have less experience than the students (see Goddard and Beard, 2007, for views from students and teachers about English Language AS/A Level). One way to shift the position of the teacher from a didactic role is to construct the learning environment as a research community; and this can work regardless of whether learning and teaching is face to face, online or blended. Here are some of the ways that you can start to build a subject community:

- tabulate and display the group results of the audit;
- based on the audit, create some interest groups to collect material and present ideas to the larger group – on, for example, sport, new technologies, gender, different 'Englishes';
- create some displays that can be added to by class members. There are many possible areas, including etymologies; new words and expressions; examples of stereotyping; creative headlines; occupational language; metaphors; political rhetoric; language puzzles, jokes and games; words in different languages

for which there are no English equivalents (see de Boinod 2005); advertising techniques (see Goddard 2002); articles about language; dialect terms; shop names; signs and symbols.

All these activities can work digitally as well as in face-to-face contexts.

The subject content for English Language AS/A Level requires students to have opportunities to 'engage creatively' as well as 'critically' with their programme of study, and to develop their skills as 'producers', as well as 'interpreters' of language. The activities described previously lend themselves well to creative production, whether that is an oral presentation from an individual or group, a formal written report or an article for the school or college newspaper, all of which could be digital outcomes. An array of skills is involved in presenting and debating ideas, including note-making, record keeping, critiquing different perspectives, working productively with others and meeting deadlines – all of which will stand students in good stead in future study and in work and life more generally.

SHOWING THE RELEVANCE OF TAUGHT KNOWLEDGE: LANGUAGE LEVELS IN PRACTICE

As with any subject, English Language AS/A Level involves new knowledge for students, in the form of academic theories about language, and research studies which test out those theories or add new ones. Regardless of the specification chosen, or the theory being explored, the language levels listed earlier form a set of 'building blocks' from which students can both construct their knowledge about theoretical areas, and deconstruct texts and discourses to reveal possible meanings. For this reason, many textbooks spend some time at the outset covering these levels (e.g. Clayton et al., 2015).

Language levels are so named because each focuses on a different level, or scale, of language use. At the smallest level is phonology, or the sounds that make up speech. At the largest level is discourse, which can refer to widespread ways of thinking and talking about topics – for example, discourses of science, or food, or sexuality (see Goddard and Carey, 2017, for more on discourse(s)). We don't think about these different levels as language users, but studying language requires a detailed focus on particular aspects; otherwise, the analytical task can be overwhelming. University courses can involve studying a single language level for a whole term. But at AS/A Level, we are simply talking about familiarising students with these language levels and – crucially – showing how they can be applied.

Post-16 students are no different from pupils at any other stage in wanting to see the relevance of what they are doing, and to understand the value of any activity. To underline the importance of this, the rest of this chapter explains the language levels, show their relevance and suggest how they can be actively approached. Because the study of spoken language is probably less familiar, that area is covered here in more detail than the other levels.

WORKING WITH SPEECH

In Linguistics, the terms phonetics, phonology and prosodics are all associated with the analysis of speech. Phonetics refers to how sounds are produced, while phonology is the study of the sound system within a language. Prosodics are the 'music' of our voices – for example, intonation and pitch.

There are different types of alphabets for representing the sounds of languages, rather than their spelling systems. A phonetic alphabet called the IPA – the International Phonetic Alphabet – covers all the languages in the world. There are also phonemic alphabets, which cover just the sounds of a specific language. The phonemic alphabet for English has many practical functions. It is used by speech therapists to analyse problems of articulation; and by drama voice coaches to help actors assume different accents. The IPA has a more global reach. It enables performers such as singers and speech-makers to express themselves in a foreign language without knowing that language. It is also a key part of dictionary listings, where words are given a phonetic representation to show pronunciations. These provide insights even for native speakers of English, because the pronunciations are based on 'Received Pronunciation' (RP), which is a socially based, prestige accent rather than a regional variety.

There are digital versions of alphabets for sound, such as the phonemic chart at the link below. Once students are used to the system, they will soon see that the symbols are a useful tool for the precise description of English sounds, rather than using the written alphabet. You can speed up this realisation by pointing to some words with similar spellings but different pronunciations, as in Activity 17.2.

Activity 17.2: Transcribing sound

Go to www.phonemicchart.com

Transcribe the spoken realisations of each of these words, focusing particularly on how the 'ough' spelling varies when spoken:

through
thorough
cough
rough
thought
bough
dough

You can capitalise on early insights into the differences between speech and writing by setting students the task of recording and transcribing some informal spoken language. To see what can be learned from this, try it for yourself in Activity 17.3.

Activity 17.3: Transcribing dialogue

Record and transcribe a small piece of informal conversation. You don't need to use phonemic symbols throughout, but you might want to highlight pronunciations that are interesting.

Even a small amount of material will touch on aspects of each of the language levels, as well as reveal some key differences between speech and writing:

- *semantics* – do we always speak in 'words' with boundaries around them, or in a stream of sound?
- *grammar* – do speakers express themselves in full sentences, as in some writing?
- *pragmatics* – how much meaning is implicit, rather than explicitly explained? How is turn-taking managed? How does the physical context shape the language use?
- *discourse* – each genre has its own characteristics and even within speech, there are many subtypes. How would you classify your material? What was the purpose of the dialogue?

In reviewing your material, think about some of the ways in which your real speech sample differs from the kinds of dialogue seen in novels and playscripts. How 'realistic' is literary dialogue?

The speech-writing interface has seen many changes since the advent of new technologies, with the emergence of new 'hybrid' forms of language – that is, those that use features of both speech and writing. Examples of new language can include subtle variants – for example, 'yes', 'yeh', 'yeah', 'yep', 'yay' and 'yess' all mean something slightly different (see Goddard, 2011). There are also new pragmatic rules. For example, how does turn-taking work on real-time digital platforms such as Zoom? Students can learn a lot from looking at computer-mediated communication (CMC). Activity 17.4 asks you to think about your own usage.

Activity 17.4: Changing conventions

Make a collection of some of your own CMC. How does your language vary in your sample? For example, do you use language differently on different platforms? Do you vary according to who the recipient is? How do you open and close messages in emails and text messages?

SEMANTICS

Working on casual speech allows some insights into informal English, particularly the everyday vocabulary that we all use. But there are also formal equivalents, allowing speakers to choose a style from their linguistic repertoire. Thesaurus work can reveal stylistic options and show the connotations of selecting one term or another: for example, what the choice of 'sweat' rather than 'perspiration' suggests about the communicators and the context. Such choices also reveal the influences of different languages in the history of English, with many Anglo-Saxon terms at the informal end of the lexicon and French or Latin terms at the formal end. A simple search of 'origin of the word X' on Google usually offers a good level of etymological information.

Formality is also a factor in the semantics of naming and labelling. This is accessible to students from their own experience of personal names and titles. Listing the different ways that people use variants of their name shows the relationship between language choices and expressions of power or intimacy. If the class includes students who know other languages, interesting comparisons can be made.

Repertoires of style are also about relationships between 'standard' or 'official' languages and non-standard varieties, where, again, students will have become familiar with ideas about the forms of language seen as appropriate in different contexts. This is an opportunity to link together the code switching that is part of life for students with regional dialects, with the choice of whole different languages by students who are operating bilingually. Of course, some students will be in both those categories, with, additionally, regional or social styles within their additional language(s).

GRAMMAR

This level often suffers from the mistaken idea that everything has to be covered. Your main aim is to show that grammar is about meaning, and that grammatical choices construct different perspectives. The focus of Activity 17.5 is on grammar and gender representation.

Activity 17.5: Grammar and gender

Goddard and Mean (2009) show how the language patterns in romantic fiction portray men as active, and women as passive recipients of men's actions. A simple process of turning the pronouns round can throw these patterns into high relief. For example, replace 'he' with 'she' and 'she with 'he' in the following:

He pulled her towards him, feeling the swish of her blonde hair against his cheek and holding her so close that he could feel her beating heart. She broke away, trembling, not able to meet his gaze that was bearing down on her, full of urgent demand.

What image is created from the grammatical reversal exercise?

Apart from the pronouns, which other terms are often associated with one sex or another?

The Twitter account 'the man who has it all' is based on this idea of role reversal, parodying the advice books that represent men and women in a certain way. Collect some of the posts and you can build an archive that reveals the way both semantic and grammatical choices construct gender representations.

SUMMARY AND KEY POINTS

- AS/A level English Language is something to be enjoyed, not feared.
- There may be areas of English Language that are new to you, but its interdisciplinarity means that many other subjects are relevant.
- Use students (and yourself) as a resource both as language users and data gatherers in a research community.
- Set up some early activities to explore the nature of spoken language.
- Try to show how aspects of subject knowledge have real-world applications and implications.
- New technologies offer useful resources for English Language and they can also be analysed as new sites for language use.

KEY RESOURCES

1. Baker, P. (2008) *Sexed Texts: Language, Gender and Sexuality*. London: Equinox. The complex connections between gender and sexuality are explained well here.
2. Carter, R. and McCarthy, M. (1997) *Exploring Spoken English*. Cambridge: CUP. A non-technical account of different types of interaction, drawing on naturally occurring speech.
3. Clayton, D. (ed.) (2018) *Language Handbook: Key Thinkers on Key Topics*. 2nd Ed. London: English & Media Centre. A set of articles about a wide range of relevant language topics.
4. Cameron, D. (1995) *Verbal Hygiene*. London: Routledge. A look at public attitudes towards language, covering areas such as 'political correctness'.
5. Crystal, D. (2005) *The Stories of English*. London: Penguin. An accessible and entertaining account of English language history.
6. Madden, M. (2005) *99 Ways to Tell a Story*. London: Penguin. The wittiest exploration of narrative perspective and genre that you will ever see.
7. Routledge Intertext series. A core text plus 25 titles covering many topics that students can research independently: www.routledge.com/Intertext/book-series/SE0313
8. Saxton, M. (2010) *Child Language Acquisition and Development*. London: SAGE. An area that can seem challenging is explained clearly here.
9. The British Library has a digital archive of speech, including different accents and dialects: https://sounds.bl.uk/Accents-and-dialects
10. The British Library site also features many written texts from different genres. This link is to a historical collection of cookery books: www.bl.uk/learning/langlit/texts/cook/cookery2.html

Chapter 18 English across the curriculum

JUDITH KNEEN

INTRODUCTION

The reason why many teachers choose to teach within the secondary – as opposed to the primary sector – is to become a specialist teacher in the subject they love. And indeed, as an English teacher, it can be fabulously rewarding to share your enthusiasm for *Of Mice and Men* or *Macbeth* or rap lyrics with young pupils. However, if you teach English in a splendid but secluded bubble, you will undoubtedly miss out on rich learning opportunities in your classroom practice and in your own professional development.

English, perhaps more than any other subject, benefits from the potential of developing powerful teaching opportunities across traditional subject boundaries. Exploring grammar and vocabulary, for example, through comparisons with other languages can bring out the elegance and sophistication of language. Recognising the types of expressive 'language' inherent in the expressive arts (e.g. art, drama, music) can support pupils' confident articulation of ideas in English. Joint exploration of contexts and concepts between English and the humanities can help pupils develop a more rounded view of a text, writer or topic.

The benefits don't stop with the pupils; collaborating with practitioners from other subjects can also develop – and sometimes challenge – our English teacher's pedagogic perspective in a way that makes us reflect more deeply on how to teach different areas within the subject. Appreciation of the potential of cross-curricular links helps provide a better understanding of English teaching and learning and opens doors to creative approaches.

At the end of this chapter you should be able to:

- appreciate that English, as a subject area, does not exist isolation but has significant connections and commonalities with other areas of the curriculum;
- recognise how cross-curricular working can enhance the learning experience for pupils;
- draw on an increasing range of different ways to work across traditional subject 'borders'.

DOI: 10.4324/9781003093060-19

WHAT DO WE MEAN BY 'CROSS-CURRICULAR'?

You may have come across a number of terms that describe working across subject boundaries, including cross-curricular, multidisciplinary, interdisciplinary and transdisciplinary. The most commonly used is probably cross-curricular, which has been defined as 'sensitivity towards, and a synthesis of, knowledge, skills and understandings from various subject areas' (Savage, 2011, p.8). Basically, all of these terms are about making connections between different areas of the curriculum, or curriculum integration, but we can make connections in different ways, and it is helpful to recognise different ways of making connections. Drake and Burns (2004) provide helpful distinctions between the terms multidisciplinary, interdisciplinary and transdisciplinary. As you can see from Table 18.1, such distinctions can indicate significant differences in learning intentions and classroom practice.

We can organise teaching and learning, then, with differing degrees of integration; the prominence of the subject is likely to be greater in a multidisciplinary approach than in a transdisciplinary approach. It is helpful to be aware of such distinctions of meaning, particularly as you work on collaborations within your school.

Within this chapter, however, the term 'cross-curricular' is used and the focus is on creating meaningful links between English and at least one other subject.

WHY BOTHER?

Is it important to forge links across the curriculum? Isn't it just a way of engaging pupils? Well, cross-curricular work is often used to provide extra motivation, but more importantly it can be used to 'offer more depth than a single subject could do' (Barnes, 2018, p.xv). It is also undoubtedly the case that we can support pupils by helping them 'join the dots' between different areas of the curriculum. Beyond the classroom, we do not see the world through discrete subject areas, but rather 'Our experience of the world is cross-curricular' (Barnes, 2015, p.1). In other words, we use many perspectives to make sense of our world. When teachers support pupils' understanding across subject areas, we are developing 'an enriched pedagogy' (Savage, 2011, pp.8–9), which supports both our own understanding and our pupils'.

It is important to have a rationale behind any cross-curricular work. You need to be clear about how it will help pupils' understanding within English. For

Table 18.1 Different types of curriculum integration

Type of link	Description	Example
Multidisciplinary	A theme is used as a linking device, but the teaching centres on the subject	A school has a special half-term focus on the climate crisis and each subject area tackles different areas of the topic, e.g. creating poetry in English
Interdisciplinary	Structuring the curriculum around learning aspects which different subjects have in common with each other	In ICT/Computing lessons, pupils learn how to use an audio-editing application so that pupils in English can then create a podcast about the climate crisis.
Transdisciplinary	The theme or topic is the main teaching focus, and subjects help explore this theme or topic	A school has organised a Climate Awareness Day, which is a day off timetable, during which all teachers work together to support pupils in creating a presentation about the topic.

Source: Derived from Drake and Burns (2004).

example, making a model of an Elizabethan theatre may be a fun thing to do with Art or History, but it only really begins to help pupils' understanding if you also teach about aspects such as the Tudor audience experience, the actor-audience relationships, how the language in the plays has to indicate night-time in an open-air theatre and so on.

Activity 18.1: Links between English and other subjects

- Identify three texts, commonly taught in English, that may benefit from closer links with other subject areas and how they might benefit (e.g. *Animal Farm* through understanding of historical and political issues in the book).
- Are there skills used in English that may benefit from cross-curricular links? (E.g. using graphs to chart tension in a text).
- What conditions are needed for successful links between subjects? (E.g. time for colleagues to do joint planning).

POEMS AND PAINTINGS

Poetry and the arts are natural companions. They often share expressive and distinctive ways of communicating thoughts and feeling. Here we consider English and art, but it could easily be dance, drama or music. *The Lady of Shalott*, by Alfred Tennyson, is an ideal choice for exploring poetry with the help of art. This nineteenth-century lyrical ballad of a medieval lady imprisoned within a tower by magical means, has unfamiliar vocabulary and language structures which can make the text difficult for pupils to access. However, the use of art can help overcome barriers to this classic text, as well as enable pupils to explore the expressive language of both poetry and painting.

A number of pre-Raphaelite artists illustrated Tennyson's poetry, and their paintings can provide support in accessing and understanding the poem. The paintings provide different depictions of the Lady at different stages in the poem. Exploring one representation of the mysterious Lady of Shalott can help pupils establish a relationship with this enigmatic figure.

Possibly the best-known painting related to the poem, John William Waterhouse's *The Lady of Shalott*, 1888, is available on the Tate website from where it can be reproduced for educational purposes (see Key Resources). If you have the technology, you can project a large colour image of this for the whole class to explore, using the language of art to describe the picture.

Possible activities for exploring the painting

1. Starter – Drawing from memory: You need a print of the painting *The Lady of Shalott*. Put your class into groups of about five. Give each group one piece of blank paper and a pencil. Call up one member from each group to the front, show them the painting for 30 seconds, then ask them to go and draw an outline of the painting on their paper. Whilst they do that, call up the next member of each group and give them 30 seconds to study the painting, and then they go back to add to the drawing. Continue until each group member has had a chance to contribute. They can then compare their version with the original before starting to talk about what the picture might be depicting.

2. Painting Talk: give pupils the opportunity to explore and to talk about the painting in pairs. Set them up with questions, considering the painting from an art perspective. Possible questions:
   a. Identify five things you can see in the painting.
   b. What genre is this picture? For example, historical, fantasy, mythical, portrait, landscape and so on.
   c. How is the painting presented? For example, realistic, exaggerated, abstract, idealised.
   d. How is colour utilised? For example, muted, vibrant, monochrome, natural.
   e. Describe the figure in the painting, for example, her pose, the body language, where she is looking, her expression, her mood and so on.
   f. Where is the main emphasis for the viewer?

Share and discuss their ideas

3. Personal response to the painting. Provide a framework for pupils to provide their ideas about what this painting is about. Possible questions:
   a. What are the tones of this painting, and how does this affect the mood? For example, dark and gloomy, light and cheery, shadowy and mysterious.
   b. How does the painting make you feel? For example, uplifted, curious, tense, optimistic, moved, forlorn.
   c. What might be the story behind this painting?
4. Video analysis of painting. View the short video on the Tate website (see Key Resources), which provides a very helpful reading of the Waterhouse paintings and an accessible outline of the key events of the poem.
5. Comparison. Once the poem has been read, pupils can return to the painting, to identify the moment from the poem that is depicted. With the extra knowledge they have gained from the text, they can reappraise the painting, identifying elements from the narrative and evaluating Waterhouse's interpretation of the Lady of Shalott.

Using images provides an alternative way to approach an understanding of a challenging text. By looking at one perspective of *The Lady of Shalott*, it helps arouse some intrigue and an interest in finding out more about her, including whether their assessment of her from the painting is accurate.

Notice, too, that the skills used to analyse the painting are very similar to the skills we would use to analyse the poem itself. This example of interdisciplinary links (Drake and Burns, 2004) shows how the skills of analysis can be transferable between arts subjects. For example, the interpretation of a figure and how it is depicted in a painting relates to the analysis of a character in literature. Looking at both can enable fresh connections, as looking at the ideas behind the painting can help clarify and enhance the pupils' understanding of the poem.

LITERATURE AND CONTEXT

Exploring context is often a significant part of studying literature, whether this be events, environment, background or ideas. In this case, working together with another subject can help enhance and deepen understanding.

The Holocaust is often a theme within texts studied in English. The import, seriousness and complexity of such a theme means that it is vitally important that it is taught with accuracy and sensitivity. A sound understanding of the Holocaust is central to any study of any text that deals with this theme and planning with the support of history colleagues is recommended.

One of the most commonly studied books by younger secondary school pupils is *The Boy in the Striped Pyjamas*. Set during World War II, it is a story of two boys who become friends on either side of the fence in a death camp. The Holocaust forms the total context for this story. A study by the University College London Centre for Holocaust Education, drawing on contributions from nearly 10,000 secondary school pupils, found that this book is 'by a large margin, the most read book and the most watched film (viewed by 84.4% of those pupils who said they had seen a film about the Holocaust)' (Foster et al., 2016, p.2), indicating that the book and film are firmly part of current popular culture.

However, there has been criticism of the historical accuracy of the story (Schickel, 2008; Gray, 2016; Randall, 2019; Holocaust Educational Trust, n.d.). Particular objections relate to the naivety of the main character, Bruno, who as

> the son of a senior SS officer [...] would have been, by law, a member of the Hitler Youth. He would have attended a German school where pupils regularly swore oaths to Hitler and where antisemitic propaganda infiltrated every part of the curriculum.
>
> (Randall, 2019)

Furthermore, Shmuel, the Jewish boy Bruno meets in the camp, would very likely 'have been sent straight to the gas chambers on arrival, just like the majority of children who arrived there, as the Nazis didn't consider them useful as forced labour' (ibid.).

As an English teacher, it is vital that you develop an informed understanding of the context of a story dealing with such important historical facts and that you consider the perspective on the topic that you create within the classroom. This might apply, for example, to literature that raises issues of bullying, racism, refugees, poverty and so on. Engaging with the history of this subject is essential and linking with history colleagues is likely to be very helpful. The Holocaust Educational Trust (HET) recommend a cross-curricular approach. Adapting the principles of the International Holocaust Remembrance Alliance (IHRA), they provide a very helpful set of principles for approaching teaching about the Holocaust, some of which can be seen in Table 18.2. (See Key Resources for further information.)

One of the principles is to avoid viewing Jewish people purely as victims and, rather, to provide pupils with a perspective of Jewish life before the Holocaust, so that they can see and relate to the everyday lives of ordinary Jewish people. Photographs can be a helpful way of doing this and they provide a valuable link between past and present. For example, Figure 18.1 shows a photograph of a little girl in 1937. Pupils can use skills of deduction and inference to describe and explain what they can see in the photography, for example, the age of the girl, how she is feeling, where she is going and so on. The little girl is called Ursula, and she is carrying a *Schultüte*, or cone full of sweets, which is traditionally given to children on their first day at school in Germany. Ursula is Jewish and is following the usual pattern of life as followed by other German families. The photograph captures a special moment in her life, highlighting it was possible to be German and Jewish.

Exploring photographs should help pupils make links with the past and understand similarities in their lives. They can help fill in the gaps there might be in

Table 18.2 Principles for studying the Holocaust, adapted from Holocaust Educational Trust derived from the International Holocaust Remembrance Alliance (IHRA)

Create a positive, pupil-centred, cross-curricular approach informed by dialogue with colleagues and supported by collaboration between departments.	Avoid defining Jewish people solely by the Holocaust – teach about Jewish life in Europe before the war.
Avoid simple, reductive answers to complex questions and issues. Adopt an approach which is rooted in the historical events of the Holocaust.	Do not romanticise history. Teaching and learning about the Holocaust should not be redemptive but challenging.
Choose resources carefully, with sensitivity to pupils, victims and survivors. This means avoiding the use of horrific imagery which can upset and desensitise pupils, dehumanise victims, and portray those who suffered in a light that would be recognisable to the perpetrators.	Make activities meaningful (no word searches or dot-to-dot games!). Similarly, avoid role-play/empathy activities – we cannot imagine or expect pupils to imagine what it was like to be in the camps or on a transport.
Be precise with language. Define the term 'Holocaust', being specific and avoiding an all-encompassing definition. Avoid stereotypical descriptions, such as seeing all Germans as Nazis.	Try to use historically authentic sources alongside works of fiction. This could, for example, entail the comparison of a survivor testimony with a novel or poem which depicts similar experiences.
Focus on individual experiences to make understanding the enormity of the experience more personal.	When teaching works of fiction, ensure that pupils are aware of their relationship to the history, whether depicting real events (e.g. *When Hitler Stole Pink Rabbit* or *Maus*) or invented characters grounded in historical reality (e.g. *Once* or *If Not Now, When*?)

Figure 18.1 Black and white image of a young girl smiling. She is smartly dressed for school with a school bag and hat, and is carrying a cone full of sweets which is almost as big as she is

Source: United States Holocaust Memorial Museum, courtesy of Janine Klipstein Gimpelman Sokolov.

stories about the Holocaust with facts about real people's lives. The HET online resources include a wide range of photographs for pupils to explore (see Key Resources).

Activity 18.2: Exploring context in literature

Below is a list of commonly taught texts in English.

- *A Christmas Carol*
- *Animal Farm*
- *Frankenstein*
- *Noughts & Crosses*
- *Of Mice and Men*
- *The Handmaid's Tale*

1. Choose one text and sketch an outline for a cross-curricular collaboration, considering aspects such as subjects involved, the content, the type of collaboration, pedagogical approaches, skills developed and so on.
2. The teaching principles in Table 18.2 relate to teaching about the Holocaust. However, you will teach other texts that refer to sensitive issues, for example, refugees, bullying, racism, poverty. Choose one such theme and create a set of teaching principles which show sensitivity to the theme. Use the IHRA/HET principles as a starting point.

ENGLISH COUNTS

Links between English and the arts or humanities are often clear to see, but it is worthwhile exploring potential cross-curricular opportunities that appear less obvious.

Maths has its own language for expressing things and this can be very useful in English too. For example, graphs and charts can express data and ideas in an immediate and accessible way. Such representations are helpful in English for encouraging readers to actively read different types of text, and for helping writers find different ways of presenting ideas. Venn diagrams can be used to explore differences and links both within and between texts. For example, they can be used to support comparison of ideas between two or more poems, or the responses of characters in a novel or play. Different types of graphs can be used to show the stages of a plot, show a character's range of emotions or chart the atmosphere in a scene. Infographics use a mixture of formats (e.g. images, graphs, limited text) to present data in an easily accessible way. They help show connections and patterns. An infographic can be an imaginative way for pupils to present data, for example, from a class survey or research on a topic. Importantly, team up with maths colleagues to ensure that the terminology you adopt is the same as that used in maths, to reinforce the accurate use of terminology across the curriculum.

But maths can also be the stimulus for some fun with both words and numbers. Listen to Harry Baker's love poem (see Key Resources), and you will never see prime numbers in the same way again. After viewing Harry's TED talk, give pupils their own numbers to research and explore, or ask them to choose a number that is significant to them, with a view to writing their own homage to that number. Another engaging number-related investigation is to set your class the challenge of working out the riddle in Sylvia Plath's poem 'Metaphors' (see Key Resources) and you will see the exquisite structuring of a poem to the rhythm of the number nine, from the letters in the title, to the number of syllables and lines, to meaning of the riddle itself. Such activities use and celebrate the beauty of both English and maths.

Activity 18.3: English in other subjects

Back in 1921, a government-commissioned report (the *Newbolt Report*) was a formative report in establishing the position of English as a school subject. A key recommendation was that 'That every teacher is a teacher of English because every teacher is a teacher in English' (Newbolt, 1921, p.348). Newbolt was advocating what is often known as language or literacy across the curriculum. Explore your understanding of this, by completing these tasks:

1. Find out if your school has a policy for literacy/language across the curriculum.
2. Ask colleagues from other subjects about what sort of English knowledge and skills may be needed in their subjects. For example, do they have a particular focus on reading, writing, or speaking and listening?
3. Gather some examples of writing in different subjects. Analyse them for different forms and purposes of writing, as well as the writing skills being used. Are there areas of commonality between the subjects? Are the same skills being used? Perhaps this could be the basis for a useful research inquiry to support whole-school literacy.

THE BENEFITS OF COLLABORATION

This chapter has mainly focused on the benefits to pupils of cross-curricular working, by providing an enhanced and deeper engagement in learning within English lessons. However, there are considerable benefits to the teacher also. Stevens (2011, p.27) points out some positive characteristics of collaboration across subjects, including:

- shared schemes of work;
- sharing of, and shared making of, apt resources;
- regular meetings to share pedagogical ideas and practices;
- mutual observation of lessons and team teaching;
- involvement in wider contexts, for example, subject associations;
- involvement in extracurricular and social activities.

Cross-curricular discussions and the sharing of ideas about content and pedagogy have benefits for new and experienced teachers alike.

Activity 18.4: Developing a philosophy

Teaching standards, in all areas of the UK, stipulate the need to work collaboratively. Establish the appropriate teaching standard(s) within your own context and address this standard(s) by articulating your own philosophy of cross-curricular collaboration in approximately 50 words. Use the ideas and Key Resources from this chapter, and your own research in school, to help shape your philosophy. If you wish, support your philosophy with a bank of evidence gleaned from your reading and your experiences. Your philosophy might be used as evidence for meeting the standards, or as a stimulus for discussion with mentors/line managers on developing your approach to cross-curricular work.

SUMMARY AND KEY POINTS

- Cross-curricular study is about making constructive links between subjects.
- Working across the curriculum should focus on supporting and enhancing pupils' engagement with and learning within English.
- There is a range of terminology, and nuances of meaning, but the focus is collaboration with and sensitivity to other areas of the curriculum.
- Create positive links with colleagues and departments across the curriculum.
- Look for opportunities to exploit and reinforce the similarities and connections in knowledge, understanding and skills between English and other subjects.
- Work with colleagues from departments that offer obvious links, but also look at the potential for links where the connections may not be so obvious.

KEY RESOURCES

1. Savage, J. (2010) *Cross-Curricular Teaching and Learning in Secondary School*. London: Routledge. This is a good general text on the principles and strategies related to cross-curricular teaching.
2. Stevens, D. (2011) *Cross-Curricular Teaching and Learning in the Secondary School: English*. London: Routledge. This text considers the nature of English within a cross-curricular context, as well as a range of pedagogic approaches. It has ideas for collaborations across different areas of the curriculum.
3. Waterhouse, J. W. (1888) *The Lady of Shalott* [oil on canvas]. Tate. [www.tate.org.uk/art/artworks/waterhouse-the-lady-of-shalott-n01543] This iconic image of the Lady of Shalott can be used to support pupils' first encounters with the poem. There is also a short video that helps unravel how the painting (and other Waterhouse images) tell the story of the Lady: www.tate.org.uk/art/artists/john-william-waterhouse-583/curse-lady-shalott
4. The Holocaust Educational Trust provide a wealth of supportive and freely available resources. They include:
   a. Teaching the Holocaust in English: www.het.org.uk/images/downloads/Resources/Teaching_the_Holocaust_in_English.pdf
   b. General principles for teaching the Holocaust: www.het.org.uk/images/downloads/Educational_principles.pdf
   c. Photographs about Jewish life: www.het.org.uk/images/downloads/Primary/Pre-war_cards.pdf

5. Baker, H. (2014) 'A Love Poem for Lonely Prime Numbers'. Available from: (www.ted.com/talks/harry_baker_a_love_poem_for_lonely_prime_numbers#t-253003). Harry Baker is a performer poet and lover of maths. They combine in this entertaining TED talk.
6. British Library (no date) Sylvia Plath. Available from: www.bl.uk/people/sylvia-plath (accessed 9 May 2020). This site provides more information about the poet. The poem 'Metaphors' can be found at: https://shenandoahliterary.org/blog/2012/01/metaphors-by-sylvia-plath/

Chapter 19 Writing well-being: Using reflective diary-writing to support English teacher well-being

LUCY KELLY

INTRODUCTION

This chapter explores reflective diary-writing as a positive tool for individual teacher well-being. In an educational climate experiencing a recruitment and retention crisis (Worth, 2018; Foster, 2019), and a profession noted as one of the 'most stressful' (Holmes, 2019, p.20), diary-writing can help you as English teachers consider a situation from a variety of perspectives, can be cathartic and celebratory, and can act as a stimulus to other forms of writing to be taken into the classroom.

It is important to note from the outset that, whilst teacher well-being must be addressed at a government and a school level (Howard, 2020), this chapter focuses on individual teacher well-being. This is because, if teachers know what positive well-being looks like at an individual level (Holmes, 2019) – and we must remember that well-being is a 'dynamic process' (ibid., p.6) that is not only bespoke, but always changing – then they can use this knowledge to make collective, structural changes in school and beyond.

As a term, well-being has multiple definitions; however, here, I use the World Health Organisation's definition of positive well-being, which defines it as 'a state [...] in which the individual realizes [sic] his or her own abilities, can cope with the normal stresses of life, can work productively and fruitfully, and is able to make a contribution to his or her community' (2018, online). Like Holmes, this definition draws attention to the individual, and the potential power they have when it comes to their own well-being. But how does this link to reflective diary-writing? Well, if reflective writing 'can tell you what you think' (Bolton et al., 1999, p.43), then perhaps it is in the pages of a diary where teachers can 'realize [sic] [their] own abilities' (WHO, 2018, online) and what positive well-being means to them personally.

At the end of this chapter you should be able to:

- recall some practical ideas on how you might approach reflective diary-writing to support your own well-being;
- apply reflective diary-writing to writing in school;
- use some of the suggestions listed to prioritise reflective diary-writing into your already busy week.

DOI: 10.4324/9781003093060-20

WHY TEACHER WELL-BEING MATTERS

Currently, many teachers are not prioritising their own well-being. Alongside the existing retention and recruitment problem in teaching, we are also facing a teacher well-being crisis (Kelly, 2020) because 'the pace and depth' (Holmes, 2019, p.8) that a lot of teachers work at is unsustainable. The recent Teacher Wellbeing Index (2019) results support this viewpoint. Their findings reveal that workload is the main reason teachers consider leaving the profession. In addition, work-related stress levels have increased, which contributes towards a negative work/life balance where teachers are unable to switch off and relax and, consequently, are sleeping less (cited in Kelly, 2020, pp.19–20). Howard (2020) puts these statistics into context:

> Teaching encourages sleep deprivation, through the endless to-do lists that fight to deprive you of any sense of satisfaction, to late night parents' evenings followed by early mornings. Terms are an endurance test in themselves – particularly the more persistent ones in the run-up to formal examinations: we push a little harder, for a little longer, and can forget that, in doing so, we are sabotaging ourselves a little in the process.
>
> (p.50)

These are hard-hitting messages that need acknowledging because if, as Howard goes on to note, 'Teachers are the most important resource of the school' (2020, p.304), then surely we need to be looking after this resource so that it flourishes?

HOW REFLECTIVE DIARY-WRITING CAN HELP TEACHER WELL-BEING

One way teachers can consider whether or not they are flourishing is through reflective diary-writing, which can be a place to find clarity in our 'extraordinarily muddled and chaotic' lives (Bolton et al., 1999, p.20). This idea was powerfully demonstrated in the pilot phase of the 'Reimagining the Diary' (2019) research project, which explores reflective diary-writing as a positive tool for teacher well-being. Working with a group of 15 teachers, who were tasked with keeping a diary for a week during term-time (plain notebook, sound jotter, kindness journal), we found that a diary gives teachers a space for catharsis, celebration and gaining perspective on an event or situation. Over 93% of participants perceived an improvement in their well-being when keeping a diary and, although time was the biggest factor to consider, 60% of participants wanted to continue their diary-writing practice, and 86.7% would advise other teachers to take it up (Kelly, 2020).

These high results could be a response to the statistics shared from the Teacher Wellbeing Index: now, more than ever, teachers need a space for reflection. Teaching is a 'full throttle' (Howard, 2020, p.44) profession without parameters; it can fill every aspect of your life, which makes it very difficult to stop. This is made harder by the fact that we are living in a world of constant connection. So, even if we do 'stop', we are still accessible and contactable. Whilst this offers many benefits (including opportunities for reflective diary-writing – see Kelly (2019) for a further discussion on this), it does pose its challenges, especially when it comes to achieving work/life balance, managing stress and switching off from the day. Indeed, having worked at such speed and intensity, we are then 'too anxious, wired and overloaded to know how to power down' (Hosbawm, 2020, pp.97–8); and, because we cannot switch-off, we live in a state of continual stress, awaiting the next ping of an email notification to pull us back into work mode. It is a vicious cycle: constant connection with others means no time for connection with yourself. Yet, if knowing yourself at a deeper level is the key to improving individual well-being, then we must break this cycle and turn inwards. As demonstrated through our project, reflective diary-writing can help teachers do this; it is a space to get to know your multiple selves and what those selves need to flourish, both personally and professionally. Investing in this relationship is paramount because, as Holmes (2019) notes:

> The more we come to understand how we work, how we respond to the situations life presents us with, and how we seek solutions for any problematic issues we face, the more likely we are to occupy the optimum stress zone. This could ultimately help us to move towards a greater sense of wellbeing than we are currently experiencing.
>
> (p.13)

APPROACHING REFLECTIVE DIARY-WRITING

Reflective diary-writing is a familiar concept: many of us have written diaries and many of us have taught diaries – think of Anne Frank, Samuel Pepys and Virginia Woolf, to name but a few. However, this familiarity with the diary as a form can be a poisoned chalice because, whilst we see the many benefits reflective diary-writing has to offer, we have also seen what a 'good' diary looks like, which makes it difficult to approach diary-writing authentically (Kelly et al., 2020, pp.4–5). Therefore, although Bolton et al. suggest that, when writing a diary, 'there will never be an imagined reader leaning over your shoulder criticising your style of grammar, or tut-tutting over the contents, or querying all the inconsistencies' (1999, p.32), I would argue otherwise. As English teachers, the iconic diarists are the 'reader[s] leaning over [our] shoulders', which makes us nervous to begin because we feel our diaries will never be as 'good' as theirs.

Yet, if we want to reap the rewards of reflective diary-writing – including 'gain[ing] clarity' and 'record[ing] precious moments' (RtD Survey, 2019) – then we must break away from our own expectations and assumptions around reflective diary-writing, questioning, instead, the real purpose of the writing and its intended audience (Kelly et al., 2020). Indeed, if the audience is solely the individual writing it, and they are writing it with the intention of getting to know themselves better in order to improve their own well-being, then surely the 'rules' around diary-writing can be discarded?

Like well-being, reflective diary-writing is bespoke: there is no 'one size fits all' approach because there is no 'one size fits all' human. So, whilst the blank page can offer some individuals the freedom to be as creative as they like, for others it is too much – they seek the comfort of a structured kindness journal, or recording their thoughts and feelings verbally in an audio jotter or, perhaps, using drawings/images to articulate their emotions and experiences. Therefore, this chapter does not include a 'success criteria' or 'WAGOLL' (What A Good One Looks Like) for the 'perfect' diary – although there are many books available with this information, if helpful. Instead, what follows is a suggestion on how you might approach your reflective diary-writing so that you get the most from it.

One way to do this is to let your 'Inner Poet' take the lead. This idea was first advanced by Mimi Thebo, Carnegie-nominated children's author, and was introduced in the 'Reimagining the Diary' project as a way for individuals to reclaim reflective diary-writing. Here, Thebo drew on ideas shared in American writer Dorothea Brande's seminal book *Becoming a Writer* (1934). Although Brande's book was written nearly a century ago and focuses on writing fiction, her concepts of the 'critic' and the 'artist' (both in Brande, 1934, p.39) – which Thebo terms the 'Inner Poet' and 'Inner Editor' – are applicable to reflective diary-writing (whether online or offline). Furthermore, these concepts can be taken into the classroom.

Brande defines the 'critic' as 'intellectually critical, detached, tolerant [and] provid[ing] suitable conditions for the artist-self', whilst the 'artist' is 'sensitive, enthusiastic, and partisan' (both Brande, 1934, p.49). For Brande, each writing personality has a part to play in the writing process; however, she emphasises that their distinct functions mean they should appear at different stages:

> When the actual writing is to be done, your elder self [or critic] must stand aside, only murmuring a suggestion now and again on such matters as your tendency to use repetitions, or to suggest that you are being too verbose, or that the dialogue is getting out of hand. Later you will call on it to consider the completed draft, or section, and with its help you will alter the manuscript to get the best possible effects. But at the time of writing, nothing is more confusing than to have the alert, critical, overscrupulous rational faculty at the forefront of your mind. The tormenting doubts of one's ability, the self-conscious muteness that drops like a pall over the best story ideas, come from consulting the judge in oneself at the moment when it is the storyteller's [artist's] turn to be in the ascendant. It is not easy at first to inhibit the running verdicts on every sentence, almost every word, that is written, but once the flow of the story has well set in, the critical faculty will be content to wait its turn.
>
> (1934, p.56)

If we think about Brande's words in relation to reflective diary-writing, then she is suggesting that the 'artist' should take centre stage first, with the 'critic' waiting in the wings. Although this approach to reflective diary-writing might feel strange to begin with, it does help us write from a place of authenticity – one that is not constrained by the famous diaries on our bookshelves or the 'SPaG Police'. Thus, rather than writing with our imposter syndrome and perfectionism at the forefront, we write from the heart, which connects us to our thoughts, feelings and emotions, and enables us to reflect on our well-being honestly. Yet, it is important to note 'that these two halves of the writing personality are [not] at war with each other' (Brande, 1934, p. 57). Rather,

> When each has found its place, when each is performing the functions which are proper to it, they play endlessly back and forth into each other's hands, strengthening, inciting, relieving each other in such a way that the resulting personality, the integral character, is made more balanced, mellow, energetic and profound.
>
> (Brande, 1934, pp.57–8)

As shown above, once the 'artist' has performed, it is then the 'critic's' turn to be in the spotlight. In terms of reflective diary-writing, the 'critic's' job is to help the writer be 'detached', which is important if we are to help diarists – in this case teachers – use reflective diary-writing as a space to consider their well-being from a critical perspective, questioning 'how we respond to the situations life presents us with, and how we seek solutions for any problematic issues we face' (Holmes, 2019, p.13). The 'critic' encourages us to sort through what the 'artist' has shared on the page or screen, which allows us to see ourselves from different angles. Without the 'critic' and the level of detachment they bring to our writing, we may not make the personal and professional changes needed to leave us feeling empowered.

Now you have been introduced to these writing personalities, Activity 19.1 invites you to visualise them and then write with your 'artist' and 'critic' in mind.

Activity 19.1

- At the launch of our project, Thebo asked us the following questions: what might your 'artist' and 'critic' wear? How might they talk? How might they walk? Note down some ideas and, if you can, draw a picture of them – you could even create a storyboard for each of your writing personalities.
- Once you have done this, approach an event from your day through the eyes of your 'artist' and write freely about it – remember that the 'critic' is waiting in the wings and will have their turn shortly! Write for as long as you need to, without editing your writing along the way. This is an opportunity for you to let the pen or keyboard flow unencumbered.
- Then, when you feel you have written all you can, let the 'critic' have their turn. Go back over your writing and make changes where necessary. These changes might be grammatical, or they might be content-driven – for example, fleshing out a particular description.
- Once the 'critic' has finished, reread it, and then step back and reflect on the process, as well as the product itself. How do you feel about the event now? Has anything new come to light?

As shown in Activity 19.1, approaching reflective diary-writing in this way helps you as an English teacher write freely, without success criteria, exemplar models and prior assumptions around reflective diary-writing – that is, the 'critic' – impeding your progress. The 'critic' does have a place in the writing process, but your 'artist' must take the lead so that you can write your own narrative as authentically as possible. If we want to make positive changes to our individual well-being, then we need to act, but first, we need to know what that action looks like and why it is important to us personally. Reflective diary-writing is certainly one place to have this conversation; it is a place for you to 'writ[e] yourself out' (Brande, 1934, p.73) and to see yourself, and your life, objectively. Once 'you' are on the page or screen, it is much easier to identify those actions.

APPLICATION TO THE CLASSROOM

Using your diary as a space to reflect on 'you' means that you probably reflect on your working life as well as your non-working life. Indeed, the diary offers the same opportunities – catharsis, celebration and perspective – to our professional selves: it is a space to release the 'School issues and worries that never seem to go away' (RtD Survey, 2019). This process gives us the mental space and energy to enjoy – and record – the moments of success we have felt during our working day; moments that are sometimes cast aside because we fixate on the black dot on the white page. A diary welcomes both, which has a positive impact on our personal and professional well-being. Moreover, it benefits our pupils because happy teachers lead to happy pupils (Howard, 2020).

Additionally, you can apply your newly discovered reflective-writing self to your classroom practice by sharing your own experiences of writing with your classes. Sometimes, pupils think English teachers find writing easy. We are quick to show our pupils the product – that is, the 'perfect' paragraph from a literary essay – but do we show them the process? Do they see the various drafts our writing has been through to get to that stage? The difficulties you have faced with your own reflective writing – such as the fear of the blank page or being judged – might help you empathise with your pupils and the struggles they face when approaching their own writing. Communicating these events with your classes could result in co-creating a bank of strategies to help you all put pen to paper.

Pupils could also think about their own 'artist' and 'critic'. You might begin this activity with a class discussion on the characteristics of each writing personality, drawing on images from popular culture and then using these to create a collage for each one. This discussion could act as a springboard into pupils drawing and describing their own, individual 'artist' and 'critic' – perhaps incorporating the storyboarding idea from earlier. Reference to these writing personalities might be made when launching future writing tasks. In Chapter 6 you were introduced to the idea of 'free-writing' as a way for pupils to generate ideas before drafting and revising their work with a more critical eye so, with this in mind, pupils could be encouraged to bring their 'artist' to the writing first and then go back to the 'critic'.

PRIORITISING REFLECTIVE DIARY-WRITING

As noted above, approaching reflective diary-writing in this way leads you towards a better understanding of yourself and the changes you can make in your daily life (both personally and professionally) to improve your own well-being. Yet, as we will explore in Activity 19.2, to get the most from your diary, you need to make it a priority.

In fact, you should treat writing in your diary as a non-negotiable date with a VIP because, otherwise, the writing will not happen. Brande advises 'that at the moment, *on the dot of the moment*, you are to be writing, and that you teach yourself that no excuse of any nature will be offered when the moment comes' (1934, p.78, italics in original text). The participants in our project identified time as the biggest factor when it came to writing in their diaries (RtD Survey, 2019); however, when they did find or make the time for it, they experienced the many benefits that reflective diary-writing had to offer them. Interestingly, those who missed a day of diary-writing felt 'bereft' and had 'a lot more thoughts charging around in [their] head[s]' (ibid.).

Activity 19.2

I now invite you to timetable your diary into your week. Will you write daily? Or weekly? This may seem very regimented for what should be a creative activity; however, in a time-pressured profession, it is very important for teachers to prioritise the activities and tasks they give their attention to (Holmes, 2019). Giving your diary time – and marking it in your calendar – makes it visible and important. As teachers we are at the mercy of endless 'to-do' lists, but where does our self-care and individual well-being feature on those lists? In my experience, it is relegated to the bottom if, indeed, it appears at all. Yet, to be the best versions of ourselves, we need to prioritise activities that help us recharge and run on full batteries (Kell, 2018). Therefore, block out time on your calendar for your diary and make it something you look forward to – perhaps invest in a new notebook and pen to help you get started, for example.

And now that you have made your diary a VIP in your life, you can begin to think about what those 'dates' might look like. In addition to what we have already discussed, part of your reflective diary-writing time might be celebrating all of the wonderful things you – and others – have done, or it might be spent looking backwards, considering how to resolve the patterns you have noticed in certain aspects of your life (Howard, 2020). Alternatively, you could use this time to look to the future. Using the page of a diary to meet your future self can be extremely powerful because it helps you identify the person you want to become and the steps you need to take in order to get there.

SUMMARY AND KEY POINTS

- This chapter has aimed to offer you, as English teachers, some practical examples of how you might use reflective diary-writing as a positive tool for your own well-being, as well as its application to the classroom.
- In a profession that 'has no endpoint' (Howard, 2020, p.93), and one that attracts perfectionists, it is easy to keep going; however, this leads to us neglecting our own well-being, which has repercussions inside and outside the classroom.
- As shown in this chapter, diaries can be a space to press pause and reaffirm the self (and the various facets that self takes). Yet, in order to get the most out of our diary-writing, we need to let go of what a 'good' diary looks like and, instead, use our inner 'artist' and 'critic' to write our own, bespoke version that suits us and our individual well-being needs.

KEY RESOURCES

1. Bolton, G., Field, V. and Thompson, K. (1999) *The Therapeutic Potential of Creative Writing: Writing Myself*. London: Jessica Kingsley Publishers. This text explores the therapeutic benefits of creative writing, offering suggestions for individuals to try, as well as tips to get started.
2. Brande, D. (1934) *Becoming a Writer*. New York: Harcourt, Brace & Company. This book focuses on the skills, habits and practices needed to become a successful writer.
3. Holmes, E. (2019) *A Practical Guide to Teacher Wellbeing*. London: SAGE. This practical book contains tips and strategies to help teachers prioritise their own well-being and avoid burnout.
4. Howard, K. (2020) *Stop Talking about Wellbeing: A Pragmatic Approach to Teacher Workload*. Woodbridge: John Catt Educational Limited. This book takes a practical approach to teacher well-being, exploring the factors and systems that affect teacher well-being within school, and how teachers and senior leadership teams can address them.
5. Kelly, L., Huxford, G. and Kelly, C. (2020) 'In our daily struggles': Diaries as a tool for teacher well-being. *Life Writing*. pp.1–16. (published online). https://doi.org/10.1080/14484528.2020.1763232. This article introduces the 'Reimagining the Diary' (2018–19) project to consider the history of reflective writing within the

teaching profession and to highlight the current problems facing teachers and educationalists looking to use self-reflection as a tool for improving well-being.

6. Kelly, L. (2020) Reclaiming teacher wellbeing through reflective diary writing. *IMPACT*, 9. Available at: https://impact.chartered.college/article/reclaiming-teacher-wellbeing-reflective-diary-writing/ [Accessed 10 July 2020]. This article explores the findings from the first phase of the 'Reimagining the Diary' (2018–19) project, alongside some of the latest Teacher Wellbeing Index (2019) results, in order to show that diary-writing could be a small but important step in the journey of teacher well-being.

References

Albright, L. and Ariail, M. (2005) Tapping the potential of teacher read-alouds in middle schools. *Journal of Adolescent & Adult Literacy*. 48 (7). pp.582–91.

Alexander, R. (2008a) *Towards Dialogic Teaching: Rethinking Classroom Talk*. 5th Ed. Cambridge: Dialogos.

Alexander, R. (2008b) *Essays on Pedagogy*. London: Routledge.

Alexander, R. (2012) Improving oracy and classroom talk in English schools: Achievements and challenges, available at: http://robin alexander.org.uk/wp-content/uploads/2019/12/DfE-oracy-120220-Alexander-FINAL0.pdf (accessed 18 March 2021).

Alexander, R. (2018) Developing dialogic teaching: Genesis, process, trial. *Research Papers in Education*. 33 (5). pp.561–98.

Alexander, R. J. (2003) Talk in teaching and learning: International perspectives. In QCA. *New Perspectives on Spoken English in the Classroom. Discussion Papers.* London: Qualifications and Curriculum Authority (QCA), pp.27–38.

Alton Towers. 'Launching Galactica', available at: www.altontowers.com/about-alton-towers/blog/launching-galactica/ (accessed 1 July 2020).

Anderson, G. (2013) Exploring *The Island*: Mapping the shifting sands in the landscape of English classroom culture and pedagogy. *Changing English*. 20 (2). pp.113–23.

Andrews, R., Torgerson, C., Beverton, S., Freeman, A., Locke, T., Low, G., Robinson, A. and Zhu, D. (2006) The effect of grammar teaching on writing development. *British Educational Research Journal*. 32 (1). pp.39–55.

Applebee, A.N. (1996) *Curriculum as Conversation: Transforming Traditions of Teaching and Learning*. Chicago and London: University of Chicago Press.

Applebee, A.N., Langer, J.A., Nystrand, M. and Gamoran, A. (2003) Discussion-based approaches to developing understanding: classroom instruction and student performance in middle and high school English. *American Educational Research Journal*. 40 (3). pp.685–730.

Armitage, A. (2016) An introduction to Tales from Ovid. British Library, available at: www.bl.uk/20th-century-literature/articles/an-introduction-to-tales-from-ovid (accessed 18 March 2021).

Armitage, S. (2014) *The Last Days of Troy*. London: Faber.

Arnold, M. (1869) *Culture and Anarchy* [ebook]. Oxford: Oxford University Press.

Assessment and Qualifications Alliance (AQA) (2018a) *GCSE English Literature, Paper 1 Shakespeare and the 19th-century novel: Report on the examination.*

Manchester: AQA, available at: https://filestore.aqa.org.uk/sample-papers-and-mark-schemes/2018/june/AQA-87021-WRE-JUN18.PDF (accessed 19 June 2020).

Assessment and Qualifications Alliance (AQA) (2018b) *GCSE English Language Specification* (8700), available at: https://filestore.aqa.org.uk/resources/english/specifications/AQA-8700-SP-2015.PDF (accessed 29 June 2020).

Atherton, C., Green, A. and Snapper, G. (2013) *Teaching English Literature 16–19*. Abingdon, Oxon: Routledge.

Atwood, M. (2006) *The Penelopiad*. Edinburgh: Canongate Books.

Bahktin, M.M. (1981) *The Dialogic Imagination*. Austin: University of Texas Press.

Barnes, D. (2008) Exploratory Talk for Learning. In Mercer, N. & Hodgkinson, S. (eds.). *Exploring Talk in School*. London: SAGE, pp. 1–15.

Barnes, J. (2015) *Cross-Curricular Learning 3–14*. London: SAGE.

Barnes, J. (2018) *Applying Cross-Curricular Approaches Creatively*. Abingdon: Routledge.

Barron, F., Montuori, A. and Barron, A. (1997) *Creators on Creating: Awakening and Cultivating the Imaginative Mind*. New York: Tarcher/Penguin.

Barry, P. (2004) Putting contexts in their place. *emagazine* issue 23, English & Media Centre, available at: www.englishandmedia.co.uk/e-magazine/ (accessed 18 March 2021).

Barry, P. (2012) *Literature in Contexts*. Manchester and New York: Manchester University Press.

BBC News (2003) Irresponsible Hodge under fire, 14 January, available at: news.bbc.co.uk/1/hi/education/2655127.stm (accessed 5 August 2020).

Beard, M. (2008) *In Our Time*. www.bbc.co.uk/programmes/b0093z1k

Beard, R. (2000) *Developing Writing 3–13*. Abingdon: Hodder & Stoughton.

Benyahia, S. and Mortimer, C. (2013) *Doing Film Studies*. Abingdon: Routledge.

Bereiter, C. (1980) Development in Writing. In Gregg, L.W. & Steinberg, E.R. (eds.). *Cognitive Processes in Writing*. Hillsdale, NJ: Lawrence Erlbaum Associates, pp.73–96.

Bereiter, C. and Scardamalia, M. (1982) From Conversation to Composition: The Role of Instruction in a Developmental Process. In Glaser, R. (ed.). *Advances in Instructional Psychology*, Vol. 2. Hillsdale, NJ: Lawrence Erlbaum Associates, pp.1–64.

Berninger, V. and Swanson, H.L. (1994) Modifying Hayes and Flower's model of skilled writing to explain beginning and developing writing. In Butterfield, E. (ed.). *Children's Writing: Toward a Process Theory of the Development of Skilled Writing*. Greenwich, CT: JAI Press, pp.57–81.

Berninger, V.W., Fuller, F. and Whittaker, D. (1996) A process model of writing development across the life span. *Educational Psychology Review*. 8 (3). pp.193–218.

Beyer, C. (2013) The stuff of legend, or unpacking cultural baggage? Introducing first year English literature and humanities students to foundational literary texts. *Changing English: Studies in Culture and Education* 20 (4). pp.395–403.

Blake, J. and Shortis, T. (2010) *Who's prepared to teach school English?* Committee for Linguistics in Education, available at: https://clie.org.uk/wp-content/uploads/2015/12/pgce-report-2010.pdf (accessed 1 July 2020).

Bleiman, B. (2019) *What do we mean by cultural capital?* EMC blog, 13 January, available at: www.englishandmedia.co.uk/blog/whose-cultural-capital (accessed 20 June 2020).

Bleiman, B. (2020) *What Matters in English Teaching: Collected Blogs and Other Writing*. London: English & Media Centre.

Bloome, D. (1986) Building literacy and the classroom community theory into practice. *Building Literacy* 25 (2). pp.71–6.

Board of Education (BoE). (1905/1912) *Suggestions for the Consideration of Teachers and Others Concerned in the Work of Public Elementary Schools.* London: Board of Education.

Bolton, G., Field, V. and Thompson, K. (1999) *The Therapeutic Potential of Creative Writing: Writing Myself.* London: Jessica Kingsley Publishers.

Bomford, K. (2018) What are (English) lessons for? *Changing English.* 26 (1). pp.3–15.

Bosman, A. (2010) Shakespeare and Globalization. In De Grazia, M. & Wells, S. (eds.). *The New Cambridge Companion to Shakespeare.* Cambridge: Cambridge University Press, pp.285–302.

Bourdieu, P. (1984) *Distinction: A Social Critique of the Judgement of Taste,* trans. Nice, R. Cambridge, MA: Harvard University Press.

Bourdieu, P. and Passeron, J. (1977) *Reproduction in Education, Society and Culture.* London: SAGE.

Braddock, R. Lloyd-Jones and Schoer, L. (1963) *Research in Written Composition.* Urbana, IL: National Council of Teachers of English.

Brand, M., & Brand, G. (2006). *Practical fluency: Classroom perspectives, grades K-6.* Portland, Maine: Stenhouse Publishers.

Brande, D. (1934) *Becoming a Writer.* New York: Harcourt, Brace & Company.

British Council (2016) *All the World's.* London: British Council.

The British Library (2020) *Learning.* [online] Available at: www.bl.uk/learning (accessed 11 March 2020).

Britton, J. (1970) *Language and Learning.* New York: Penguin Books.

Britton, J. (1982) *Prospect and Retrospect: Selected Essays of James Britton,* edited by Gordon M. Pradl. Montclair, NJ: Boynton/Cook; London: Heinemann, available online at: https://sites.google.com/a/nyu.edu/gordonpradl/resources (accessed 18 March 2021).

Brown, P.C., Roediger III, H.L. and McDaniel, M.A. (2014) *Make It Stick.* Cambridge, MA: Harvard University Press.

Buckingham, D. (2003) *Media Education.* London: Polity Press.

Buckingham, D. (2019) *The Media Education Manifesto.* Cambridge: Polity Press.

Bullock, A. (1975) *A Language for Life: Report of the Committee of Enquiry appointed by the Secretary of State for Education and Science under the Chairmanship of Sir Alan Bullock F.B.A.* London: HMSO.

Bunyan, P. and Moore, R. (2005) *NATE Drama Packs Introductory Pack: Drama within English 11–16.* London: National Association for the Teaching of English

Burn, A. (2011) From Beowulf to Batman: Connecting English and media. In Davison, J., Daly, C. & Moss, J. (eds.). *Debates in English Teaching.* Abingdon: Routledge, pp.117–30.

Burn, A. (2013) Six arguments for the media arts. *Teaching English.* 2. pp.55–60.

Burn, A. (2018) Reflections on the Cinema Hypothesis: A response to Alain Bergala. *Film Education Journal.* 1 (1). pp.51–63.

Burn, A. and Connolly, S. (2020) Unable to Go It Alone: Re-stating the Case for a Strengthened English/Media Relationship. In Davison J. & Daly C. (eds.). *Debates in English Teaching.* 2nd Ed. Abingdon: Routledge, chapter 3.

Burns, R. (2018) Applying the 'powerful knowledge' principle to curriculum development in disadvantaged contexts. *Impact,* available online at: https://impact.chartered.college/article/applying-powerful-knowledge-principle-curriculum-development-disadvantaged-contexts/ (accessed 18 March 2021).

Capel, S., Leask, M. and Younie, S. (eds.) (2019) *Learning to Teach in the Secondary School: A Companion to School Experience.* Abingdon: Routledge.

Carter, R. and Goddard, A. (2016) *How to Analyse Texts: A Toolkit for Students of English.* London: Routledge.

Carter, R. and McCarthy, M. (2006) *Cambridge Grammar of English: A Comprehensive Guide. Spoken and Written English Grammar and Usage*. Cambridge: Cambridge University Press.

Centre for Literacy in Primary Education (CLPE) (2018) *Reflecting Realities Report Year 2: Survey of Ethnic Representation within UK Children's Literature 2018*, available at: https://clpe.org.uk/RR (accessed 1 January 2021).

Chanquoy, L. (2001) How to make it easier for children to revise their writing: A study of text revision from 3rd to 5th grades. *British Journal of Educational Psychology*. 71. pp.15–41.

Chenoweth, N.A. and Hayes, J.R. (2001) Fluency in writing: Generating text in L1 and L2. *Written Communication*. 18, pp.80–98.

Clark, C. and Teravainen-Goff, A. (2018) *Mental Wellbeing, Reading and Writing: How Children and Young People's Mental Wellbeing Is Related to Their Reading and Writing Experiences*. London: National Literacy Trust.

Clayton, D., Goddard, A., Kemp, B. and Titjen, F. (2015) *AQA English Language: A Level and AS*. Oxford: OUP.

Cliff Hodges, G. (2010) Rivers of reading: Using critical incident collages to learn about adolescent readers and their readership. *English in Education*. 44 (3). pp.181–200.

Cliff Hodges, G. (2011) Textual drama: The value of reading aloud. *EnglishDramaMedia*. Feb 2011.

Cliff-Hodges, G. (2016) *Researching and Teaching Reading: Developing Pedagogy through Critical Inquiry*. Abingdon: Routledge.

Coles, J. (2013) 'Every child's birthright'? Democratic entitlement and the role of canonical literature in the English National Curriculum. *Curriculum Journal* 24 (1). pp. 50–66.

Compton, D., Miller, A.C., Elleman, A.M. and Steacy, L.M. (2014) Have we forsaken reading theory in the name of 'quick fix' interventions for children with reading disability? *Scientific Studies of Reading* 18 (1). pp.55–73.

Council for Curriculum, Examinations and Assessment (CCEA) (2007) *Northern Ireland Curriculum*, available at: https://ccea.org.uk/ (accessed 18 March 2021).

Council for the Curriculum, Examinations and Assessment (CCEA) (2017). GCSE English Language 2017 https://ccea.org.uk/key-stage-4/gcse/subjects/gcse-english-language-2017 (accessed 30 September 2020).

Cox, B. (1989a) *English for Ages 5 to 16: Proposals of the Secretary of State for Education and Science and the Secretary of State for Wales*. London: Department of Education and Science and the Welsh Office.

Cox, B. (1989b) *Appendix 6: Approaches to the Class Novel in English for Ages 5–16*, available at: www.educationengland.org.uk/documents/cox1989/cox89.html (accessed 18 March 2021).

Craft, A. (2003) Creative thinking in the early years of education. *Early Years: An International Journal of Research and Development*. 23 (2). pp.143–54.

Cremin, T. (2009a) *Teachers as Readers: Building Communities of Readers*. Milton Keynes: Open University.

Cremin, T. (2009b) *Teaching English Creatively*. London: Routledge.

Cremin T. (2019) Reading communities: why, what and how? *NATE Primary Matters*, available at: https://researchrichpedagogies.org/_downloads/Reading_Communities_TCremin_2019.pdf (accessed 18 March 2021)

Cremin, T. (2020). Reading for pleasure: Challenges and opportunities. In Davison, J. & Daly, C. (eds.). *Debates in English Teaching*. London: Routledge. pp.92–102.

Cremin, T. and Myhill, D. (2012) *Writing Voices: Creating Communities of Writers*. Abingdon: Routledge.

Cremin, T., Mottram, M., Powell, S., Collins, R. and Safford, K. (2014) *Building Communities of Engaged Readers: Reading for Pleasure*. London: Routledge.

Cummins, J. (1991) Language development and academic learning. In Malave, L. & Duquette, G. (eds.). *Language, Culture and Cognition*. Clevedon: Multilingual Matters, pp.161–75.

Cunningham, A.E. (2005) Vocabulary growth through independent reading and reading aloud to children. In Hiebert, E.H. & Kamil, M.L. (eds.). *Teaching and Learning Vocabulary: Bringing Research to Practice*. Mahwah, NJ: Lawrence Erlbaum Associates, pp.45–68.

Cunningham, A. and Stanovich, K. (1998) What reading does for the mind. *American Educator*. 22. pp.8–17.

Cunningham, A. and Stanovich, K. (2003) Reading can make you smarter. *Principal*. 83 (2). pp.34–9.

Curran, J. (2013) Mickey Mouse Squeaks Back: Defending Media Studies. Keynote address to the MeCCSA conference, Derry 2013, available at: www.meccsa.org.uk/news/mickey-mouse-squeaks-back-defending-media-studies/ (accessed 5 August 2020).

Curriculum for Wales (CfW) (2016) *Programme of Study for English, Key Stages 2–4*, available at: https://hwb.gov.wales/curriculum-for-wales-2008/key-stages-2-to-4/english-programme-of-study-key-stages-2-4 (accessed 18 March 2021).

Cushing, I. (2018) 'Suddenly, I am part of the poem': Texts as worlds, reader-response and grammar in teaching poetry. *English in Education*. 52 (1). pp.7–19.

Czerniewska, P. (1992) *Learning about Writing*. Oxford: Blackwell.

Dahl, R. (1979) *Tales of the Unexpected*. London: Penguin.

Datchuk, S.M. (2017) A direct instruction and precision teaching intervention to improve sentence construction of middle school students with writing difficulties. *Journal of Special Education*. 51. pp.62–71.

Davison, J. and Daly, C. (2014) *Learning to Teach English in the Secondary School*. Abingdon: Routledge.

Dawes, L. (2001) Interthinking – the power of productive discourse. In Goodwin, P. (ed.). *The Articulate Classroom: Talking and Learning in the Primary School*. London: David Fulton, pp.125–32.

De Boinod, A.J. (2005) *The Meaning of Tingo*. London: Penguin.

Dean, G. (2003) *Teaching Reading in Secondary Schools*. 2nd Ed. London: David Fulton.

Dellerman, P., Coirier, P. and Marchand, E. (1996) Planning and expertise in argumentative composition. In Rijlaarsdam, G., van den Bergh, H. & Couzijn, M. (eds.). *Theories, Models and Methodology in Writing Research*. Amsterdam: Amsterdam University Press, pp.182–95.

Department for Children, Schools and Families (DCFS)/Qualifications and Curriculum Authority (QCA) (2007) *The National Curriculum: Statutory Requirements for Key Stages 3 and 4*. London: DCSF/QCA.

Department for Digital, Culture, Media and Sport (DCMS) (2016) *The Culture White Paper*. London: HMSO.

Department for Education (DfE) (2011) *Teachers' Standards*, available at: www.gov.uk/government/publications/teachers-standards (accessed 29 June 2020).

Department for Education (DfE) (2013a) *English Programmes of Study: Key Stages 1 and 2 National Curriculum in England*, available at: https://assets.publishing.service.gov.uk/government/uploads/system/uploads/attachment_data/file/335186/PRIMARY_national_curriculum_-_English_220714.pdf (accessed 18 March 2021).

Department for Education (DfE) (2013b) *English language GCSE Subject Content and Assessment Objectives*, available at: https://assets.publishing.service.gov.uk/government/uploads/system/uploads/attachment_data/file/254497/GCSE_English_language.pdf (accessed 18 March 2021).

Department for Education (DfE) (2013c) *History Programmes of Study: Key Stages 1 and 2 National Curriculum in England*, available at www.gov.uk/government/publications/national-curriculum-in-england-history-programmes-of-study (accessed 28 March 2021).

Department for Education (DfE) (2013d) *English Programmes of Study: Key Stage 3 National Curriculum in England*, available at: https://assets.publishing.service.gov.uk/government/uploads/system/uploads/attachment_data/file/244215/SECONDARY_national_curriculum_-_English2.pdf, (accessed 20 March 2021).

Department for Education (DfE) (2013e) *The National Curriculum in England: Key stages 1 and 2 framework document*. London: Department for Education, available at: https://assets.publishing.service.gov.uk/government/uploads/system/uploads/attachment_data/file/425601/PRIMARY_national_curriculum.pdf (accessed 1 March 2020).

Department for Education (DfE) (2014a) *The National Curriculum in England Framework Document*, available at: https://assets.publishing.service.gov.uk/government/uploads/system/uploads/attachment_data/file/381344/Master_final_national_curriculum_28_Nov.pdf (accessed 18 March 2021).

Department for Education (DfE) (2014b) *National Curriculum in England: English Programmes of Study*, available at: www.gov.uk/government/publications/national-curriculum-in-england-english-programmes-of-study (accessed 18 March 2021).

Department for Education (DfE) (2014c) *English Programmes of Study: Key Stage 4 National Curriculum in England*, available at: www.gov.uk/government/uploads/system/ uploads/attachment_data/file/331877/KS4_English_PoS_FINAL_170714.pdf (accessed 12 March 2021).

Department for Education (DfE) (2014d) *GCE AS and A Level Subject Content for English Language*, available at: www.gov.uk/government/uploads/system/uploads/attachment_data/file/302109/A_level_English_language_subject_content.pdf chapter 17 (accessed 18 March 2021).

Department for Education (DfE) (2019) *National Statistics, Key Stage 4 performance, 2019 (provisional)*, available at: www.gov.uk/government/statistics/key-stage-4-performance-2019-provisional (accessed 13 June 2020).

Department for Education and Employment (DfEE) (1999) *The National Curriculum: English*. London: HMSO.

Department for Education and Skills/Qualifications and Curriculum Authority (2004) *The National Curriculum: A Handbook for Teachers*. London: HMSO.

Department for Education and the Welsh Office (1995) *English in the National Curriculum*. London: HMSO.

Department of Education and Science (DES) (1975) *A Language for Life (The Bullock Report)*. London: HMSO.

Dickens, C. (1854) *Hard Times*, available online at: www.gutenberg.org/ebooks/786 (accessed 24 March 2015).

Dickson, A. (2015) *Worlds Elsewhere: Journeys Around Shakespeare's Globe*. London: The Bodley Head.

Dixon, J. (1967) *Growth through English*. Sheffield: National Association for the Teaching of English.

Dixon, J. (1975) *Growth through English: Set in the Perspective of the Seventies*. 3rd Ed. Yorkshire: National Association for the Teaching of English/Oxford University Press.

Dobson, T. and Stephenson, L. (2020) Challenging boundaries to cross: primary teachers exploring drama pedagogy for creative writing with theatre educators in the landscape of performativity. *Professional Development in Education*. 46 (2). pp.245–55.

Drake, S.M. and Burns, R.C. (2004) *Meeting Standards through Integrated Curriculum*. Alexandria, VA: Association for Supervision and Curriculum Development (ASCD).

Dreher, S. (2003) A novel idea: Reading aloud in a high school English classroom. *The English Journal*. 93 (1). pp.50–3.

Duncan, S. (2012) *Reading Circles, Novels and Adult Reading Development*. London: Bloomsbury.

Dunn, J., Harden, A. and Marino, S. (2013) Drama and Writing: Overcoming the Hurdle the Blank Page. In Anderson, M., & Dunn, J. (eds.). *How Drama Activates Learning: Contemporary Research and Practice*. London: Bloomsbury, pp.245–59.

Dymoke, S. (2003) *Drafting and Assessing Poetry: A Guide for Teachers*. London: SAGE.

Dymoke, S. (2009) *Teaching English Texts 11–18*. London: Continuum.

Dymoke, S., Lambirth, A. and Wilson, A. (2013) *Making Poetry Matter: International Research on Poetry Pedagogy*. London: Bloomsbury Academic.

Eaglestone, R. (2009) *Doing English*. New York: Routledge.

Eaglestone, R. (2017) *Doing English: A Guide for Literature Students*. Abingdon: Routledge.

Eaglestone, R. (2019) *Literature: Why It Matters*. Cambridge: Polity Press.

Education, Audio-Visual and Culture Executive Agency of the European Commission (EACEA) (2011) *Teaching Reading in Europe: Contexts, Policies and Practices*. Brussels: EACEA, Eurydice.

Education Scotland (2010) *Curriculum for Excellence*, available at: https://education.gov.scot/education-scotland/, (accessed 18 March 2021).

Education Support (2019) *Teacher Wellbeing Index 2019*. London: Education Support, available at: www.educationsupport.org.uk/resources/research-reports/teacher-wellbeing-index-2019 (accessed 17 May 2020).

Elbow, P. (1998) *Writing without Teachers*. 2nd Ed. New York: Oxford University Press.

Elbow, P. and Belanoff, P. (2000) *A Community of Writers: A Workshop Course in Writing*. 3rd Ed. Boston: McGraw-Hill.

Eliot, G. (1861) *Silas Marner: The Weaver of Raveloe*. Available online at: Silas Marner, by George Eliot (gutenberg) www.gutenberg.org/files/550/550-h/550-h.htm.org) (accessed 1 August 2020).

Elliott, V. and Olive, S. (2019) Secondary Shakespeare in the UK: What gets taught and why? *English in Education*, online, available at: www.tandfonline.com/doi/full/10.1080/04250494.2019.1690952 (accessed 20 June 2020).

English & Media Centre (2013) *KS3 Language Laboratory*. London: English & Media Centre.

English, F. (2011) *Pupil Writing and Genre: Reconfiguring Academic Knowledge*. London and New York: Continuum.

English Speaking Union (ESU) (2020) *The English-Speaking Union Has Been Discovering Voices for 100 Years*, available at: www.esu.org/ (accessed 25 June 2020).

Etymonline.com (2020) text (n.), available at: www.etymonline.com/search?q=text (accessed 1 August 2020).

Fleming, M. (2017) *Starting Drama Teaching*. 4th Ed. Abingdon: Routledge.

Fleming, M. and Stevens, D. (2015) Drama. In Fleming, M. & Stevens, D. (eds.). *English Teaching in the Secondary School*. 4th Ed. Abingdon: Routledge, pp.156–76.

Fletcher, J. (2014) A review of 'effective' reading literacy practices for young, adolescent 11-to-13-year-old students. *Educational Review*. 66 (3). pp.293–310.

Flower, L. and Hayes, J. (1981) A cognitive process theory of writing. *College Composition and Communication*. 32 (4). pp.365–87.

Fontich, X. and Garcia-Folgado, M. (2018) Grammar instruction in the Hispanic area: The case of Spain with attention to empirical studies on metalinguistic activity. *L1 Educational Studies in Language and Literature*. 18. pp.1–39.

Foster, D. (2019) *Teacher Recruitment and Retention in England*. House of Commons Briefing Paper (no. 7222. 12 February). House of Commons Library.

Foster, S., Pettigrew, A., Pearce, A., Hale, R., Burgess, A., Salmons, P. and Lenga, R. (2016) *What Do Students Know and Understand about the Holocaust? Evidence from English Secondary Schools*. London: UCL.

Fountas, I. and Pinnell, G. (1996) *Guided Reading: Good First Teaching for All Children*. Portsmouth, NH: Heinemann.

Fowler, J. (1910) English Literature in Secondary Schools. In *The Pamphlets on the Teaching of English* (1907–21), available at: https://archive.org/details/pamphletsonteach00engl (accessed 12 January 2016).

Franks, A. and Bryer, T. (2014) Drama in Teaching and Learning English. In Davison, J. (ed.). *Learning to Teach English in the Secondary School*. 4th Ed. Abingdon: Routledge.

Franks, A., Durran, J. and Burn, A. (2006) Stories of the three-legged stool: English, media, drama, from critique to production. *English in Education*. 40 (1). pp.64–79.

Frayer, D., Frederick, W.C. and Klausmeier, H.J. (1969) *A Schema for Testing the Level of Cognitive Mastery*. Madison: Wisconsin Center for Education Research.

Freire, P. (1985) *The Politics of Education: Culture, Power, and Liberation*. Westport, CT and London: Greenwood Publishing Group.

Gallagher, K. (2009) *Readicide: How Schools Are Killing Reading and What You Can Do About It*. Portland, OR: Stenhouse Publishers.

Gerson, M. (2011) Harry Potter and the power of myth. *The Washington Post*, 18 July, available at: www.washingtonpost.com/opinions/harry-potter-and-the-power-of-myth/2011/07/18/gIQArUChMI_story.html (accessed 18 March 2021).

Gibb, N. (2015) How E.D. Hirsch Came to Shape UK Government Policy. In Simons, J. and Porter, N. *Knowledge and the Curriculum: A Collection of Essays to Accompany E.D. Hirsch's Lecture at Policy Exchange*, available at: https://policyexchange.org.uk/wp-content/uploads/2016/09/knowledge-and-the-curriculum.pdf (accessed 5 August 2020).

Gibbons, S. (2013) *The London Association for the Teaching of English 1947–67: A history*. London: Trentham Books.

Gibbons, S. (2019) 'Death by PEEL?' The teaching of writing in the secondary English classroom in England. *English in Education*. 53 (1). pp.36–45.

Gibson, R. (1998) *Teaching Shakespeare*. Cambridge: CUP.

Gillard, D. (2018) Education in England: A History of Our Schools, available at: www.educationengland.org.uk/history/ (accessed 17 July 2020).

Gillespie, A. and Graham, S. (2014) A meta-analysis of writing interventions for students with learning disabilities. *Exceptional Children*. 80. pp.454–73.

Giovanelli, M. (2016) Text World theory as cognitive grammatics: A pedagogical application in the secondary classroom. In Lahey, E. & Gavins, J. (eds). *World Building: Discourse in the Mind*. London and New York: Bloomsbury Academic, pp.109–26.

Giovanelli, M. and Mason, J. (2015) 'Well I don't feel that': Schemas, worlds and authentic reading in the classroom. *English in Education*. 49 (1). pp.41–56.

Goddard, A. (2002) *The Language of Advertising*. London: Routledge.

Goddard, A. (2011) 'Type you soon!' A stylistic approach to language use in a virtual learning environment. *Language and Literature*. 20 (3). pp.184–200.

Goddard, A. (2012) *Doing English Language*. Abingdon: Routledge.

Goddard, A. and Beard, A. (2007) *As Simple as ABC? Issues of Transition for Students of English Language A Level Going On to Study English Language/Linguistics in Higher Education*, Report Series No. 14, The Higher Education Academy English Subject Centre, https://issuu.com/englishsubjectcentre/docs/abc_language (accessed 1 August 2020).

Goddard, A. and Carey, N. (2017) *Discourse: The Basics*. Abingdon and New York: Routledge.

Goddard, A. and Mean, L. (2009) *Language and Gender*. London: Routledge.

Golding, P. (2019) Media studies in the UK. *Publizistik*. 64 (4). pp.503–15.

Goldsmith, K. (2011) *Uncreative Writing: Managing Language in the Digital Age*. New York: Columbia University Press.

Goldsmith, K. (2013) *Seven American Deaths and Disasters*. New York: Powerhouse Books.

Goodwyn, A. (2011) Literary Reading: The Challenge of Getting Young People to Experience Poetry. In Michael, L. (ed.). *Bringing Poetry Alive*. London: SAGE, pp.129–42.

Goodwyn, A. (2016) Still growing after all these years? The resilience of the Personal Growth model of English in England and also internationally. *English Teaching: Practice and Critique*. 15 (1). pp.7–21.

Gordon, J. (2019a) Pedagogic literary narration in theory and action. *L1-Educational Studies in Language and Literature*. 19. pp.1–31.

Gordon, J. (2019b) the turn of the page: Spoken quotation in shared reading. *Classroom Discourse*. 11 (4). pp.366–87.

Gordon, J. (2020) *Researching Interpretive Talk around Literary Narrative Texts: Shared Novel Reading*. New York: Routledge.

Graesser, A., Singer, M. and Trabasso, T. (1994) Constructing inferences during narrative text comprehension. *Psychological Review*. 101 (3). pp.371–95.

Graham, J. (2018) Bringing it all back home: Putting media back into the English curriculum. *Teaching English*. 17. pp.35–9.

Graham, J. and Green, A. (2011) Media in English. In Green, A. (ed.). *Becoming a Reflective English Teacher*. Maidenhead: Open University Press, pp.140–55.

Graham, S. and Perin, D. (2007) A meta-analysis of writing instruction for adolescent pupils. *Journal of Educational Psychology*. 99 (3). pp.445–76.

Graham, S., Bollinger, A., Booth Olson, C., D'Aoust, C., MacArthur, C., McCutchen, D. and Olinghouse, N. (2012) *Teaching Elementary School Students to Be Effective Writers: A Practice Guide* (NCEE 2012–4058). Washington, DC: National Center for Education Evaluation and Regional Assistance, Institute of Education Sciences, U.S. Department of Education, available at: https://ies.ed.gov/ncee/wwc/Docs/PracticeGuide/writing_pg_062612.pdf (accessed 10 June 2020).

Gray, M. (2016) *Boy in the Striped Pyjamas*: A blessing or curse for Holocaust education? *Holocaust Studies*. 20 (3). pp.109–36.

Greene, M. (2014) Teaching the art of 'wide-awakeness'. *Independent School*. 74 (1). pp.122–6.

Guthrie, J.T. and Wigfield, A. (2000) Engagement and motivation in eading. In Kamil, Mosenthal, P.B., Pearson P.D. & Barr, R. (eds.). *Handbook of Reading Research*, Vol. 3. Mahwah, NJ: Lawrence Erlbaum Associates, pp.403–22.

Hacker, D.J., Keener, M.C. and Kircher, J.C. (2009) Writing is applied metacognition. In Hacker, D.J., Dunlosky, J. & Graesser, A.C. (eds.). *Handbook of Metacognition in Education*. New York and Abingdon: Routledge, pp.154–72.

Haddon, M. (2004) B is for bestseller. *The Guardian*, 11 April, available at: www.theguardian.com/books/2004/apr/11/booksforchildrenandteenagers.features3 (accessed 29 May 2020).

Hall, C. (2015) Understanding Reading. In Brindley, S. & Marshall, B. (ed.). London: Bloomsbury, pp.61–71.

Halliday, M.A.K. (1978) *Language as Social Semiotic: The Social Interpretation of Language and Meaning*. London: Edward Arnold.

Halliday, M.A.K. (2003) Introduction: On the 'architecture' of human language. In Webster, J. J. (ed.). *On Language and Linguistics*, Vol. 3 in *Collected Works of MAK Halliday*. London: Continuum, pp.1–29.

Halliday, M.A.K. and Matthiessen, C. (2004) *An Introduction to Functional Grammar*. 3rd Ed. London: Edward Arnold.

Halliday, M.A.K. (1993) Towards a language-based theory of learning. *Linguistics in Education*. 5. pp.93–116.

Harris, K.R., Graham, S. and Atkins, M. (2015) Tier 2, Teacher implemented writing strategies instruction following practice-based, professional development. *Contemporary Educational Psychology*. 40. pp.5–16.

Hasbrouk, J. and Tindal, G. (2006) Oral reading fluency norms: A valuable assessment tool for reading teachers. *The Reading Teacher*. 59 (7). pp.636–44.

Hayes, J.R. (1996) A New Framework for Understanding Cognition and Affect in Writing. In Levy, C.M. & Ransdell, S. (eds.). *The Science of Writing: Theories, Methods, Individual Differences and Applications*. Mahwah, NJ: Lawrence Erlbaum Associates, pp.1–27.

Hayes, J.R. and Flower, L.S. (1980a) Identifying the Organisation of Writing Process. In Gregg, L.W. & Steinberg, E.R. (eds.). *Cognitive Processes in Writing*. Hillsdale, NJ: Lawrence Erlbaum Associates, pp.3–30.

Hayes, J.R. and Flower, L.S. (1980b) The dynamics of composing. In Gregg, L.W. & Steinberg, E.R. (eds.). *Cognitive Processes in Writing*. Hillsdale, NJ: Lawrence Erlbaum Associates, pp.31–50.

Haynes, N. (2016) The myths and folktales behind Harry Potter, BBC, available at: www.bbc.com/culture/article/20161122-the-myths-and-folktales-behind-harry-potter (accessed 18 March 2021).

Herbert, T. (2018) *WW1 Facts and Numbers*, available at www.standard.co.uk/lifestyle/ww1-soldiers-in-numbers-how-many-died-world-war-one-facts-for-armistice-day-a3986761.html (accessed 8 April 2020).

Hessel, A. and Murphy, V. (2019) Understanding how time flies and what it means to be on cloud nine: English as an Additional Language (EAL) learners' metaphor comprehension. *Journal of Child Language*. 46 (2). pp.265–91.

Hibbin, R. (2016) Oral storytelling, speaking and listening and the hegemony of literacy: Non-Instrumental language use and transactional talk in the primary classroom. *Changing English Studies in Culture and Education*. 23 (1). pp.52–64.

Hier, B.O., Eckert, T.L., Viney, E.A. and Meisinger, E. (2019) Generalization and maintenance effects of writing fluency intervention strategies for elementary-age students: A randomized controlled trial. *School Psychology Review*. 48 (4). pp.377–82.

Hillocks, G. (1984) What works in teaching composition: A meta-analysis of experimental treatment studies. *American Journal of Education*. 93 (1). pp.133–70.

Hillocks, G. and Smith, M. (1991) Grammar and Usage. In Flood, J., Jensen, J., Lapp, D. & Squire, J. (eds.). *Handbook of Research on Teaching the English Language Arts*. New York: Macmillan, pp.591–603.

Holbrook, D. (1967) *English for Maturity*. 2nd Ed. Cambridge: Cambridge University Press.

Holmes, E. (2019) *A Practical Guide to Teacher Wellbeing*. London: SAGE.

Holocaust Educational Trust (n.d.) *Teaching the Holocaust in English*, available at: www.het.org.uk/images/downloads/Resources/Teaching_the_Holocaust_in_English.pdf (accessed 3 May 2020).

Hosbawm, J. (2020) *The Simplicity Principle: Six Steps Towards Clarity in a Complex World*. London: Kogan Page.

Howard, K. (2020) *Stop Talking About Wellbeing: A Pragmatic Approach to Teacher Workload*. Woodbridge: John Catt Educational.

Howe, A. (1992) *Making Talk Work*. London: Hodder and Stoughton.

Hughes, T. (1967) *Poetry in the Making: An Anthology of Poems and Programmes from Listening to Writing*. London. Faber.

Hughes, T. (1987) To parse or not to parse: The poet's answer. *The Sunday Times*, 22 November 1987.

Hunt, C.T. (1909). The teaching of Shakespeare in schools. *The Practical Teacher*. 29 (8). pp.396–7.

Hwb (2020) *The Curriculum for Wales*, available at: https://hwb.gov.wales/curriculum-for-wales/ (accessed 18 March 2021).

Janks, H. (2009) Writing: A critical literacy perspective. In Beard, R., Myhill, D., Riley, J. & Nystrand, M. (eds.). *The SAGE Handbook of Writing Development*. London: SAGE, pp.126–36.

Johnson, K.R. and Street, E.M. (2013) *Response to Intervention and Precision Teaching: Creating Synergy in the Classroom*. New York: Guilford.

Jones, D. (2017) Talking about talk: Reviewing oracy in English primary education. *Early Child Development and Care*. 187 (3–4). pp.498–508.

Jones, P. and Chen, H. (2016) The role of dialogic pedagogy in teaching grammar. *Research Papers in Education*. 31 (1). pp.45–69.

Jones, S., Myhill, D. and Bailey, T. (2013) Grammar for writing? An investigation into the effect of contextualised grammar teaching on pupil writing. *Reading and Writing*. 26 (8). pp.1241–63.

Kamler, B. (1995) The grammar wars or what do teachers need to know about grammar? *English in Australia*. 114. pp.3–15.

Keen, J. (2017) Teaching the writing process. *Changing English*. 24 (94). pp.372–385.

Keen, J. (2020) Writing revision: evidence for learning. *Changing English*. 27 (2). pp.121–36.

Kell, E. (2018) *How to Survive in Teaching without Imploding, Exploding or Walking Away*. London: Bloomsbury.

Kellogg, R.T. (1994) *The Psychology of Writing*. Oxford: Oxford University Press.

Kellogg, R.T. (1996) A Model of Working Memory in Writing. In Levy C.M. & S. Ransdell (eds.). *The Science of Writing: Theories, Methods, Individual Differences, and Applications*. Mahwah, NJ: Lawrence Erlbaum Associates, pp.57–71.

Kelly, A.V. (2009) *The Curriculum: Theory and Practice*. 6th Ed. London: SAGE.

Kelly, L. (2019) Private lives, public selves. *TEAN*. 11 (2). pp.82–9.

Kelly, L. (2020) Reclaiming teacher wellbeing through reflective diary writing. *Impact*, 9, available at: https://impact.chartered.college/article/reclaiming-teacher-wellbeing-reflective-diary-writing/ (accessed 10 July 2020).

Kelly, L., Huxford, G. and Kelly, C. (2020) 'In our daily struggles': Diaries as a tool for teacher well-being. *Life Writing* (published online). https://doi.org/10.1080/14484528.2020.1763232

Kelman, S. (2011) *Pigeon English*. London: Bloomsbury.

Kendeou, P., Bohn Gettler, C., White, M.J. and van den Broek, P. (2008) Children's inference generation across different media. *Journal of Research in Reading*. 31. pp.259–72.

King, S. (2000) *On Writing: A Memoir of the Craft*. New York: Scribner.

Kingman, J. (1988) *Report of the Committee of Inquiry into the Teaching of English Language*. London: Her Majesty's Stationery Office.

Kintsch, W. (1998) *Comprehension: A Paradigm for Cognition*. Cambridge: Cambridge University Press.

Klingelhofer, R. and Schleppegrell, M. (2016) Functional grammar analysis in support of dialogic instruction with text: Scaffolding purposeful, cumulative dialogue with English learners. *Research Papers in Education*. 31 (1). pp.70–88.

Knights, B. and Thurgar-Dawson, C. (2008) *Active Reading*. London: Bloomsbury.

Kolln, M. and Gray, L. (2016) *Rhetorical Grammar: Grammatical Choices, Grammatical Effects*. New York: Pearson.

Kolln, M. and Hancock, C. (2005) The story of English grammar in US schools. *English Teaching: Practice and Critique*. 4 (3). pp.11–31.

Kress, G. (1994) *Learning to Write*. London: Routledge.

Kress, G. and Van Leeuwen T. (2001) *Multimodal Discourse: The Modes and Media of Contemporary Communication*. London: Bloomsbury.

Kucan, L. and Beck, I. (1997) Four fourth graders thinking aloud: An investigation of genre effects. *Journal of Literacy Research*. 28. pp.259–88.

Kuhn, M., Schwanenflugen, P. and Meisinger, E. (2010) Aligning theory and assessment of reading fluency: Automaticity, prosody, and definitions of fluency. *Reading Research Quarterly*. 45 (2). pp.230–51.

Land, S. (2015) Skilled reading in isiZulu: What can we learn from it? *Journal of Education*. 63. pp.57–87.

Laurenson, P. et al. (2015) From national policy to classroom practice: Promoting reading for pleasure in post-primary English classrooms. *English in Education*. 49 (1). pp.5–24.

Le Guin, U. (2015) *Steering the Craft*. New York: Houghton Mifflin Harcourt.

Lea, M. and Street, B. (2006) The 'academic literacies' model: Theory and applications. *Theory into Practice*. 45 (4). pp.368–77.

Leavis, F. (1930) *Mass Civilisation and Minority Culture*. Cambridge: Minority Press.

Leavis, F. (1948) *The Great Tradition*. London: Chatto and Windus.

Leavis, Q. (1932) *Fiction and the Reading Public*. London: Chatto and Windus.

Lefstein, A. (2009) Rhetorical grammar and the grammar of schooling: Teaching 'powerful verbs' in the English National Literacy Strategy. *Linguistics and Education*. 20. pp.378–400.

Lentricchia, F. and DuBois, A. (2003) *Close Reading*. Durham, NC: Duke University Press.

Lethem, J. (2013) The Ecstasy of Influence. In Jonathan Lethem, *The Ecstasy of Influence: NonFictions etc*. London: Vintage Books.

Lister, B. (2007) *Changing Classics in Schools*. Cambridge: Cambridge University Press.

Lister, B. (2009) Bringing Classical Literature to Life in the Classroom. Libre Conference Paper: International Perspectives on the Teaching of Latin, available at: www.academia.edu/1556422/Bringing_classical_literature_to_life_in_the_classroom (accessed 20 May 2014).

Lister, B. (2012) Telling tales. *English, Drama and Media*. 22. pp.16–22.

Littleton, K. and Mercer, N. (2013) *Interthinking: Putting Talk to Work*. Abingdon: Routledge.

Lively, P. (1973) *The Ghost of Thomas Kempe*. London: Heinemann.

London School of Economics. The Brexit Collection, available: https://digital.library.lse.ac.uk/collections/brexit (accessed 1 July 2020).

The Man Who Has It All. https://twitter.com/manwhohasitall

Macken-Horarik, M. and Sandiford, C. (2016) Diagnosing development: A grammatics for tracking student progress in narrative composition. *International Journal of Language Studies*. 10 (3). pp.61–94.

Mansell, W. (2012) The new national curriculum: Made to order? *The Guardian*, 12 November, available at: www.theguardian.com/education/2012/nov/12/primary-national-curriculum-review (accessed 11 September 2019).

Marshall, B. (2000) *English Teachers – The Unofficial Guide: Researching the Philosophies of English Teachers*. London: Routledge.

Martin, J. (1989) *Factual Writing: Exploring and Challenging Social Reality*. 2nd Ed. Oxford: Oxford University Press.

May, R. (1975/1994) *The Courage to Create*. New York: W.W. Norton.

McCallum, A. (2012) *Creativity and Learning in Secondary English*. Abingdon and New York: Routledge.

McLuhan, M. (1964) *Understanding Media: The Extensions of Man*. London: Routledge.

Medway, P. et al. (2014) *English Teachers in a Postwar Democracy: Emerging Choice in London Schools, 1945–1965*. New York: Palgrave Macmillan.

Meek, M (1991) *On Being Literate: Living with Difference*. London: Bodley Head.

Mercer, N. (2000) *Word and Minds*. London: Routledge.

Mercer, N. (2015) Why oracy must be in the curriculum (and group work in the classroom). *FORUM: For Promoting 3–19 Comprehensive Education*. 57 (1). pp.67–74.

Mercer, N. and Edwards, D. (1987) Ground rules for mutual understanding: Towards a social psychological approach to classroom knowledge. In Mercer, N. (ed.). *Language in School and Community*. London: Edward Arnold, pp.34–46.

Mercer, N. and Hodgkinson, S. (eds.) (2008) *Exploring Talk in School: Inspired by the Work of Douglas Barnes*. London: SAGE.

Mercer, N. and Littleton, K., (2007) *Dialogue and the Development of Children's Thinking: A Sociocultural Approach*. Abingdon: Routledge.

Merga, M. (2013) Should silent reading feature in a secondary school English programme? West Australian students' perspectives on silent reading. *English in Education*. 47 (3). pp.229–44.

Merga, M. (2019) *Librarians in Schools as Literacy Educators: Advocates for Reaching beyond the Classroom*. London: Palgrave Macmillan.

Merga, M.K. (2017) Interactive reading opportunities beyond the early years: What educators need to consider. *Australian Journal of Education*. 61 (3). pp.328–343.

Micciche, L. (2004) Making the case for rhetorical grammar. *College Composition and Communication*. 55 (4). pp.716–37.

Moats, L. (2009) Knowledge foundations for teaching reading and spelling. *Reading & Writing*. 22. pp.379–99.

Mol, S. and Bus, A. (2011) To read or not to read: A meta-analysis of print exposure from infancy to early adulthood. *Psychological Bulletin*. 137 (2). pp.267–96.

Moo, J. (2006) Reading and writing. *The Atlantic*, August, available at: www.theatlantic.com/magazine/archive/2006/08/reading-and-writing/305075/ (accessed 18 March 2021).

Morgan, J. (2014) Michael Young and the politics of the school curriculum. *British Journal of Educational Studies*. 63 (1). pp.5–22.

Morpurgo, M. (2003) *Private Peaceful*. London: HarperCollins.

Myhill, D. (2005a) Testing times: The impact of prior knowledge on written genres produced in examination settings. *Assessment in Education: Principles, Policy & Practice*. 12 (3). pp.289–300.

Myhill, D. (2005b) Ways of knowing: Writing with grammar in mind. *English Teaching: Practice and Critique*. 4 (3). pp.77–96.

Myhill, D. (2011) The ordeal of deliberate choice: Metalinguistic development in secondary writers. In Berninger, V. (ed.). *Past, Present and Future Contributions of Cognitive Writing Research to Cognitive Psychology*. London and New York: Psychology Press, pp.247–74.

Myhill, D. (2018). Grammar as a meaning-making resource for improving writing. Contribution to a special issue: Working on Grammar at School. L1-Education: Empirical Research across Linguistic Regions. *L1-Educational Studies in Language and Literature*. 18. pp.1–21.

Myhill, D. and Newman, R. (2019) Writing talk – developing metalinguistic understanding through dialogic teaching. In Mercer, N., Wegerif, R. & Major, L. (eds.). *International Handbook of Research on Dialogic Education*. Abingdon: Routledge, pp.360–72.

Myhill, D. and Watson, A. (2017) 'The dress of thought': Analysing literature through a linguistic lens. In Goodwyn, A., Durrant, C., Reid, L. & Scherff, L. (eds.). *International Perspectives on the Teaching of Literature in Schools Global Principles and Practices*. London: Routledge, pp.18–28.

Myhill, D. and Watson, A. (2019) The Dartmouth conference revisited: Changing views of grammar – or not? In Goodwyn, A., Durrant, C., Sawyer, W., Scherff L. & Zancanella, D. (eds.). *The Future of English Teaching Worldwide: Celebrating 50 Years from the Dartmouth Conference*. London: Routledge, pp.241–53.

Myhill, D., Jones, S. and Lines, H. (2018) Supporting less-proficient writers through linguistically-aware teaching. *Language and Education*. 32 (4). pp.333–49.

Myhill, D., Jones, S. and Watson, A. (2013) Grammar matters: How teachers' grammatical subject knowledge impacts on the teaching of writing. *Teaching and Teacher Education*. 36. pp.77–91.

Myhill, D., Jones, S., Lines, H. and Watson A. (2012) Re-thinking grammar: The impact of embedded grammar teaching on pupils' writing and pupils' metalinguistic understanding. *Research Papers in Education*. 27 (2). pp.139–66.

Myhill, D., Jones, S., Watson, A. and Lines, H. (2013) Playful explicitness with grammar: A pedagogy for writing. *Literacy*. 47 (2). pp.103–11.

Myhill, D., Lines, H. and Jones, S. (2018) Texts that teach: Examining the efficacy of using texts as models. *L1-Educational Studies in Language and Literature*. 18. pp.1–24.

Myhill, D., Lines, H. and Watson, A. (2011) Making meaning with grammar: A repertoire of possibilities. *English in Australia*. 47 (3). pp.1–10.

Myhill, D., Newman, R. and Watson, A. (2020) Going meta: Dialogic talk in the writing classroom. *Australian Journal of Language and Literacy*. 43 (1). pp.5–16.

Myhill, D.A., Jones, S.M., Watson, A. and Lines, H.E (2016) *Essential Primary Grammar*. Oxford: OUP.

Nadeau, M. (2017) Implementing a new pedagogical grammar: Obstacles and opportunities from the experience in francophone Québec. *Caplletra. Revista Internacional de Filologia*. 32 (2). pp.189–216.

Nag, S., Chiat, S., Torgerson, C. and Snowling M.J. (2014) *Literacy, Foundation Learning and Assessment in Developing Countries: Final Report. Education Rigorous Literature Review.* Department for International Development, available at www.gov.uk/research-for-development-outputs/assessment-of-literacy-and-foundational-learning-in-developing-countries (accessed 22 March 2021).

Nagy, W. and Scott, J. (1990) Word schemas: Expectations about the form and meaning of new words. *Cognition & Instruction*. 7. pp.105–27.

The National Advisory Committee on Creative and Cultural Education (NACCCE) (1999) *All Our Futures: Creativity, Culture and Education,* available at: http://sirkenrobinson.com/pdf/allourfutures.pdf (accessed 2 March 2021).

National Council of Teachers of English (NCTE) (1992) *A Position Statement from the Committee on Storytelling*, 1992. Available online at https://ncte.org/statement/teachingstorytelling/ (accessed 1 August 2021).

National Foundation for Educational Research (2019) *Achievement of 15 Year-Olds in England: PISA 2018 Results Research Report*. London: DfE, available at https://assets.publishing.service.gov.uk/government/uploads/system/uploads/attachment_data/file/855985/PISA_2018_England_national_report_accessible.pdf (last accessed 17 July 2020).

Newbolt, J.H. et al. (1921/1934) *The Teaching of English in England (being the Report of the Departmental Committee Appointed by the President of the Board of Education to Inquire into the Position of English in the Educational System of England).* London: HMSO, available at: www.educationengland.org.uk/documents/newbolt/newbolt1921.html (accessed 26 April 2020).

Newman, R. (2017) Let's talk talk: Utilising metatalk for the development of productive collaborative dialogues. *Thinking Skills and Creativity*. 26 . pp.1–12.

Newman, R. and Watson, A. (2020) Shaping spaces: Teachers' orchestration of metatalk about written text. *Linguistics and Education*. 60. 100860.

Nystrand, M. (1989) A social-interactive model of writing. *Written Communication*. 6. pp.66–85.

Nystrand, M. (2006) Research on the role of classroom discourse as it affects reading comprehension. *Research in the Teaching of English*. 40 (4). pp.392–412.

Nystrand, M. and Gamoran, A. (1991) Instructional discourse, pupil engagement, and literature achievement. *Research in the Teaching of English*. 25. pp.261–90.

Oakhill, J. and Cain, K. (2012) The precursors of reading ability in young readers: Evidence from a four-year longitudinal study. *Scientific Studies of Reading*. 16 (2). pp.91–121.

Oakhill, J., Cain, K. and Elbro, C. (2015) *Understanding and Teaching Reading Comprehension: A Handbook.* Abingdon: Routledge.

Office for Standards in Education (Ofsted), (2019). *The School Inspection Handbook.* Available at: www.gov.uk/government/organisations/ofsted (accessed 1 January 2020).

Okkinga, M., van Steensel, R., van Gelderen, A.J.S. and Sleegers, P.J.C. (2018) Effects of Reciprocal teaching on reading comprehension of low-achieving adolescents: The importance of specific teacher skills. *Journal of Research in Reading*. 41 (1). pp.20–41.

Olive, S. (2015) *Shakespeare Valued: Education Policy and Pedagogy 1989–2009.* Bristol: Intellect.

Organisation for Economic Co-operation and Development (OECD) (2019) *PISA 2018 Results.* Vol. 1: *What Students Know and Can Do.* Paris: PISA, OECD Publishing, available at www.oecd.org/education/pisa-2018-results-volume-i-5f07c754-en.htm (accessed 22 March 2021).

Osundare, N. (1990) *Songs of the Season*. Ibadan, Nigeria: Heinemann Educational Books.

O'Toole, J. and Stinson, M. (2013) Drama, speaking and listening: The treasure of oracy. In Anderson, M. & Dunn, J. (eds.). *How Drama Activates Learning: Contemporary Research and Practice*. London: Bloomsbury.

Oxford University Press (2018) *Why Closing the Word Gap Matters: Oxford Language Report*, available at: https://global.oup.com/education/content/dictionaries/key-issues/word-gap/?region=uk (accessed 22 March 2021).

Paraskevas, C. (2006) Grammar apprenticeship. *English Journal*. 95 (5). pp.65–9.

Perera, K. (1987) *Understanding Language*. London: NAAE.

Perfetti, C. and Stafura, J. (2014) Word knowledge in a theory of reading comprehension. *Scientific Studies of Reading*. 18 (1). pp.22–37.

Perloff, M. (2012) *Unoriginal Genius: Poetry by Other Means in the New Century*. Chicago: University of Chicago Press.

Perryman, J. and Calvert, G. (2020) What motivates people to teach, and why do they leave? Accountability, performativity and teacher retention. *British Journal of Educational Studies*. 68 (1). pp.3–23.

Petty, G. (2006) *Evidence Based Teaching: A Practical Approach*. Cheltenham: Nelson Thornes.

Phillips, L. (2013) Storytelling as pedagogy. *Practical Strategies Literacy Learning: The Middle Years*. 21 (2). pp.ii–iv.

Philpot, D. (2005) Children's metafiction, readers and reading: Building thematic models of narrative comprehension. *Children's Literature in Education*. 36 (2). pp.141–59.

Phonemic Chart, available at: www.phonemicchart.com (accessed 22 March 2021).

Pipher, M. (2006) *Writing to Change the World*. New York: Penguin.

Polan, D. (2007) *Scenes of Instruction: The Beginnings of the US Study of Film*. Berkeley: University of California Press.

Polanyi, M. (1966) *The Tacit Dimension*. Chicago: University of Chicago Press.

Pope, R. (2013) *Textual Intervention: Critical and Creative Strategies for Literary Studies*. Abingdon: Routledge.

Potter, J. (2020) Reading and Writing Media Texts: Critical Digital Literacy in the Making. In Davison, J. & Daly, C. (eds.). *Debates in English Teaching*. Abingdon: Routledge, pp.53–65.

Prescott, P. (2010) Shakespeare and popular culture. In De Grazia, M. & Wells, S. (eds.). *The New Cambridge Companion to Shakespeare*. Cambridge: Cambridge University Press, pp.269–84

Purewal, S. (2017) Shakespeare in the classroom: To be or not to be. *Warwick Journal of Education*. 1. pp.20–35.

Qualifications and Curriculum Authority (QCA) (2007a) *English: Programme of Study for Key Stage 3 [and 4] and Attainment Targets*. London: QCA.

Qualifications and Curriculum Authority (QCA) (2007b) *The National Curriculum Statutory Requirements for Key Stages 3 and 4*. London: HMSO. http://archive.teachfind.com/qcda/orderline.qcda.gov.uk/gempdf/184721553X.PDF (accessed 3 March 2021).

Quality Assurance Agency (QAA) (2019) *Subject Benchmark Statement: English*, available online at www.qaa.ac.uk/docs/qaa/subject-benchmark-statements/subject-benchmark-statement-english.pdf?sfvrsn=47e2cb81_4 (accessed 6 August 2020).

Railton, N. (2015) Lessons in culture: Oral storytelling in a literature classroom. *Changing English*. 22 (1). pp.50–9.

Randall, H. (2019) *The Problem with 'The Boy in the Striped Pyjamas'*. The Holocaust Exhibition and Learning Centre, available at: https://holocaustlearning.org.uk/latest/the-problem-with-the-boy-in-the-striped-pyjamas/ (accessed 3 May 2020).

Rank, T., Millum, T. and Warren, C. (2011) *Teaching English Using ICT: A Practical Guide for Secondary School Teachers*. London: Bloomsbury.

Recht, D. and Leslie, L. (1988) Effect of prior knowledge on good and poor readers' memory of text. *Journal of Educational Psychology*. 80. pp.16–20.

Reid, M., (2015) Film, Literacy and Participation. In Brindley, S. & Marshall, B. (eds.). *Masterclass in English Education*. London: Bloomsbury, pp.84–96.

Reimagining the Diary (RtD) Survey (2019) P1, *Reimagining the Diary*, University of Bristol, April 2019. Data available on formal request.

Resnick, L.B. and Schantz, F. (2015) Talking to learn: The promise and challenge of dialogic teaching. In Resnick, L., Asterhan, C. & Clarke, S. (eds.). *Socializing Intelligence through Academic Talk and Dialogue*, Washington, DC: American Educational Research Association, pp.441–50.

Retelsdorf, J., Köller, O. and Möller, J. (2014) Reading achievement and reading self-concept: Testing the reciprocal effects model. *Learning and Instruction*. 29. pp.21–30.

Reynolds, R., Taylor, M., Steffensen, M., Shirey, L. and Anderson, R. (1982) Cultural schemata and reading comprehension. *Reading Research Quarterly*. 17. pp.353–66.

Roberts, R. (2020) A 'Godlike Science': English Teaching in Secondary Schools. In Hall, C.J. & Wicaksono, R. (eds.). *Ontologies of English: Conceptualising the Language for Learning, Teaching, and Assessment*. Cambridge: Cambridge University Press, pp.122–41.

Rosen, M. (2019) Why reading aloud is a vital bridge to literacy. *The Guardian*, 9 March, available at: www.theguardian.com/books/2019/mar/09/why-reading-aloud-is-a-vital-bridge-to-literacy (accessed 1 July 2020).

Rosenblatt, L. (1970/1995) *Literature as Exploration*. London: Heinemann.

Rosenblatt, L. (1978) *The Reader, the Text, the Poem*. Carbondale: Southern Illinois University Press.

RtD Survey, *Reimagining the Diary*, University of Bristol, April 2019. Data available on formal request. See https://research-information.bris.ac.uk/en/projects/re-imagining-the-diary-writing-and-well-being-for-busy-people

Sacks, S. (2013) Bring back the illustrated book! *The New Yorker*, 22 February, available at: www.newyorker.com/books/page-turner/bring-back-the-illustrated-book (accessed 1 July 2020).

Savage, J. (2011) *Cross-Curricular Approaches to Teaching and Learning in Secondary Education*. London: Routledge.

Sawyer, R.K. (2011) *Structure and Improvisation in Creative Teaching*. Cambridge: Cambridge University Press.

Scammacca, N.K., Roberts, G.J., Cho, U., Williams, K.J., Roberts, G., Vaughn, S. and Carroll, M. (2016) A century of progress: Reading interventions for students in grades 4–12, 1914–2014. *Review of Educational Research*. 86 (3). pp.756–800.

Scardamalia, M. and Bereiter, C. (1987). Knowledge telling and knowledge transforming in written composition. *Advances in applied psycholinguistics*. 2. pp. 142–175.

Schickel, R. (2008) *The Boy in the Striped Pajamas*: A failed Holocaust fable. *TIME*, 7 November, available at: http://content.time.com/time/arts/article/0,8599,1857440,00.html (accessed 3 May 2020).

Schleppegrell, M. and Moore, J. (2018) Linguistic tools for Supporting Emergent Critical Language Awareness in the Elementary School. In Harman, R. (ed.).

Bilingual Learners and Social Equity: Critical Approaches to Systemic Functional Linguistics. New York: Springer, pp.23–43.

Scottish Government. (2019) *Scotland's Curriculum for Excellence: Putting Learners at the Heart of Education*, available at https://scotlandscurriculum.scot (accessed 20 June 2020).

Shakespeare, W. and Alexander, P. (1953) *Complete Works*. London: Collins.

Sharples, M. (1999) *How We Write: Writing as Creative Design*. London: Routledge.

Shayer, D. (1972) *The Teaching of English in Schools 1900–1970*. London: Routledge.

Shelley, P.B. (1840) *Essays, Letters from Abroad, Translations and Fragments*. In two volumes, edited by Mary Shelley. London: Edward Moxon.

Sigvardsson, A. (2020) Don't fear poetry! Secondary teachers' key strategies for engaging pupils with poetic texts. *Scandinavian Journal of Educational Research*. 64 (6). pp.953–66.

Smagorinsky, P. (2009) EJ Extra: Is it time to abandon the idea of 'best practices' in the teaching of English? *The English Journal*. 98 (6). pp.15–22.

Smith, E. (2019) *This Is Shakespeare: How to Read the World's Greatest Playwright*. London: Pelican Books.

Smith, L. (2018) 'We're not building worker bees'. What has happened to creative practice in England since the Dartmouth Conference of 1966? *Changing English*. 26 (1). pp.48–62.

Smith, L. (2019) The role of English in the conversation of humankind: Humanism and creativity in Newbolt (1921) and the National Curriculum (2014). *English in Education*. 53 (3). pp.253–65.

Smith, L. (2020) Top ten texts: A survey of commonly-taught KS3 class readers. *Teaching English*. 23. pp.30–3.

Sommers, N. (1980) Revision strategies of student writers and experienced adult writers. *College Composition and Communication*. 31 (4). pp.378–88.

Soter, A.O., Wilkinson, I.A., Murphy, P.K., Rudge, L., Reninger, K. and Edwards, M. (2008) What the discourse tells us: Talk and indicators of high-level comprehension. *International Journal of Educational Research*. 47. pp.372–91.

Springhall, J. (1999) *Youth, Popular Culture and Moral Panics*. London: Palgrave.

Stanovich, K.E. (1986) Matthew effects in reading: some consequences of individual differences in the acquisition of literacy. *Reading Research Quarterly*. 21 (4). pp.360–407.

Steele, S. (2015) Lifting Poetry off the Page. In Dymoke, S., Barrs, M., Lambirth, A. & Wilson, A. (eds.). *Making Poetry Happen: Transforming the Poetry Classroom*. London and New York: Bloomsbury, pp.17–28.

Stevens, D. (2011) *Cross-Curricular Teaching and Learning in the Secondary School: English*. London: Routledge.

Summerfield, G. (ed.) (1968) *Creativity in English: Papers relating to the Anglo-American Seminar on the Teaching of English (Dartmouth College, New Hampshire, 1966): The Dartmouth Seminar Papers*. Champaign, IL: NCTE.

Sutherland, J. (2006) Promoting group talk and higher-order thinking in pupils, by coaching secondary English trainee teachers. *Literacy*. 40 (2). pp.106–14.

Sutherland, J. (2015) 'Going meta': Using a metadiscoursal approach to develop secondary students' dialogic talk in small groups. *Research Papers in Education*. 30 (1). pp.44–69.

Sutherland, J., Westbrook, J., Oakhill, J. and Sullivan, S. (2020) A 'faster read': A mixed-method, pilot study enhancing whole-text comprehension, using high-quality discourse, with a focus on inference. (under review).

Swales, J. (1990) *Genre Analysis*. Cambridge: Cambridge University Press.

Tan, S. (2007) *The Arrival*. London: Hodder Children's Books.

Thomas, D. (2011) *Deconstructing Digital Natives*. London: Routledge.

Thompson, D. (1943) *Voice of Civilisation: An Enquiry into Advertising*. London: F. Muller.

Tracey, L. Boehnke, J., Elliott, L., Thorley, K. Ellison, S. and Bowyer-Crane, C. (2019) *Grammar for Writing Evaluation: Report and Executive Summary*. London: Education Endowment Foundation.

Turner, C. (2019) English A-level suffers collapse in student numbers as teachers blame tougher GCSEs. *The Telegraph*, 13 August, available at www.telegraph.co.uk/news/2019/08/13/english-a-level-suffers-collapse-student-numbers-teachers-blame/ (accessed 10 October 2020).

Van den Bergh, H. and Rijlaarsdam, G. (1996) The Dynamics of Composing: Modelling Writing Process Data. In Levy, C.M. & Ransdell, S. (eds.). *The Science of Writing: Theories, Methods, Individual Differences, and Applications*. Mahwah, NJ: Lawrence Erlbaum Associates, pp.207–32.

Victoria State Government. (2020) *Literacy Teaching Toolkit: Guided Reading*, available at: www.education.vic.gov.au/school/teachers/teachingresources/discipline/english/literacy/readingviewing/Pages/teachingpracguided.aspx#link94 (accessed 22 March 2020).

Videbaek, S. (2020) PISA: Beyond the league tables and the headlines, available online at: www.sec-ed.'co.uk/best-practice/pisa-beyond-the-league-tables-and-the-headlines/ (accessed 1 February 2021).

Vygotsky, L. (1991) *Thought and Language*. Cambridge, MA: The MIT Press.

Vygotsky, L. (1998) Imagination and Creativity in the Adolescent. In Reiber, R. (ed.). *The Collected Words of L.S. Vygotsky*, Vol. 5. New York: Plenum Press, pp.151–66.

Vygotsky, L.S. (1978) *Mind in Society: The Development of Higher Psychological Processes.* Cambridge, MA: Harvard University Press.

Walker, A. (1973) 'The flowers'. In Walker, A. (ed.). *Love & Trouble; Stories of Black Women*. New York: Harcourt Brace Jovanovich, pp.119–120.

Waters, S. (2011) *The Secret Life of Plays*. London: Nick Hern Books.

Watson, A. (2012) Navigating 'the pit of doom': Affective responses to teaching 'grammar'. *English in Education*. 46 (1). pp.22–37.

Watson, A.M. and Newman, R.M.C. (2017) Talking grammatically: L1 adolescent metalinguistic reflection on writing. *Language Awareness*. 26 (4). pp.381–98.

Welsh Government (2016) *Curriculum for Wales: Programme of Study for English, Key Stages 2–4*, available at: https://hwb.gov.wales/curriculum-for-wales-2008/key-stages-2-to-4/english-programme-of-study-key-stages-2-4 (accessed 23 March 2021).

Westbrook, J. (2011) Access, Choice and Time. In Davison, J., Daly, C. & Moss, J. (eds.). *Debates in English Teaching*. London: Routledge, pp.104–16.

Westbrook, J. (2013) Reading as a hermeneutical endeavour: Whole-class approaches to teaching narrative with low-attaining adolescent readers. *Literacy*. 47 (1). pp.42–9.

Westbrook, J., Sutherland, J., Oakhill, J. and Sullivan, S. (2019) Just reading: the impact of a faster pace of reading narratives on the comprehension of poorer adolescent readers in English classrooms. *Literacy UKLA*. 53 (2). pp.60–8.

White, J. and Brown, M. (2012) An unstable framework: Critical perspectives on The Framework for the National Curriculum. *New Visions for Education Group*, 5.

Whittaker, F. (2019) Russell Group ditches 'facilitating subjects' A-level list. *Schoolsweek*, 23 May, available at: https://schoolsweek.co.uk/russell-group-ditches-facilitating-subjects-a-level-list/ (accessed 5 August 2020).

Wigram-Evans, C. (2020) Tales of the tiger: Searching for big cats in India's wildest state, *National Geographic*, 2 April, available at: www.nationalgeographic.co.uk/travel/2020/04/tales-of-tiger-searching-big-cats-indias-wildest-state (accessed 1 July 2020).

Wilkinson, A. (1965) *Spoken English* (Educational Review occasional publications, No 2). Birmingham: University of Birmingham.

Williams, M. (2012) *Now Is the Time for Running*. London: Tamarind.

Williams, R. (2015) *Keywords: A Vocabulary of Culture and Society*. 3rd Ed. Oxford: Oxford University Press.

Wilson, G.C. (1964) The structure of English. In Ford, G.W. & Pugno, L. (eds.). *The Structure of Knowledge and the Curriculum*. Chicago: Rand McNally, pp. 71–86.

Wintour, P. (2012) Michael Gove accused of major gaps in draft national curriculum for English, *The Guardian*, 31 October, available at: www.theguardian.com/politics/2012/oct/31/michael-gove-draft-national-curriculum (accessed 4 September 2019).

World Health Organisation (WHO) (2018) *Mental Health: Strengthening Our Response*, available at: www.who.int/news-room/fact-sheets/detail/mental-health-strengthening-our-response (accessed 17 May 2020).

Worth, J. (2018) Latest teacher retention statistics paint a bleak picture for teacher supply in England', *NFER*, 28 June, available at: www.nfer.ac.uk/news-events/nfer-blogs/latest-teacher-retention-statistics-paint-a-bleak-picture-for-teacher-supply-in-england/ (accessed 17 May 2020).

Wray, D. (2004) *Critical Literacy*. Reading: National Centre for Language and Literacy.

Yandell, J. and Brady, M. (2016) English and the politics of knowledge. *English in Education*. 50 (1). pp.44–59.

Yandell, J. and Franks, A. (2019) Approaching Shakespeare. In Davison, J. & Daly, C. (eds.). *Learning to Teach English in the Secondary School*. 5th Ed. Abingdon: Routledge, pp. 166–181.

Yekovich, F., Walker, C., Ogle, L. and Thompson, M. (1990) The influence of domain knowledge on inferencing in low aptitude individuals. In Graesser A., & Bower, G. (eds.). *The Psychology of Learning and Motivation*, Vol. 25. New York: Academic Press, pp.175–96.

Index

Note: Page numbers in *italics* refer to figures and those in **bold** refer to tables. The letter n after a page number denotes an endnote.